Sunset Travel Guide to
Washington

By the Editors of Sunset Books and Sunset Magazine

Lane Publishing Co. • Menlo Park, California

Table of Contents

Introducing the Evergreen State 7

The City of Seattle 10

Puget Sound 32

The Olympic Peninsula 44

Southwest Corner 60

The Cascade Mountains 72

Columbia River Gorge 96

Central Washington 104

The Inland Empire 116

Index 127

Hours, admission fees, prices, telephone numbers, and highway designations in this book are accurate as of June 1978. Maps have been provided in each chapter for the special purpose of highlighting significant regions, routes, or attractions in the state. More detailed maps of Washington are available from auto clubs, oil companies, or the Washington State Highway Commission, Olympia, WA 98501.

Editor, Sunset Books: David E. Clark

Second Printing May 1979

Research and Text: Bob Thompson
Supervising Editor:
  Maureen Williams Zimmerman

Design: Cynthia Hanson

Cover: Churning through blue water, ferry makes Edmonds to Kingston run. Ahead, Kitsap Peninsula foothills dense with Douglas fir step up to high Olympic Mountains. Washington State Ferries photograph by Steven C. Wilson.

Special Features

Salmon . . . King of
    Washington's Sport Fish   **13**
Washington's Clams   **20**
The Old-fashioned Pleasures
    of Fairs   **29**
Puget Sound Ferry Routes   **36**
Digging Razor Clams   **68**
Hints for High Country
    Hikers   **80**
Indian History in
    Washington   **85**
Paul Bunyan Games   **89**
Freshwater Fishing   **92**
The Cowboy at His Best   **113**

Undimmed by time are Seattle Space Needle, Pacific Science Center—1962 fair legacies.

Acknowledgments

The following individuals and agencies were of great help in putting together this book: Lon Backman, Bobbi Bennett, Diana Comini, Jon Comini, Robert Cumbow, Michael Galvin, Pat McKelheer, Ray Pittman, Don Richardson, Harolyn Thompson, Ralph White, Harold Zwaschka, Washington Department of Commerce and Economic Development, Department of Fisheries, Department of Game, Department of Natural Resources, State Parks Department, and all of the visitor information bureaus and chambers of commerce that responded generously to our requests for information.

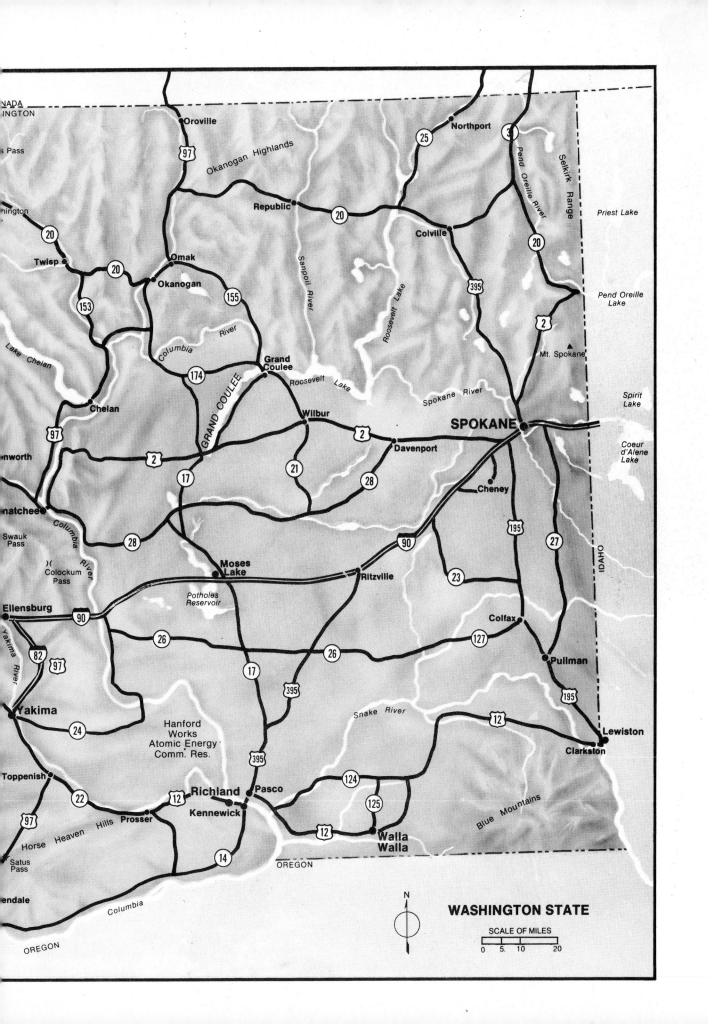

WASHINGTON STATE

SCALE OF MILES

0   5.   10   20

Two states in one

In the cool, wet western half of Washington (below), a far-ranging ferry system is a vital part of the highway network where Puget Sound cannot be bridged. In warm, dry eastern Washington (right), wheels can go almost anywhere one cares to drive them. Nothing symbolizes better the sharp divisions caused by the towering Cascade Mountain range. For residents and visitors alike, the split yields an astonishing diversity of recreational pursuits.

Introducing the Evergreen State

Every now and again some literal-minded geographer tries to tell the world that Washington and Oregon are designed all wrong—that the western halves of the two should be combined into one coastal state while the easterly halves should be united as the second state.

Unofficially, some things work out along these lines. Portland serves as the metropolitan center for much of southwest Washington, while Spokane plays a major urban role for many eastern Oregonians.

The literal-minded geographers draw their conclusion upon the spine of the Cascade Mountains. The mountains form a high, nearly unbroken barrier to passage between east and west in Washington. More important, they break the flow of sea air from the Pacific toward the interior so sharply that the west side has true climax rain forest, the east side true desert.

Because of the Cascades, little Washington—330 miles north-south by 460 miles east-west—has more diversity of terrain and climate than entire nations on smoother parts of the earth's crust. Within this diversity is every possibility for the outdoor recreationist: deep-sea fishing and glacial lake fishing, skiing on snow or water, light air or deep-sea sailing, hiking, and more.

Because of this, no sensible redefinition of state boundaries is likely. The natives, happy with two states for the price of one, would revolt.

Where to Go? What to Do?

Washington is to a tremendous degree an outdoor state: a mecca for hikers, skiers, hunters, campers, fishermen, boaters, divers, bicyclists, even golfers and tennis players.

The range of choice for each of these activists is made broad by the state's implausible range of terrain and climate. There is, for example, an annual ski race on the Fourth of July, and a mid-winter series of sailing races.

Washington divides itself into eight readily definable regions: Seattle, Puget Sound basin, the Olympic Peninsula, Southwest Washington, the Cascades, the Columbia Gorge, Central Washington, and Eastern Washington—the latter sometimes called the Inland Empire.

Of the eight, only Seattle has any reputation at all for urbanity. And still, while the city is home to an internationally praised opera company, a superior collection of Asian art, and a first-rate, left-handed National Football League quarterback, Seattle is still a comfortable place for an outdoorsman. Local businessmen commute from suburbs to work—or to University of Washington football games—aboard their boats. It is possible to fish for salmon within direct sight of downtown office windows. And long hiking trails depart from well within the city limits.

The other seven regions share some characteristics, but remain sharply distinct each from the others. Predictably, the basic differences stem from terrain and climate.

The Puget Sound basin outside Seattle, from Olympia north to the Canadian border, is the most populous region of the state. Nonetheless, it guards an outdoorsy character. Fishing—mostly salt, but with ample freshwater opportunities—is, along with boating, the major attraction.

The Olympic Peninsula, between Puget Sound and the ocean, takes a long step further in the direction of unspoiled wilderness. In a way, it is a microcosm of the whole state. A high range of mountains in the middle parallels the Cascades, leaving a shoreline ranging from rocky open ocean to placid sheltered arms in Puget Sound. The mountains create a rain shadow that requires irrigation on a small plain in the northeast corner, though it also produces a true rain forest on the ocean side.

Southwest Washington in many ways bridges the small gap between the Puget Sound basin and the Olympic Peninsula. Not only is it neighbor to both, but its qualities fall between those of the other regions. Its Pacific shoreline is gentler and more accessible than that of the peninsula. Its interior, on the other hand, is a shade more rugged and less populous than the Puget Sound country. Its prime vacation attractions are ocean fishing for salmon, razor clamming, every kind of freshwater fishing, and hunting.

The Cascades are the special province of hikers and campers in summer, skiers in winter. Parklands in this lofty, seldom-broken range are well developed for both purposes. Curiously, Mt. Rainier National Park has some of the gentlest, most accessible hiking and camping of any part of the range, which generally grows more rugged from south to north. The true seeker of wilderness solitude goes straight to North Cascades National Park. For skiers, every mountain pass has opportunity.

The Columbia Gorge is, in everyday terms, a practical corridor for commerce, the easiest all-year route between the coast and the interior. More important, it is a special place—an awesome gap carved through immovable mountains by the irresistible force of the Columbia River at its fullest. There is some fine fishing to be done in the river and in the mountains rising above it, but just looking around can be reward enough.

Central Washington—the great basin of the Columbia—holds most of the state's cowboys and Indians. In more recent times, since Grand Coulee and other dams brought irrigation water to the parched hillsides, it has become home also to agriculturalists of every stripe, but especially apple growers, vineyardists, and wheat ranchers. In this sprawling region are most of the state's dude ranches, wilderness packers, and other horse-borne enterprises. Rivers and lakes provide some of the most reliable freshwater fishing in the state. Hunters favor the region, in some places for deer, in others for upland game birds.

Eastern Washington is the quiet edge. South of Spokane, it is much like Central Washington except that its farmers work their land dry instead of with irrigation. North of Spokane, surprisingly rugged mountains focus recreation in a few places—fishing water and ski slopes being the primary possibilities.

As easy as the state is to see in geographic blocks, it is even easier to consider activity by activity. The following quick summary is meant to guide readers with particular interests to more detailed information within the book.

Golf. Golf has been a popular recreation in every corner of Washington for decades. Nowhere are courses entirely absent; in few places are they even scarce. In green and growing western Washington, most mature courses are tightly treed. The emphasis is on accuracy rather than distance (which is hard for high handicappers to get on rain-softened fairways). In eastern Washington, courses tend to be more open and not so much longer.

Seattle has the greatest number of courses. Some of the toughest tests are at Port Ludlow (page 48), Sequim (page 50), and Leavenworth (page 86). Spokane's municipal system has two outstanding courses (page 119). Courses are noted throughout the book, usually within the descriptions of towns.

Tennis. Again, Seattle and environs offer the greatest number of public play courts and clubs, including some indoor complexes (page 26). Most of the towns along interstate freeways have good courts, many of them lighted to extend the short northwest season.

Bicycling. Bicyclists may shudder to think of mountainous Washington as a place to ride. In fact, the state is full of cycling enthusiasts who have developed a substantial number of trails in varied terrain. Seattle and its suburbs (especially those east of Lake Washington) have a host of marked trails, many in relatively open countryside. Also, the town of Redmond is a center for both road and velodrome racing.

Away from the urban environment, favored cycling areas include the surprisingly hilly San Juan Islands (page 33) and the surprisingly flat northeast corner of the Olympic Peninsula (page 50).

Hiking. Three national parks, five national forests, and uncounted state, county, and local parks hold at least 2,000 miles of marked trails, ranging from the Pacific Crest Trail down to the epic seashore hike in the Olympic National Park.

Because of their extent and their huge parklands, the Cascades hold the best-known and most used areas. However, they are far from alone. The whole Olympic Peninsula is crisscrossed with trails. Less known is the Wenaha wilderness in the Blue Mountains, in the extreme southeast of the state (page 121).

Newcomers to the northwest and/or to wilderness hiking might profit from reading the cautionary notes on page 80.

Camping. All the same parks and regions that make hiking a major recreation in Washington state allow camping of every sort, from roadside-with-trailer to deep wilderness tent camping.

Mounds of oyster shells *are evidence of oyster industry's continuing importance in Willapa Bay. Estuary waters also hold salmon, steelhead, crabs, clams.*

In summer, pressure on the more accessible parks can be intense. The National Park, National Forest, and State Park systems reservation policies all are essentially first-come, first-served. National Park and National Forest information comes from individual units. The Washington State Department of Parks has a central office at P.O. Box 1128, Olympia 98504.

Skiing. Every Cascade pass has one or more ski resorts (pages 77, 78, 84, 86, 89). Others are on Mt. Rainier (page 75), near Wenatchee (page 86), and—with the deepest powder—near Colville (page 125).

For cross-country skiers, the passes listed above are launch points. Other fine cross-country skiing is in the Methow Valley (page 93). Snowshoers tend to work the same areas.

Fishing. Few states offer a more varied fishery than does Washington. Salmon is the main game for many, especially at Westport (page 63) and Ilwaco (page 63), but also all around the Olympic Peninsula and in Puget Sound. Winter steelheading is another major sport. Again, the Olympic Peninsula and Puget Sound are the prime spots, although in rivers rather than in salt water. The Columbia, from its mouth all the way up to the British Columbia border, is a major freshwater fishery.

Trout and kokanee are planted in every lake and stream that does not support a native population.

The Washington Department of Fisheries (115 General Administration Bldg., Olympia 98504) controls all fishing for salmon, shad, and sturgeon no matter where caught, and all other salt-water food fish and shellfish. The State of Washington Department of Game (600 N. Capitol Way, Olympia 98504) governs fishing for steelhead, trout, bass, and all other freshwater food fish. Anyone thinking to fish should contact both agencies about licenses, permits, and seasons. The requirements are more complicated than the rules of golf—and more strictly enforced.

Boating. Puget Sound, from one end to the other, is the great boating capital of Washington. Rental craft are available at marinas along both shores. The other great waterway is the Columbia, with its tributary the Snake. Using these two rivers, a boater can put in at the Columbia mouth and not leave the water until the craft reaches Lewiston, Idaho. The area around the Tri-Cities (page 100) is a sunny hub for Columbia and Snake boating. In addition to these waterways, there are hundreds of lakes ranging from 55-mile-long Chelan down to modest ponds; boat launches and rental agencies on these make a long enough list to fill a telephone book for, say, Tacoma.

The City

Increasingly sophisticated, the city still guards its close ties to the great outdoors

Ask one group of Seattleites what the city is all about and they will say Boeing, football, and fishing. Ask the same question of the neighbors and the response will be opera and sailing. A good many other answers would also be correct, for this northwesternmost of large United States cities (550,000 within incorporated limits; 1.4 million in the metropolitan area) is remarkable for both outdoor and indoor attractions.

Seattle fits tightly between a lake and an inland sea, and not much more loosely between two towering mountain ranges. In the long twilights of summer, boats by the thousands move easily on calm water until 9 P.M. or even later. In winter, office workers escape after the workday to any of several areas to ski away their cares on lighted slopes, with an hour's drive or less as the price of being there.

For a long time this benign outdoors overwhelmed most would-be urbanity. In the early 1960s a tightly knit colony of painters flourished in the city, but sold its canvases elsewhere. A slim but steady stream of jazz musicians has called Seattle home between road trips since the 1940s. The Seattle Symphony enjoyed a quiet reputation for excellence, but only enough listeners to support a short season.

However, with the World's Fair of 1962 came a blossoming of the arts. The first great sign was in 1970, when the now famous Seattle Opera Company outdrew the now infamous Seattle Pilots baseball team for a whole season.

The pace of life in a steadily growing city has quickened with each passing year. Fair-year visitors have a whole new skyline to look at from the Space Needle. The Smith Tower, for decades trumpeted to all comers as the tallest building west of the Mississippi, is now just the tallest building on its block. Seattle is big and bustling enough now to please people who think elevators are a logical form of transportation, yet the city is still well-wedded to its great outdoors. The combination is most attractive.

Weather. Outsiders are pleased to tell other outsiders that Seattle's principal product is rain. In sheer volume, the rain is not so impressive. The annual average is 34 inches; however, the modest total spreads itself around. In a typical year, Seattle accepts measurable precipitation on 152 days. As the figures hint, only a few howling storms come along each winter. Most Seattle rain falls too softly to interfere with gardening, golfing, weekend sailing, or bicycling.

Almost all Seattle weather is as temperate as its rainfall. The temperature crests into the 90° F. range only about twice each summer, while the average winter's maximum fails to reach 32° on just two days. (Overnight frosts occur an average of 15 times downtown, 40 in the open suburbs.)

There is a dry season. When the year lives up to the averages, only five July days see rain, and only six in August. Between them, these two months have 22 of the city's annual ration of 71 cloudless days.

Winter visitors must know that it can snow. Seattle, all hills, gets its snow wet. When packed it becomes slippery; a great many cars are left in awkward places by demoralized owners.

Highways. Interstate Highway 5 slices Seattle in half along its long, skinny north-south axis. The freeway is nonstop except during the rush hours. Beyond all doubt I-5 is the most efficient way into the city from Vancouver, British Columbia, to the north, or Portland, Oregon, to the south.

Approaching Seattle from the east, Interstate 90 is a freeway as far as the Lake Washington Floating Bridge. From there it dwindles to expressway and finally to four-lane city street (Dearborn Avenue) just before its link with I-5 on the south edge of the main business district.

From the Seattle-Tacoma International Airport (Sea-Tac), I-405 cuts east to an intersection with I-5 for traffic bound downtown. I-405 then loops around the east side of Lake Washington, rejoining I-5 some miles north of the city. This route is a good bypass for anyone wishing to avoid congestion on the downtown stretches of I-5. Fast, frequent bus service on I-405 and I-5 links the airport with a downtown terminal at Sixth Avenue and Seneca Street.

See additional maps on pages 12 and 28.

# of Seattle

Aside from these interstate freeways, Seattle has few expressways. For north-south traffic, old U.S. Highway 99 (now State Highway 99) can be a useful alternative to I-5. It is called Marginal Way in the industrial south end of the city, the Alaskan Way Viaduct in midcity, and Aurora Avenue in the residential-commercial north end.

Crosstown traffic gets along on arterial streets. The downtown area is a grid of one-way streets.

The city and all of sprawling King County are served by a unified bus system, Metro Transit, that not only serves the downtown area, but has routes leading well into the Cascades.

Accommodations. Seattle's major hotels cluster together on or close to Fifth Avenue in the main shopping district. To the north, between that district and the Seattle Center—site of the 1962 Seattle World's Fair—are several sizable motels. Smaller, more modest motels string out still farther to the north along Aurora Avenue. The largest of Seattle's motels—several of them—flank Seattle-Tacoma International Airport on old U.S. 99. The only other sizable group of suburban motels is in the town of Bellevue, near exits from I-405.

But this does not exhaust the list by any means. One large, luxury motel perches on a waterfront pier. The University of Washington district has a large hotel and several smaller motels. However, no districts but those noted above have concentrated accommodations giving a range of choices.

The Urban Core

Although Seattle stretches almost 20 miles south to north, its urban attractions cluster together in a remarkably compact core area.

The center of the business and downtown shopping district can be placed at Fifth Avenue and Pine Street. Four major hotels and several fine restaurants are within 4 blocks. Most of the city's old-line luxury shops are on Fifth, or just off it. Several first-run motion picture houses are also in this neighborhood.

From Fifth and Pine, the Seattle Center is but 9 blocks north (and brought closer by the nonstop, 15-cents-a-ride monorail connecting the two points). Revitalized Pioneer Square and spanking-new Kingdome are only 12 and 17 blocks south, respectively. The grand old Pike Place Market lies a mere 5 blocks west, with the waterfront 3 blocks beyond it.

Most of this area is served free by Metro Transit buses. All riders board free. Those who debark within the "Magic Carpet" zone pay nothing. The boundaries are Stewart and Jackson streets, the waterfront, and Sixth Avenue.

The Seattle Center

Though the spiritual legacy of Expo 1962 pervades all Seattle, the concrete reminders cluster on the original 74-acre site just north of the main business district. It is one of the great urban attractions in the West and one of the great rainy-day refuges in all the world.

In quick summary, the grounds hold the Space Needle, the Pacific Science Center, a museum of firefighting, an art museum and gallery, a multicultural food circus, and an amusement park. Here also are the Coliseum (for basketball, trade shows, and popular concerts), the Opera House, the Playhouse, an ice arena, and a high school football stadium.

The handsomely landscaped grounds also hold several heroic fountains—beautiful in any kind of weather but especially heartening in the rain, when they give Seattleites a definite sense of fighting back.

The Space Needle has a lofty observation deck (520 feet above the ground) and a revolving restaurant almost as high. Both are reached by a high-speed toll elevator.

The Pacific Science Center is the most diverse and absorbing attraction on the grounds. In a city where the Boeing Company figures largely, it is no particular surprise that aerospace occupies a great proportion of this hands-on museum, but

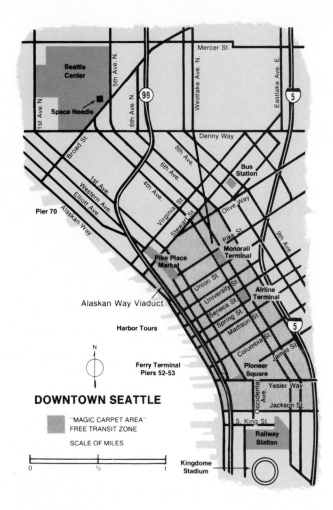

DOWNTOWN SEATTLE

"MAGIC CARPET AREA" FREE TRANSIT ZONE

SCALE OF MILES

0   ½   1

the exhibits also cover other realms of technology, as well as the natural sciences and regional human history.

For nonscientific types, the most reassuring place to start is with a machine that demonstrates the law of probability. This device dumps thousands of balls through a clear-walled maze. Individual balls take crazily bouncing journeys down the vertical labyrinth, yet taken as a whole they always conform precisely to a curve painted on the wall. It makes anything believable.

The art museum here is the modern art division of the Seattle Art Museum. For further notes on the museum, the opera, and other cultural activities, see page 18.

The center maintains a general information telephone number, 625-4234, from 8 A.M. to 9 P.M.

Pike Place Market

Slowly but inevitably, Seattle's Pike Place Market is changing. From its founding in 1907 through the 1950s, it was a classic street market after the European model. Scores of farmers from truck gardens in the rich river valleys south of town

rented stalls at 25 cents a day at the foot of Pike Street and sold fresh produce to downtown office workers. Fish and meat markets added their wares. A handful of offbeat restaurants fed the farmers and their customers from dawn through the lunch hour. A sparse scattering of secondhand stores filled in the nooks and crannies.

Now the truck gardens are nearly all gone, replaced by suburban housing. The main market building is part produce market, part flea market, and part arts and crafts fair. Other buildings facing the market contain sophisticated shops—a bookstore, a wine merchant, a game and toy shop—all handsomely housed because of a thoughtful renewal project for the whole district.

Though things aren't what they used to be, the rambling market building remains a good place for kids to find out about unusual vegetables and meats, as well as some of the more curious edibles from the sea. Its maze of ramps and stairs makes it a great place for losing mothers for a while.

Like the Seattle Center, the market was planned for the rainy climate. You can explore for hours under a single roof, and for hours more under another roof just across the street.

The Waterfront

Seattle, like San Francisco, has two waterfronts: the old one, built for the smaller ships of an earlier day, is turning into a superior recreational resource, while the newer, working waterfront hides away farther from the visitor's city.

Seattle's recreational waterfront stretches from Pier 48 to Pier 70—roughly from the lower end of the main business district north to the top end. It is less than a mile from the major downtown hotels. The stroll from one end to the other offers diverse charms in a short distance.

Pier 48 belongs to the Alaska Ferries. The information office there provides arrival and departure schedules. (Don't assume that you can buy passage on a whim; advance reservations are required.) A park dedicated to Alaska fronts the pier.

Next door, at the foot of Washington Street, is a public boat landing.

On Pier 51, Ye Olde Curiosity Shop bulges with souvenirs. It also has museum-quality Indian and Eskimo art and artifacts.

The Washington State Ferries have their headquarters at Pier 52, which is also the dock for the Bremerton (see page 47) and Bainbridge Island (see page 48) runs. For a complete roster of ferry routes, see page 36.

Adjoining Pier 54 is Firehouse 5, home to Seattle's fireboats and to a small museum of local firefighting. The fireboats stage weekly pumping drills just off the pier, usually on Monday mornings.

Salmon . . . King of Washington's Sport Fish

The salmon in all its varieties is one of nature's great enigmas, and in most of those varieties is one of the most delicious fish in the world.

The salmon is anadromous, which is to say it spawns in fresh water but swims most of its adult life in salt water. That is not so uncommon. However, the Pacific salmon virtually disappears from the time it hatches and drifts down to the sea to the time it returns—2 to 5 years later—as an adult fish ready to spawn in its turn. It is known that the schools swim vast distances, but the exact routes are unknown.

The other peculiarity of this fish is that it spawns only once, inevitably dying as the concluding gesture of spawning. When it does spawn, it chooses the precise place of its birth, down to a matter of feet in a natural stream. How salmon find their own source is not known exactly, but it appears to have some relationship to the exact chemical composition of the home water. They seem to smell their way home. Hatchery fish can be observed trying to swim into inlet pipes bringing water into the pond from which they hatched.

Five species are commonly found in Washington waters. They are known to science by their common Russian names. *Orcorhynchus tschawytscha* is the great Chinook (also known as king, tyee, spring, and quinnat). This is the largest of salmon, averaging 20 pounds but capable of thrice that weight. The other great edible salmon is *O. kisutch*, better known as the silver or coho. In addition to these there are the pink (also called the humpie), the sockeye (also called red), and chum (also called dog salmon because the Indians of old reserved it for dog food). Fishermen also refer to the blackmouth, but it is an immature Chinook.

The great seasons for fishermen are winter and spring, when the fish gather from all across the Pacific for their annual spawning runs up dozens of rivers, but especially the Columbia. However, man is spreading the season out to a year-round one through unseasonal releases of hatchery-raised fish which do not follow the migratory patterns of fish released in the natural cycle, but stay in Puget Sound.

Inland saltwater areas east of the entrance to the Strait of Juan de Fuca are open to fishing the year around. The sheltered waters are calm even in winter. From November through April, schools of salmon mill around and feed in the areas around the Strait, the San Juan Islands, and Puget Sound, including Hood Canal and Elliott Bay directly in front of Seattle.

Both Chinook and coho are in these regions in winter. Typically, their weights range from a couple of pounds for coho and yearling Chinooks up to 20 pounds for 4th-year Chinooks.

Outside the Strait and along the Pacific Coast of Washington, the ocean season begins in May and extends through June.

The great spring runs of spawning fish bring coho in the 4 and 5-pound range and Chinooks weighing as much as 40 pounds. (Once in a while, somebody brings in a giant Chinook at 60, even 70 pounds.)

Westport and Ilwaco are the two great ports for charter boats working the Columbia River runs. They are supplemented by small fleets at Tokeland and Ocean Shores. Upcoast, small charter fleets operate at LaPush, Neah Bay, Sekiu, and Port Angeles. These latter also offer small rental boats called kickers for near-shore fishing.

Inside Puget Sound there are few charter boats, but many opportunities to rent kickers. Particularly active spots are Ballard and West Seattle in Seattle, Hansville on the Kitsap Peninsula, Anacortes, and the San Juan resorts. Most of the shoreside cities north of Seattle on Puget Sound have at least one marina with rental boats.

Day-trip charters run from $20 to $30 per person, with rental gear available for a small extra charge. Kickers with outboards usually rent for $25 a day, give or take a few dollars.

Washington does not require a license for salmon, but anglers must have in their possession a punch card (obtainable at most sporting goods stores and marinas).

Bag limits and seasonal closures of waters are strictly enforced. Also, there are some underwater marine parks closed at all times. Any angler should have a current copy of *Sportfishing Regulations for Salmon, Shellfish and Other Foodfish*, available along with punch cards or by writing the Washington Department of Fisheries, 115 General Administration Building, Olympia 98504.

Salmon also may be taken in certain freshwater lakes and streams; the seasonal closures and boundaries of these are quite complex, but are described in the pamphlet.

Pier 55 contains a ship's chandlery.

Pier 56, at the foot of Seneca Street, is the home dock of Seattle Harbor Tour boats. In addition to conventional tours of the old waterfront and the newer working one, the company operates two excursions daily to Blake Island, where an Indian style salmon bake is the main attraction of a visit to Tillicum Village.

Pier 57 is a waterfront park and public fishing pier. The deck has holes cut in it for drop-line artists. An old barge hull floats alongside for those who wish to get close to their work. Indoor and outdoor benches and picnic tables make this an excellent point to tarry.

Next door, Pier 59 houses Seattle's aquarium, opened in 1977. Designed to get people alongside fish in their natural habitat, the aquarium became an instant local success. It is worth waiting in line for if that's necessary. Hours are 9 A.M. to dusk.

After a spate of working piers comes Pier 69, home to *Princess Marguerite*, the British Columbia Ferry System's day boat to Victoria and back. It runs throughout the summer season, May through Labor Day. The *Marguerite* is a most agreeable environment in itself; Victoria, though no longer the isolated bit of Olde England it was two decades ago, is still a matchless change of pace.

Pier 70, the most northerly of the publicly accessible piers, is a complex of specialty shops and restaurants at the foot of Elliott Avenue.

Other shops and restaurants are threaded all along the route.

A large metered parking area adjoins Pier 70. Metered parking is also available all along the waterfront beneath the Alaskan Way Viaduct. Pier 70 has garage parking. All these areas are not enough on a fine summer's day, but the walk from town is not far for anyone in reasonably good physical condition.

The newer, working waterfront does not lend itself well to visits. The harbor tour provides closer views than any from the landward side, but the persistently curious can get a fairly clear picture of the container terminals from Spokane Street below the viaduct leading to West Seattle from Old U.S. 99.

Pioneer Square: History Revived

Pioneer Square was the heart of Seattle in its rowdiest days—the era of the Alaska Gold Rush.

Variety is Seattle's spice
The clustered skyscrapers downtown and the looming heights of Mt. Rainier guarantee a mix of urbanity and the outdoors.

The fledgling city began to grow on that spot much earlier, when Henry Yesler's mill gave rise to the original definition of "skid road": a road on which logs were skidded to a mill. With the gold rush, Pioneer Square grew into the sort of place where a political quarrel could be settled on the street with pistols, where a great vaudeville circuit—the Pantages—would be born, and, finally, where stolid burghers preferred not to go.

As a new, more sober city center emerged uptown, Pioneer Square developed the secondary, more durable definition of "skid road": a quarter for derelicts.

But today, after a long, drab interim, the ornate buildings are full of life again. Though by gentler modern definition there is a hint of rowdiness at times, the main purposes of contemporary Pioneer Square are distinctive shopping and eating.

Nearly 100 businesses belong to the Pioneer Square Association, with restaurants leading in numbers. Art galleries, bookstores, and antique, home furnishing, and apparel shops are plentiful. Also on the roster are such esoteric specialties as a kite store, a player piano shop, and an antique card shop.

The quarter encompasses the 12 square blocks from the waterfront east to Second Avenue, and from South King Street north to Yesler Way. Bits and pieces lap over those boundaries, however, especially on the north. A map showing the location of each member firm in the association is available in most shops in the quarter.

One bit of the old days still remains, though it cannot accurately be said to live. The original buildings were built in a boggy spot, and the current streets and structures were simply added on top of the old. Some of the musty, dusty originals can now be seen on a private tour called Seattle Underground. Tours depart from Doc Maynard's Public House, which faces into Pioneer Square proper from First Avenue and Yesler Way. The guides provide a witty, literate history of old Seattle as they lead groups through the dim caverns of another era. There is a charge.

One other touch of nostalgia may be found in the Western Union office at South Main Street and Occidental Avenue, where old-fashioned and brand-new pieces of equipment are on display in the lobby. Would-be telegraphers can have a go at Morse Code on a sending key.

The Pioneer Square region is attractive the year around, but notably so in summer, when several sidewalk cafes blossom and two parks fill up with midday sunbathers, street artists, and leg-weary shoppers glad to see benches. The smaller park is Pioneer Square itself, at First Avenue and Yesler Way. The larger one runs 2 blocks along Occidental Avenue, from South Washington Street to South Jackson.

The Kingdome

For major events, as many as 60,000 people crowd into the King County Domed Stadium, or, as it is more commonly called, the Kingdome. But even when nothing is going on, the giant stadium on the south edge of the Pioneer Square district attracts a considerable flow of visitors.

The management runs three tours daily, unless events conflict. For a modest fee, the 45-minute tour rambles through the structure, then pauses for a leisurely look at a sports museum.

The Asian Community

Officially it is the International District. Informally (and inaccurately) it is Chinatown. By whatever name, the area just east of the Kingdome—from Sixth Avenue South to Eighth Avenue, and from Yesler Way to Weller Street—is home to people from many cultures across the Pacific.

Within these few blocks a diligent looker can find cultural centers and museums, excellent ethnic eating, a farmer's market (Fridays and Saturdays during summer in Hing Hay Park), a fortune cooky factory, a hardware store with Japanese woodworking tools, a one-time gambling den, martial arts emporiums, and—most characteristic—an herbalist or two.

A walking tour departs from the Center for Asian Arts at 622 South Washington Street. For the required reservation, call (206) 624-6342 or write the above address. The ZIP is 98104.

Of particular note for those who decline a formal tour are the Center itself, the Wing Luke Museum at 414 Eighth Avenue South, the International District Arts and Crafts Cooperative at 623 South Jackson Street, and Hing Hay Park at South King Street and Maynard Avenue South.

Proximity to the Kingdome makes the quarter notably handy for diversion and dining before events, but its riches merit more exploration.

Freeway Park

The last of Seattle's central city attractions is pure oasis: a park built across the top of Interstate 5.

Technically, the park is a huge concrete and steel machine, complete with piping systems that deliver irrigation water and nutrients to plants, pump and recirculate fountain waters, and drain away rainwater.

Practically, it is a walker's park, a viewer's park, and a picnicker's park.

A concrete canyon holds a torrential waterfall that drowns out traffic noise. Within concrete retaining walls, trees give shade and lawns give repose. An area of plants in concrete walls—called

Waterfront Park *zigzags along Elliott Bay in spacious counterpoint to Seattle's skyscrapers.*

the Great Box Garden—lies between Sixth and Seventh avenues and between Spring and Seneca streets. The canyon and waterfall is between Seventh and Eighth, and between Seneca and University. A big lawn and children's play area flanks the freeway east of Eighth.

The whole park—5.7 acres—lies close to major hotels and the heart of Seattle's downtown shopping district.

The Neighborhoods

By and large, Seattle lacks exotic neighborhoods. One exception—the Asian quarter—has already been noted. Another is the largely Black neighborhood on First Hill just east of downtown. The only remaining ethnic or national enclave is predominantly Scandinavian Ballard, in the northwest quarter of the city.

For all the lack of exotic quarters, at least two Seattle neighborhoods bear some exploration. Foremost is the University of Washington campus and its environs. Second is the Seattle-Tacoma International Airport and the area around it.

The University of Washington

Like all great university campuses—and this one has one of the largest enrollments of any single campus in the country, some 35,000 students—the University of Washington offers a number of subtle, understated attractions for visitors, not to mention the fiercer joys of a full schedule of Pac-10 athletics.

The sprawling campus is bounded on the south by the Lake Washington Ship Canal, on the east by the lake itself, and on the north by NE 45th Street. The western boundary is 15th Avenue NE, which runs parallel to (and not far from) I-5.

Old grads seeking to stroll down memory lane will find their progress oft impeded by buildings they do not remember. Large expanses of one-time lawn have given way to new halls. Still, this campus remains beautiful enough and architecturally interesting enough to merit a leisurely stroll before or after a visit to some specific attraction.

A visitor center at NE 40th Street and University Way will furnish information (operating hours of museums, calendars of events) and a walker's map. Some public parking is available in the northwest corner of campus, along the 17th Avenue entrance off of NE 45th Street.

In the northwest corner of the campus, the Thomas Burke Memorial–Washington State Museum focuses upon men and beasts of the Pacific Rim and the often shaky ground they live on. Exhibits combining zoology and geology reach back in time to the age of dinosaurs. The view of humanity is not as long but emphasizes early times.

Not far away, the Ethnic Cultural Center and Theater has public displays, mainly of contemporary materials by or about American Indians, Asian Americans, Blacks, and Chicanos.

Henry Art Gallery rounds out the list of museums on campus. It houses a permanent collection of 19th century and older paintings donated by the philanthropist for whom the museum is named. It also has contemporary works in every medium by established regional artists, faculty, and students. Its collection of tactile arts for the blind is among its most prized.

Also on campus are three theaters run by the School of Drama. One of these was the first theater-in-the-round in the U.S.

University property also contains two great gardens (see page 25) and the athletic plant (see page 21).

One block west of campus, University Avenue runs parallel to the west boundary. From NE 42nd Street north to NE 47th Street, "the Ave" and its cross streets are the commercial center and one of the social centers of student life. Here is a useful observation point for the latest youthful fashions in clothing, food, music, and movies. Its plethora of new and used bookstores is unequaled elsewhere in the city, although Shorey's on Pike Street has the greatest single collection.

Seattle-Tacoma International Airport

Like most modern metropolitan airports, Sea-Tac has developed a world of its own. As a hub for business travelers, the terminal has given rise to a ring of major motels, restaurants, and other amenities for travelers. A sizable residential population nearby has produced a gigantic shopping center—Southgate—less than 3 miles away. Finally, several nearby parks offer salt-water beaches, tennis, and other ways to stay fit.

The terminal itself is not without interest. It contains a permanent collection of 16 art works in media ranging from sculpture to light-and-sound. (A catalog with map is available at the information booth in the central lobby.) In addition to the art, semipermanent displays treat such subjects as pioneer travel. The airport also has a meditation room, which is both that and a peaceful refuge from page calls and canned music for those who do not meditate formally. Last, there is an automated subway train linking the main and satellite terminals. A great many children enjoy the train more than the airplanes.

Sea-Tac flanks Pacific Highway South—old U.S. 99—between South 154th Street and South 188th Street. The direct entrance to the terminal is from the highway. A connector road joins the terminal with I-405.

South Center, with more than 100 stores and shops, includes major retail stores and specialized boutiques among its diverse businesses. It is located in the intersection formed by I-5 and I-405, slightly more than 2 miles east of the airport.

As recreation in the area, the beach parks are Ed Munro Seahurst and Saltwater State Park (see page 24). Tyee Valley Golf Course is just south of the landing strip (see page 26). For tennis players, three county courts and, right next to them, three high school campus courts are located on South 188th Street near I-5.

Scattered Points of Interest

Seattle and its suburbs offer a number of small enchantments: offbeat museums, industrial tours, and kindred enterprises.

Chateau Ste. Michelle faithfully re-creates the facade of a French wine chateau. Behind the facade lies an up-to-date winemaking facility, Washington's largest and one of its most prestigious. A well-planned tour explains every step of winemaking, from picking grapes to corking bottles. The last stop is a tasting room. Tours run daily during business hours.

A small picnic lawn is in one corner of the handsomely landscaped grounds.

The winery is near the town of Woodinville, northeast of Seattle. The simplest route is on I-405 to the State 522 exit, east less than a mile on 522 to the Woodinville exit, then south for slightly more than a mile on State 202.

All the grapes for Ste. Michelle wines come from the east side of the Cascades.

The Rainier Brewery, maker of other distinctive fermented beverages, is open for tours and tasting daily during business hours. The brewery is in the industrial south end of Seattle, at 3100 Airport Way South. (Airport Way South parallels Interstate 5; the brewery is near Exit 163A.)

The Museum of Science and Industry, near the University of Washington campus, is just off Montlake Boulevard on the south side of the Lake Washington Ship Canal. It harbors diverse reminders of Seattle history, from the tools of pioneer doctors ("instruments" is too fine a word) to the unlimited hydroplane *Slo-Mo-Shun.* The museum also houses the Boeing Company's first airplane. (None of Boeing's Seattle installations have tours, but the 747 assembly plant near Everett does; see page 40.)

The museum is also the departure point for a nature trail that winds along the edge of Lake Washington and out onto marshy islands. The trail extends into the University of Washington Arboretum (see page 25).

An entirely different shoreline presents itself toward the west end of the ship canal, first at Salmon Bay Terminal, then at Chittenden Locks.

Salmon Bay Terminal is home port to both small boats that work local waters and to big trawlers that go north to Alaska's salmon-rich seas. As a working port, it remains an unvarnished and honest site for watching how a commercial fisherman goes about readying his craft for a trip, and what is involved in cleaning up on return to port. Not infrequently the piers are covered with gear in varying stages of repair. The variety of vessel designs is always a treat to the eye. Access to the terminal is from 15th Avenue West, at the south end of the Ballard Bridge across the ship canal.

Chittenden Locks comes more under the heading of a social experience. At 825 feet long by 80 feet wide, and with a maximum lift of 26 feet, Chittenden handles an astonishing 78,000 vessels each year. For sheer numbers, late afternoon on a summer weekend is the time to go. Then harried lockkeepers load the huge trough as full as they can

get it of everything from outboards to regal sailboats for each operation of the locks. A good day's work is 1,200 vessels. The wide range of skills among skippers brings about wider ranges of emotion as the jostling gets tighter and tighter. Visitors can look directly down into the locks from either side or from the walkways across the tops of the lock gates themselves. Those who would live the experience can find rental boats at several locations (see page 31).

At one side of the locks is a modern fish ladder, through which a highly visible salmon run passes each fall en route to spawning grounds in the Cedar River.

Also on the locks' grounds is an exotic garden (see page 25).

NW Market Street leads through Ballard to a parking lot at the main entrance to the grounds.

Waterfront Park, across Lake Washington in the suburban community of Kirkland, offers one last chance to look at ships. Its focal point is the old three-masted schooner *Wawona,* a 136-footer designed to carry huge cargoes with small crews. Her supporting cast includes an ancient tug—the *Arthur Foss*—and the lightship *Relief.* The vessels are open for visiting June through September, noon until 5 P.M. weekdays, later weekends. There is a nominal admission fee.

Central Way leads from the I-405 exit marked Kirkland directly to the moorage.

The historic vessels are only part of an extensive lakefront park that otherwise includes swimming beaches, fishing piers, picnic sites, and lawns scaled for Frisbee throwing.

Getting back and forth across Lake Washington is done, for the most part, on a pair of floating bridges. The older and more southerly one, Lake Washington Floating Bridge, has no toll. The more northerly Evergreen Point Floating Bridge, relatively new, still carries a modest toll.

Northwesterners have long since gotten used to the idea of bridges that float on the water instead of soaring above it, but outlanders still approach these bridges gingerly. The system is simple enough—the bridges float on air-filled concrete pontoons.

Casual drives across the bridges are best scheduled to avoid rush hours.

Art, Music, Theater

Seattle is no longer the city Sir Thomas Beecham so confidently called a "cultural dustbin." Beginning with its much-praised World's Fair of 1962, Seattle has built a substantial community of performing artists to go with an old, established group

Timely and timeless

A shiny new uptown skyscraper (below) coexists quite happily with a row of revitalized brick buildings in Pioneer Square, the heart of early Seattle, and not so far from being its heart again in an era when urban planning favors rehabilitation over the bulldozer. Pike Place Market is another enchanting legacy of an earlier Seattle . . . and a matchless place to learn how to shop (left).

Washington's Clams

One good thing about clams is steaming them in a bucket over a beach fire, dipping them in butter, and eating them right there. Another good thing, with larger species, is canning ground clam meat for thick, steaming winter-night chowders. But one of the best things about clams is digging them.

Clam digging on Washington's sheltered beaches is a vigorous but safe exercise for a loner, a picnic crowd, or a family of all ages. There are enough different kinds of clams on enough different kinds of beaches to guarantee some digging to anybody who can get to a representative strip of salt-water beach. Even some Seattle-area beaches still hold clam populations, though the richest beds are now farther afield.

The equipment consists of a gunny sack or other carrying device, sneakers, and a rake, hoe, trowel, or shovel—depending on the species sought. A caisson—a metal ring to shore up the sides of a deep hole while digging—may prove useful. A change of clothes for later is a good idea.

Shovels are the usual tool for digging in sandy or muddy beaches. Rakes, hoes, and trowels serve more efficiently in gravel.

All digging is most productive on minus tides, from 1 hour before low tide to 1 hour after. It is possible to dig on any low tide, but easily reached beds usually are kept thinly populated.

Although Washington does not require a license for shellfish, the state does impose bag limits. Also, some areas are seasonal, mostly because of possible red tide poisoning. Every digging party should have a current copy of *Sportfishing Regulations for Salmon, Shellfish and Other Foodfish* from the Washington Department of Fisheries, 115 General Administration Building, Olympia 98504.

The following is a roster of commonly dug clams from Puget Sound and the Strait of Juan de Fuca, and also Grays and Willapa harbors.

Bent-nosed clam. Averaging 2 inches across, it is tough, and often can be found where other varieties cannot endure. It inhabits muddy bays. It can be raked out or dug with shovels. Most are found at a 6 to 8-inch depth. The meat has a good flavor; use it whole in bouillabaisse or other stews, or chopped in chowder. (If used whole, it needs 2 days in salt water to flush mud from its stomach.)

Gaper clam. More commonly known as the horse clam or horseneck in the Northwest, it weighs as much as 3 pounds. It lives in firm, clean bay sand, usually at a depth of 2 feet or more. Its long siphon can retract quickly from the surface, giving the impression that it is digging down. It must be dug with a shovel. In wet sand a caisson may be needed to shore up the edges of a hole long enough to get down to the shell. The siphon is the edible part; its tough layer of skin must be peeled away before cooking. Most people grind or dice the meat.

Geoduck. (pronounced *gooey-duck*). Largest of Washington's clams, it ranges from a modest 3 pounds up to a record 10. It lives in muddy bay bottoms, frequently near or in eel grass, at depths ranging to 3 feet. Like the gaper, it retracts a long siphon when disturbed. Holes must be supported by caissons. The meat is much like that of the gaper.

Razor. Washington's great coastal clam, the razor, is described on page 68.

Rock cockle. Ranging up to 2 inches across, it lives in bays all along the coast, frequently near the mouth, usually in gravel. It lives at a depth of 2 to 8 inches. Rakes work in fine gravel; trowels are useful where gravel mixes with larger rock. This is the steamed clam of northwest restaurants, and that is the way it tastes best. Locally it is sometimes known as the littleneck.

Softshell clam. It burrows in muddy bays—ones still enough for the tideflats to be malodorous. The clam must be dug with gentle horizontal swipes of a shovel to avoid crushing the delicate shell. It is a clam for stews, requiring cleaning and skinning to be pleasant in flavor.

Washington clam. Also called the Martha Washington, this sweet-meated clam grows to 5 inches across, lives in slightly muddier sand than the gaper (see above) at a depth of 8 inches or slightly more. It is most efficiently dug with a shovel. The meat is tasty enough to steam, but the slick texture causes it to be more likable in chowders or other stews.

The Department of Fisheries (address above) offers a fine set of maps showing publicly accessible Puget Sound beaches and their possible edibles (clams, oysters, crabs, etc.). These maps are excellent planning aids.

of painters. Today, galleries, museums, theaters, and music halls both great and small dot the city and its suburbs.

Art

The city has several fine museums and a remarkable number of art galleries.

Seattle Art Museum, in Volunteer Park at 14th Avenue East and East Prospect Street, has major collections of Asian art. According to some collectors, its finest jade pieces are unparalleled in any other collection on the North American continent. The museum also has works by major Pacific northwest painters, including Mark Tobey.

Seattle Art Museum Pavilion, in Seattle Center, is essentially the contemporary art wing of the Seattle Art Museum. An attached gallery sells regional art.

Frye Art Museum, 704 Terry Avenue (Terry is the equivalent of 10th Avenue) houses the collection of 18th and 19th-century European and American paintings gathered and donated by Charles and Emma Frye. The museum also hosts traveling exhibits.

Pacific Northwest Arts Center, at 95 Yesler Way in the Pioneer Square district, is a museum of Northwestern arts of all sorts, from prehistoric to contemporary.

In addition to these centers, the Henry Art Gallery and the Thomas Burke Memorial—Washington State Museum house fine art. Both are on the University of Washington Campus (see page 17).

The largest group of galleries in the city is in the Pioneer Square area; they focus particularly, but not exclusively, on northwest Indian and Eskimo art.

Music

Opera leads the league in Seattle music, but it is far from alone.

The Seattle Opera Association maintains a regular season through the winter, ending in May. Then, in July, the company produces a Wagner Festival in both German and English. All performances take place in the Opera House at the Seattle Center. For schedule and ticket information, write P.O. Box 9248, Seattle 98109. Telephone: (206) 447-4752.

The Seattle Symphony Orchestra also performs its annual series of concerts in the Seattle Center Opera House. For years the symphony has enjoyed a fine reputation (and recording contracts) as a polished small orchestra. For information: 305 Harrison Street, Seattle 98109. Telephone: (206) 447-4752.

The city's universities and colleges, particularly the University of Washington, have active schedules of music by groups ranging from string quartets to symphony orchestras. The University of Washington information number is (206) 543-4880.

Classic and symphonic music aside, Seattle also has a long friendship with jazz. Medium oldtimers may remember a saxophonist named Corky Corcoran or a fine piano player named Elmer Gill. In the 1940s, both lived and played in Seattle when not on tour with big bands. Pony Poindexter spent some of the 1950s in Seattle. And such talented locals as Gerald Brashears never left home.

The best places for visitors to find out what is going on in local jazz clubs are the Friday newspapers. The morning *Post-Intelligencer* has a section called "206"; the afternoon *Times* has one called "Tempo." Both outline the weekend entertainment scene.

Theater

Seattle supports two professional repertory companies.

A Contemporary Theater (ACT) presents its season in a theater near the Seattle Center grounds. The location of the theater and the source of ticket information is 709 First Avenue West, Seattle 98119. Telephone: (206) 285-3220.

Seattle Repertory Theater, an old-line local company, performs in The Playhouse on the Seattle Center grounds. The company also operates a downtown theater, Second Stage. For information: 225 Mercer Street, Seattle 98109. Telephone: (206) 447-4764.

University of Washington student actors have three on-campus stages to work from. The Penthouse, the first theater-in-the-round built as such in the U.S., is still in regular use. The school also has a Showboat Theater patterned after an old riverboat, and one conventional proscenium arch theater. The University information number is (206) 543-4880.

Spectator Sports

After years of living or dying with the University of Washington Huskies, Seattle has recently acquired a number of professional franchises to spread the living and dying around. The city has also acquired a domed stadium that makes the process very comfortable.

On game day, tickets for any sport can be hard to come by in a sports-minded city. Writing ahead for seats is usually a good idea.

The National Basketball Association's Seattle Supersonics play their home schedule in the Coliseum, on the Seattle Center grounds. For ticket information: 221 West Harrison Street, Seattle 98109. Telephone: (206) 281-3450.

The World Team Tennis Sea-Port Cascades play the Seattle half of their home schedule in the Coliseum. For information: 300 Vine Street, Seattle 98111. Telephone: (206) 622-3943.

The North American Soccer League's Seattle Sounders play in the Kingdome. Mailing address for ticket information is 300 Metropole Building, Seattle 98104. Telephone: (206) 628-3454.

The National Football League's Seattle Seahawks play in the Kingdome. Mailing address is 5305 Lake Washington Boulevard, Kirkland 98033. Telephone: (206) 827-9766.

The American League's Seattle Mariners play baseball in the domed stadium. Mailing address is P.O. Box 411, Seattle 98104. Telephone: (206) 628-3300.

University of Washington football and basketball teams compete in the Pacific-10. The football stadium and basketball pavilion are adjacent to each other on the campus, along Montlake Boulevard just north of the Lake Washington Ship Canal. Mailing address is Intercollegiate Athletic Ticket Office, Tubby Graves Building, University of Washington, Seattle 98105. Telephone: (206) 543-2200.

Seattle University's Chieftains basketball team competes as a member of the West Coast Athletic Conference, playing home games in a gym on campus. For information: Athletic Department, Seattle University, 550 Fourteenth Avenue, Seattle 98112. Telephone: (206) 626-5305.

Finally, among the collegians, Seattle Pacific College's basketball teams compete effectively in the NCAA small schools division. The home court is on the Seattle Pacific campus, near the Lake Washington Ship Canal. For information: Athletic Department, Seattle Pacific College, Third Avenue West and West Nickerson, Seattle 98119. Telephone: (206) 281-2085.

These schools also compete in spring sports. The most notable events are eight-oared crew races, in which Washington's Huskies are perennial power-houses. Baseball, track, and tennis are also scheduled by one or more of the three schools. Tickets for these events are no problem. Schedule information is available at the addresses noted above.

Stylish cap for a freeway

In an ingenious recapture of green space, Seattle built almost 6 acres of downtown park atop Interstate 5.

Seattle Outdoors

Seattle does not have a great, all-in-one urban playground to compare with Vancouver's Stanley Park or Tacoma's Point Defiance. As a whole, however, Seattle's 5,000-acre system—consisting of 400 separate parks—has no match in the region. Coupled with nearby suburban municipal parks and the ranging King County system, Seattle's parks leave out virtually no type of terrain or outdoor activity.

Family picnic parks

Each quarter of the city has one excellent picnic park with varied attractions for whole families.

Two potentially great Seattle parks are now in their beginning stages. Both are "retired" military installations.

Much of what used to be Fort Lawton is now Discovery Park. For the moment (1978) it offers fine beach walks and a fitness course modeled on the European parcourse.

The old Sand Point Naval Air Station is also on its way to becoming a major park. The Seattle Parks & Recreation Department can provide up-to-date information on both sites.

Woodland Park, the most diverse of all Seattle's family outing parks, is also among the city's handiest for visitors. Within its spacious confines are a zoo, an old-fashioned rose garden, abundant picnic grounds, and courts and fields for all manner of games. Adjoining Green Lake has swimming beaches, rental boats, kids' fishing piers, and the city's most popular jogging and bicycling path.

The park straddles Aurora Avenue between North 50th and North 59th streets. The zoo and rose garden are in upper Woodland, west of Aurora. The picnic areas and sports fields are in lower Woodland, east of Aurora. Green Lake flanks lower Woodland.

Gasworks Park, on the north shore of Lake Union, might be the first choice of families with kids of grammar school age who need to blow off steam. The park is literally an old gas works. Much of the old machinery has been cleaned and painted so children can crawl on, in, and through it. The gear is covered by a roof. So is a small cluster of picnic tables.

The park's other attraction is a fine kite hill, which looks right into the Seattle Police Department's busy heliport. (The hill is good for rolling down, too.)

Gasworks is slightly more than a mile closer to downtown than Woodland Park–Green Lake, and almost a mile east of Aurora Boulevard.

Seward Park is Seattle's greatest recreational resource on Lake Washington. A peninsula, it has flat play lawns and swimming beaches at its base, but toward its outer end it is hilly and wooded. An expansive picnic area hides, serene, up in the woods. A trout hatchery within the park is open to visitors. The shoreline of the peninsula has pathways for walkers, joggers, and bicyclists. (For the latter, a narrow band of lakeshore extends the possibilities 2 miles north, almost to the Lake Washington Floating Bridge. Lake Washington Boulevard provides access along the lake from either north or south.)

Lincoln Park, in West Seattle, has salt-water beaches (and, for the less hardy, a heated saltwater pool), tree-shaded picnic grounds, and a variety of sports courts and fields. Somewhat remote from the rest of the city, Lincoln compensates with an atmosphere at once groomed and unspoiled. The beaches and a bluff above them are serene, more natural than not. The upper levels of the park are landscaped lawns dotted with mature trees.

From the Spokane Street access bridge into West Seattle, Fauntleroy Avenue extends directly to the front gate of the park.

Alki Beach Park. Also in West Seattle, the long beach from Alki Point to Duwamish Head supplements Lincoln Park's shore. This beach yields superb views across Elliott Bay to the downtown skyline and across Puget Sound to the Olympic Mountains. It is also the premier locale in town for beach fire picnics. Divers use the beach as a launch point for forays after diverse quarry, but especially the giant octopus.

A perimeter road around West Seattle hugs the backshore all the way.

Carkeek Park, on Puget Sound near the north city limits, has a beachfront much like Lincoln Park's, but the rest of Carkeek is essentially natural northwest woods. Many hikers use this park as a convenient short-notice retreat or conditioning ground.

Suburban Picnic Parks

Communities around Seattle—especially those on the east side of Lake Washington—are prosperous commuter suburbs but still have a life of their own. Some have excellent shopping centers and other urbane pleasures, yet their great value for visitors to the city is outdoor recreation.

The following brief list names only a few major suburban parks that have enough capacity to accept large crowds.

Ed Munro Seahurst Park, a King County park, is fairly well developed. Much of its front on Puget Sound, near the community of Burien, is a sea

wall—a favorite perch for fishermen. The park also has ample picnic grounds—the usual northwestern blend of open tables with barbecues and sheltered tables with cookstoves. Also on the grounds are a teaching center dealing with marine biology and a fish ladder and holding pond.

The park is located in the vicinity of SW 144th Street. Access requires a detailed local map.

Saltwater State Park, farther south along the Puget Sound shore, has much the same mixture of beach and picnic area, plus some campsites sheltered in trees well inshore. It is the closest state camping park to Seattle.

Luther Burbank Park, another part of the King County system, occupies the northeastern tip of Mercer Island. The park has a day boat moorage, a fishing pier, tennis courts, and a swimming beach. However, its finest feature for parents with grammar-school-age children is a play area of such imagination that it remains memorable to kids a year after they visit. The park is reached from I-90 along North Mercer Way.

Marymoor County Park touches the north end of Lake Sammamish near the town of Redmond. It is not a beach park at all, but rather a vast playground for all ages. Among its facilities are a velodrome, archery ranges, tennis courts, model airplane fields, soccer pitches, softball fields, a museum displaying pioneer folk art, and more.

Lake Sammamish State Park. Sprawling picnic lawns and a fine swimming beach have made this 430-acre unit one of the most heavily used of the Seattle region's summer parks. There is a boat launch for those who would fish the lake, waterski, or otherwise get away from the beachbound throngs.

The park, at the south end of the lake, also is a favorite beginning point for bicyclists riding north to Redmond (see page 25).

Parks Featuring Plants

Seattle's year-round mild climate lends itself to cultivation of a wide range of plants from around the world. Five major public gardens, all in a tidy row across the north end of town, invite thoughtful exploration by people who enjoy plants.

Volunteer Park features a conservatory and fine formal gardens surrounding the Seattle Art Museum. The park also has a water tower with a lofty viewing platform. Plaques on the platform identify principal peaks in both the Olympic and Cascade mountain ranges, and the perspective of the gardens below is a joy to the eye.

The main entrance is on 15th Avenue East at East Galer Street in the Capitol Hill district, south of the Lake Washington Ship Canal, east of I-5.

The University of Washington Arboretum is the greatest treasure trove for serious gardeners. The narrow park fronts on the Lake Washington Ship Canal just across from Husky Stadium, then runs more than a mile south across gently rolling terrain. Lake Washington Boulevard slips through the arboretum, which also has some pokeabout roads of its own.

At the north end of Arboretum Drive East are the offices of the garden, where visitors may pick up a map of the plantings and other information.

The arboretum contains large collections of rhododendrons, azaleas, dogwoods, hollies, magnolias, crabapples, brooms, tree peonies, flowering cherries, and flowering quinces.

Within the arboretum grounds is a 4-acre Japanese tea garden with an authentic tea house. From spring through fall the garden is open daily, 10 A.M. to sunset. In winter it is open on weekends only. The modest admission fee goes toward maintenance.

A pharmaceutical garden, across the ship canal on the main campus of the University of Washington, is filled with rare (and mostly toxic) plants such as foxglove, periwinkle, cascara, and horehound, plus such sweet-smelling ones as jasmine, lavender, and mint. The 2 acres of garden, enclosed by English tea hedge, are between Frosh Pond and the Medical School. For directions and a walking map, go to the University Visitors' Information Center at NE 40th Street and University.

Woodland Park has an extensive collection of old-fashioned roses, along with many newer ones, in a garden just inside the gate at North 50th Street and Fremont Avenue, 2 blocks west of Aurora Avenue. (Also see page 23.)

Chittenden Locks, last but not least, has a collection of well-labeled trees and shrubs on its grounds near the public parking lot. Many of the specimens are Asian exotics gathered since 1940. A six-page leaflet and guide map to the 7-acre garden are available at the gatehouse. The garden is open daily from 7 A.M. to 9 P.M. (For more information about the locks, see page 18.)

Bicycling and Jogging

Seattle and the surrounding communities have done much to make life pleasant for both bicyclists and joggers, who usually share the same routes.

The most popular run-or-ride route in Seattle circles Green Lake. The fairly level, asphalted 3-mile track carries so much traffic that the park department painted a white line down the middle. Signs show which side is for whom.

Not far behind in popularity among joggers is the waterfront. Downtown office workers and

Canoeists paddle *under Waterfront Trail footbridge in the arboretum.*

hotel guests pick up the waterside walkway at a handy point and run north. Beyond the piers, grassy Myrtle Edwards Park extends the run almost 2 miles. (Why, nonjoggers may ask, bother to go down to the waterfront? Because, joggers respond, there are no signal lights or cross streets to break the rhythm.)

The Burke-Gilman hiking and bicycling trail starts at Gasworks Park, on the shore of Lake Union near the University of Washington campus, and runs generally northward all the way to Kenmore's Logboom Park on the Lake Washington shore at NE 145th Street, a jaunt of 12½ miles one way in varied terrain. The surroundings range from shopping districts to open countryside.

Somewhat farther from the central hotel area, Lake Washington Boulevard follows the lakeshore, mostly in parklike surroundings, for several miles from the Lake Washington Floating Bridge south to Seward Park. Although the route is popular with local runners, it is out of the way as a fitness course for visitors. The fine scenery recommends this route to cyclists.

Similarly, a marked and paved bicycle route rims West Seattle's Puget Sound shoreline for several miles around Duwamish Head and out to Alki Point. The marked trail ends there, but lightly traveled local streets make an extended ride to Lincoln Park enjoyable.

Over on the east side of Lake Washington, the town of Redmond became a red-hot center of competitive bicycling early in the 1950s and has never lost its enthusiasm. Like Bellevue, it has a well-developed system of street routes (Bellevue's park department has a fine map), but it also holds two extraordinary pleasures for bicyclists.

The first is a beautifully scenic though dog-ridden road course along Lake Sammamish, leaving Lake Sammamish State Park near I-90 and following the westerly shore to Marymoor County Park at the north end of the lake. The second great place for bicycling is a velodrome in Marymoor Park. When no scheduled competitions are in progress, all comers can get onto the track and enjoy its 25° banked turns.

Four bicycle rental shops are in the region. One is at 7007 Woodlawn Avenue NE near Green Lake; another is at 5026 University Way near the campus. A third is at 2722 Alki Avenue SW in West Seattle. Finally, another shop is at 16205 Redmond Way.

Tennis

Three sizable public tennis centers are in Seattle. A fourth is across the lake in Bellevue.

The major one is a 13-court municipal complex—5 indoor courts, 8 outdoor—at Rainier Avenue and McClellan Street in the southeast quarter of town. (Long-time Pacific Coast League baseball fans will recognize the address as Sicks Stadium. The courts are in what was the parking lot.) The 13 courts built in 1977 are only the first step. Another four indoor and four outdoor courts are to be added soon. The complete plan calls for 30 courts.

Play is by the hour, for a fee; reservations are required.

North of downtown are 10 lighted outdoor courts at Lower Woodland Park, just off West Green Lake Way. Two of these can be reserved; the others are on a first-come basis.

The Seattle Park Department's other major center hides away in West Seattle, across Fauntleroy Avenue from the northeast corner of Lincoln Park. The center has six lighted courts, all outdoors.

The city of Bellevue's park department operates an eight-court tennis center called Robinswood, at 2400 151st Place SE. The courts are in the open air in summer, under bubbles in winter. During winter, play is by the hour for a fee, with reservations required. (Finding Robinswood is a job for a Sherpa. The best bet is to call (206) 455-7690 for reservations and road instructions.)

Six courts are located near Seattle-Tacoma International Airport, on South 188th Street near I-5—three on a high school campus and three in an adjacent county park.

Much of Seattle's tennis is played at private clubs. U.S.T.A. members with reciprocal privileges have seven choices, all listed in local telephone books.

Golf

Seattle has far more golfers than its courses can handle. To get in regular rounds, locals range as far north as Everett and as far south as Tacoma. Still, vacationers who can get out on weekdays can find starting times without undue trouble.

In town are three good municipal courses. Nearby are another 12 courses open to public play.

In town. Jefferson Municipal (18 holes; 6,056 yards; par 70) is on Beacon Avenue south of downtown. Thick trees on a round-backed ridge make the course play longer than the card. West Seattle Municipal (18 holes; 6,054 yards; par 71) is just off Fauntleroy Avenue, the district's main stem. Brushy ravines and rolling terrain make life miserable for hackers. Jackson Park Municipal (18 holes; 6,070 yards; par 71) is just east of I-5 at exit 174, near the north boundary of the city. Thick stands of conifers make this rolling layout the tightest test of the three municipals.

South of town. Four courses come fairly close together. Earlington (18 holes; 5,218 yards; par 69) is a flat course in bottomlands on the opposite side of I-405 from Longacres Race Track. Foster (18 holes; 5,388 yards; par 68) is another low-lying course, but all wrapped up in a curve of the Duwamish River. It is on Interurban Avenue just south of I-5 Exit 156. Maplewood (18 holes; 5,625 yards; par 68) tucks away south of Renton on the Maple Valley Highway. It is hilly in front, flat in back. Tyee Valley (18 holes; 6,100 yards; par 71) is just off old U.S. 99 on South 192nd Avenue, 4 blocks south of Sea-Tac airport. The course rolls through stands of mature trees. It takes real concentration to putt in the shadow of a descending 747.

North of town. Here the roster is short; so are the courses. Brookside (9 holes, 18 tees; 5,800 yards; par 71) is east of Woodinville on NE 156th Street. Wellington Hills (9 holes; 2,735 yards; par 34) is close by State 522, the route from Bothell to Monroe. Wayne (18 holes; 4,812 yards; par 65) flanks Bothell Way at the south city limits of Bothell. The course is physically taxing because of its steep hills and the relentless presence of Sammamish Slough at the bottom of all those hills.

The key to fine boating
Chittenden Locks connect Lake Washington with Puget Sound for 2,000 boaters on any warm weekend.

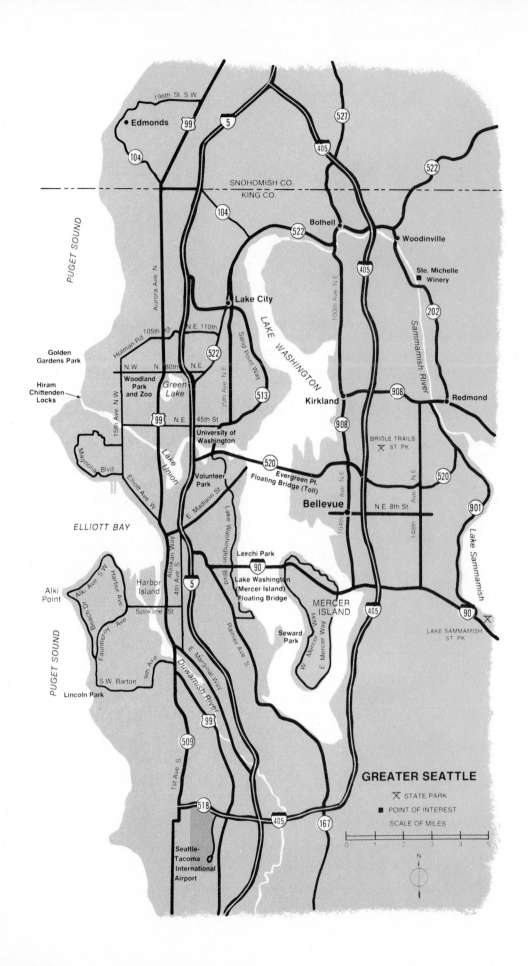

GREATER SEATTLE

✕ STATE PARK

■ POINT OF INTEREST

SCALE OF MILES

N

East of town. Bellevue Municipal (18 holes; 5,800 yards; par 70), on 140th Avenue NE, well north of the main shopping district, rolls gently through mature trees. Village Greens (18 holes; 2,239 yards; par 54) is a gentle, open layout due east of town on 156th Avenue NE. Finally, Redmond Golf Links (18 holes; 5,600 yards; par 69) is pool-table flat and quite open. It is near the main intersection in Redmond, adjacent to Marymoor County Park.

These courses are about as far from downtown Seattle as most visitors to the city would care to go for a casual round. Collectors of golf courses can look slightly farther afield with real profit. The Snoqualmie–North Bend area, on I-90, has some fine courses (Snoqualmie Falls, Tallchief, and three others). Snohomish, on the Stevens Pass Highway, has two of the most challenging layouts in the region (Kenwanda and Snohomish).

The Old-fashioned Pleasures of Fairs

The good old state or county fair continues to be the most colorful and authentic place to see folk arts and crafts. Washington has a full roster of fairs at which pies, preserves, quilting, needlework, and woodwork vie for attention with prize crops and animals. There is no forgetting the tawdry charm of the carnival, either, for it is an equally vital tradition of these happy events.

In Washington, the season begins with the first fair days of spring and does not end until well after the last of the hay is in the barn. Though this roster may not be complete, it does list most of the well-established fairs. To be sure of scheduled dates, it is best to write a regional chamber of commerce or visitor bureau for the current year's information.

APRIL
Asotin County Fair, Asotin, last weekend.

JULY
King County Fair, Enumclaw, 3rd week.
Castle Rock Fair, Castle Rock, last weekend.

AUGUST
Cowlitz County Fair and Rodeo, Longview, 1st week.
Thurston County Fair, Lacey, 1st weekend.
Stanwood Camano Fair, Stanwood, 1st wknd.
Southwest Washington Fair, Chehalis, 2nd week.
Clark County Fair, Ridgefield, 2nd week.
Pierce County Fair, Graham, 2nd weekend.
Skagit County Fair, Mount Vernon, 2nd wknd.
Jefferson County Fair, Port Townsend, 2nd wknd.
Northwest Washington Fair, Lynden, 3rd week.
Yakima Valley Junior Fair, Grandview, 3rd wk.
Grant County Fair & Rodeo, Moses Lake, 3rd week.
Grays Harbor County Fair, Elma, 3rd week.

Wahkiakum County Fair, Skamokawa, 3rd wknd.
San Juan County Fair, Friday Harbor, 3rd wknd.
Mason County Fair, Shelton, 3rd weekend.
Kitsap County Fair and Rodeo, Bremerton, last week.
Benton/Franklin Counties Fair and Rodeo, Kennewick, last week.
Skamania County Fair, Stevenson, last wknd.
Pend Oreille County Fair, Cusick, last weekend.
Island County Fair, Langley, last weekend.
Pacific County Fair, Menlo, last weekend.
Clallam County Fair, Port Angeles, last wknd.
Evergreen State Fair, Monroe, last weekend of August, first week of September.
Southeastern Washington Fair, Walla Walla, last weekend of August, first week September.

SEPTEMBER
Adams County Fair, Ritzville, 1st weekend.
Ferry County Fair, Republic, 1st weekend.
Kittitas County Fair, Ellensburg, 1st weekend.
Lincoln County Fair, Davenport, 2nd weekend.
Chelan County Fair, Cashmere, 2nd weekend.
Okanogan County Fair, Okanogan, 2nd wknd.
Northeastern Washington Fair, Colville, 2nd weekend.
Palouse Empire Fair, Colfax, 2nd weekend.
Columbia County Fair, Dayton, 2nd weekend.
Darrington Community Fair, Darrington, 2nd weekend.
Klickitat County Fair, Goldendale, 2nd wknd.
Spokane Interstate Fair, Spokane, 2nd week.
Adams County Fair, West, Othello, 2nd wknd.
North Central Washington Fair, Waterville, 3rd weekend.
Garfield County Fair, Pomeroy, 3rd weekend.
Western Washington Fair, Puyallup, 3rd week.

OCTOBER
Central Washington State Fair, Yakima, 1st week.

Parks to taste

Seattle's array of city parks ranges from wide open spaces to urbane pockets. Green Lake (above) is one sort, home to child anglers, ducks, joggers, and eight-oared crews. An entirely different approach is Gasworks (right), where scrubbed-up machinery is an almost infinite monkey jungle for kids. Both are north of downtown.

U.S.G.A. members with reciprocal privileges will also find excellent courses among the private clubs in and around Seattle.

Boating

Seattle has as good a claim as anyplace to the title of pleasure boating capital of the world. Its 40 miles of Puget Sound shoreline and 100 miles of lakefront are rife with marinas and private docks, most of them booked to capacity.

For just looking, the huge marina at Shilshole Bay in the Ballard district offers the most convincing panorama. The next largest complex is at Des Moines, a suburb south of the city.

Visitors with their own craft can launch at dozens of public ramps, either on Puget Sound or Lake Washington.

For those who come without, rentals can be had in all sizes and styles.

Canoes can be rented at Green Lake (next to Evans Pool on East Green Lake Way) for leisurely paddling on that small surface, or at the University of Washington Canoe House (just behind the football stadium) for more ambitious exploring in the channels to the north or the marshy lagoons across the mouth of the ship canal.

On Lake Union, a boathouse at 2770-C Westlake Avenue North rents rowboats for tours of that industrial waterfront or sailboats for deep-water cruises. Nearby, two other marinas also rent sailboats. One is at 2470 Westlake Avenue North, the other at 2148 Westlake North.

On the Puget Sound side, marinas with sailboats for rent are at 3030 West Commodore Way near Fort Lawton and in Ballard at 7001 Seaview Avenue NW. Lake Washington's sailboat rental marina is at 130 Lakeside Avenue, near the foot of Yesler Way.

Water skiers looking for powerful runabouts can rent them at 4500 Lake Washington Boulevard South, near Seward Park, or at 8th and Waterway in Renton, the suburb at the southern tip of Lake Washington.

Fishermen, who have less need for speed, can rent salt-water outboards in Ballard (6049 Seaview Avenue NW, 5503 Seaview NW), in West Seattle (1660 Harbor Avenue SW), or in the southerly suburb of Des Moines (22634 6th Avenue South). For freshwater fishing in Lake Washington, the resource is, again, 4500 Lake Washington Boulevard South.

Fishing

Washington State's famous fishing waters lie well away from Seattle, but the city has some reasonably productive areas, both fresh and salt water, right at its doorstep.

Elliott Bay, the water directly off the waterfront, is a fair source of blackmouth salmon (immature Chinooks up to 20 pounds) during the winter months. It takes a hardy soul to venture out in the dawn light of a chill, ofttimes rainy day in an open outboard.

Ballard's Shilshole Bay has some salmon in its offshore waters.

More casual anglers can work for perch, flounder, and other smaller fry from the Shilshole breakwater, from Pier 57 on the downtown waterfront, from sea walls along Alki Drive in West Seattle, and from the sea wall in Ed Munro Seahurst Park in Burien.

Lake Washington supports bass, catfish, perch, and kokanee (landlocked sockeye salmon). The bass tend to be plentiful along the marshy shore of the University of Washington Arboretum as early as March. They also can be caught from public fishing piers in parks from Seward Park north to the Lake Washington Floating Bridge. Kokanee, running to half a pound, also begin to be active as early as March. The other species come a little later.

The lake is open the year around for elusive trout (mostly cutthroat and rainbow).

Useful Addresses in Seattle

- Seattle–King County
  Visitors Bureau
  1815 Seventh Ave.
  Seattle, WA 98101

- King County–East Visitors Bureau
  201-116th Ave. NE
  Bellevue, WA 98004

- Metro Transit Customer Assistance
  P.O. Box 4325
  Seattle, WA 98104

- King County Dept. of Planning
  & Community Development
  Parks Division
  W226 King County Courthouse
  516 Third Ave.
  Seattle, WA 98104

- Seattle Parks & Recreation
  5201 Green Lake Way N.
  Seattle, WA 98103

- Bellevue Dept. of Parks & Recreation
  P.O. Box 1768
  Bellevue, WA 98009

- For addresses of music, theater, and sports organizations, see pages 21 and 23.

Logging towns, fishing
villages, and islands in
the sun give quiet pleasure

Outside Seattle, to both north and south, the Puget Sound basin holds a diversity of easy, friendly things to do.

This is Washington State's closest approach to a conurbation—a nose-to-tail string of cities. Tacoma almost runs into Seattle from the south; a long chain of suburbs reaches north from Seattle to Everett. And yet an old-time flavor still pervades this region. It grew up on fishing, farming, and logging. Though petroleum refining and aircraft manufacturing are important industries today, the original occupations continue to play major roles.

A variety of islands gives Puget Sound much of its particular charm. The San Juans are the most numerous as well as most famous, but they are far from the only offshore retreats from a madding mainland. Enough islands separate themselves from the mainland by narrow, bridgeable gaps to give broad choice even to the boatless. The superior Washington State ferry system brings several more islands within reach of all; many more can be reached only by boat.

With literally 1,000 miles of Puget Sound shoreline, salt-water boating and fishing naturally lead the list of recreational pursuits. Their allies—clamming, tide pooling, and drift hunting—follow closely. In addition there are fine stream fishing for steelhead and trout, good watching for bald eagles and other birds, and a surprising amount of year-round hiking and bicycling.

Indoorsmen are not altogether finished with western Washington once they leave Seattle. Tacoma and Bellingham in particular have merit for the urbanite, and some quaint shoreside towns demand urbane exploration for their architectural and occupational nostalgia.

Weather. With minor variations, the climate patterns parallel those of Seattle. July and August are reliably dry and sunny. October through March is a period of frequent rain and even more frequent clouds. Spring and fall vary not only from day to day, but also hour to hour.

Temperatures hover within a narrow, mild range. In a typical year, a shoreside station records only three maximum temperatures in the 90s.

Rainfall varies more than temperature because of rain shadow effects from the Olympics.

Almost none of the precipitation comes as snow at sea level, though the rare exceptions cause some wonderful traffic tie-ups. A mere 300 feet of elevation is enough to change a good deal of January and February precipitation to snow.

Highways. Interstate 5 cuts a wide, straight swath north and south. Outside of Seattle, Tacoma is the only spot with a regular rush-hour slowdown on the freeway, though Everett sometimes clogs up for a few minutes. All freeway exits are numbered to correspond as closely as possible to mileposts. The numbers increase from south to north, beginning with 119 at Fort Lewis near Tacoma and ending with 276 between Blaine and Canada.

Those who will accept a turtle's pace as the price for great scenery can detour on two loops west of I-5. One byroad runs the length of Whidbey Island and part of Fidalgo Island, requiring a ferry ride at the south end. The other—State Highway 11, the Chuckanut Drive—runs along a high bluff overlooking Rosario Strait south of Bellingham. It connects with I-5 at each end.

The cross-Cascades highways—State 20, U.S. 2, Interstate 90, and U.S. 12—are discussed in the Cascades chapter (page 72).

The San Juan Islands

Seattle thinks of itself as the boating capital of the world. By extension, all Puget Sounders think of their region as the global center for pleasure craft. The San Juan Islands are their mecca.

Clustered in the throat of Puget Sound are 192 islands—plus or minus a few, depending on the tide. These are the San Juans. A number are uninhabitable dots of rock. Most are thickly wooded, with fine beaches. More than a dozen have boat-in state beach parks, but only four are relatively developed, with towns, resorts, and campsites.

The accessible islands and the narrow waters

Sound

between them are an inexhaustible source of recreation for regional boaters, especially those who care to fish, dig clams, explore tidepools, hunt drift, or picnic on unspoiled beaches.

People who depend on wheels or wings for transport can use the San Juans, too. The state ferry system serves the four developed islands—Orcas, Lopez, Shaw, and San Juan—from Anacortes. The town of Friday Harbor on San Juan Island has an airstrip; a feeder airline offers connecting flights to Seattle-Tacoma Airport.

Vacationers who arrive by ferry or air have the choice of staying with their original transport or renting boats for wider exploration. Major charter services on San Juan and Lopez Islands and at Anacortes rent houseboats, cabin cruisers, and sailboats. A number of resorts rent open boats.

Much of the fishing in season is for salmon, mostly kings and silvers; halibut and rockfish of various kinds are also abundant.

Narrow, usually rocky beaches have rock cockles, softshells, and other "steamers."

In addition to attracting the water-oriented, the main islands are a major destination for bicyclists.

Finally, resorts on these forested islands invite the urban weary to laze around unabashed. Night life is practically nonexistent, and no recreation director drafts teams for funny hat competitions or mambo lessons.

In quick summary, the four principal islands:

Orcas Island. Largest of the four, Orcas has both a large number of resorts and a large camping park, Moran State Park. One of the resorts (Rosario) is posh, with tennis courts and other refinements to go with a handsome old lodge. The others are more rustic, more like beach cottages. Six are at Eastsound; another five spread across the roughly M-shaped island.

Moran State Park has 124 campsites, sheltered kitchens, picnic tables with stoves, hot showers, and other comforts. Miles of hiking trails crisscross its 5,000 acres. There is trout fishing in Cascade, Mountain, and Twin lakes. Cascade has rental rowboats and a swimming beach. Moran State Park does not have a salt-water beach.

Nearby, Mount Constitution rises 2,400 feet above the surrounding sea, giving 360° panoramas of the islands, the Cascades, and the Olympic Mountains. A paved road to the top is popular with hardy bicyclists, who swarm to this hilly island for its 80 miles of roads.

One of the two golf courses in the San Juans is 6 miles from the ferry, on the road to Eastsound and the state park. Wooded and hilly, Orcas Island Golf Club is 9 holes; 2,780 yards; par 35.

San Juan Island. The economic and administrative center of Island County, San Juan has a park commemorating some comic-opera history to go with its county camping park and 10 resorts. Friday Harbor—county seat, customs harbor, ferry terminal, and commercial center—is the anchor point.

Back in 1859, this island was the unlikely site of an unlikely war. San Juan Island National Historic Park commemorates the Pig War, so called because the only casualty was an English-owned porker shot by an American. This incident brought to a head the dispute between British and Americans over San Juan Island. Kaiser Wilhelm of Germany (of all people) mediated, pushing the island onto the American side of the then uncertain boundary.

The national historic park comprises the campsites of the two rival garrisons. English camp, northwest of Friday Harbor, has an old blockhouse surviving from the war days; otherwise it is a beach and picnic ground. American Camp, on the south side of Friday Harbor, also has beach and picnic grounds, but only markers—no permanent buildings—of the era.

San Juan County Park, about 15 miles from the ferry terminal along Roche Harbor and Marine View Drive, has 30 campsites in the main park and another 10 for cyclists at some distance off the road. Picnic tables and fireplaces are available; a store is adjacent.

Five resorts are at the town of Friday Harbor, with another four in more isolated parts.

Friday Harbor is also the site of San Juan Golf & Country Club (9 holes; 3,600 yards; par 36), which permits visitor play with reservations.

SAN JUAN ISLANDS

✗ STATE PARK
⋯⋯ FERRY ROUTE
■ POINT OF INTEREST
SCALE OF MILES

0   N   5

Lopez Island. Lopez has two camping parks, one resort, and several stores near the ferry dock at the community of Lopez.

Odlin County Park, a mile southwest of the ferry dock via Ferry Road, has 20 campsites, a cook stove, picnic tables, water, and toilets. Spencer Spit State Park, 4.4 miles southwest of the ferry dock on Baker View Road, has 14 primitive campsites, water, and toilets. Spencer Spit offers one of the few swimming beaches in the San Juans.

The lone resort is Islander Lopez, at Lopez.

Flatter than the other islands, with half of its 50 miles of roads paved, Lopez is a particular favorite of easy-going bicyclists.

Several beaches at the ends of stub roads are sandy, agreeable for picnicking and sunbathing. It takes a great deal of courage to swim in these deep, cold waters. However, Hummel Lake has easy swimming and some catchable trout.

Shaw Island. The ultimate escape among the islands served by ferries, Shaw has 10 miles of paved, hilly roads, one six-unit county camping

Water, water everywhere

Big, gentle ferries (below) are an imperative part of transportation on broad Puget Sound, as well as a stately pleasure. Sailboats (left) in a spanking breeze are an elective part of outdoor recreation. The choice rests between those who favor steady decks underfoot and those who walk a slant with joy.

park at Indian Cove, 2 miles southwest of the ferry landing, and no resorts at all. Thick woods cover much of the island. No fresh water is available.

Another 18 islands of the San Juan group have state park beaches accessible only by small boat. Of these, Stuart, Sucia, Matia, and Jones are most used, with well-developed onshore camping and picnicking grounds. Sucia and Stuart have beaches with enough shoals to tempt hardy swimmers into the water. However, as is the case on most of the islands, swimming is chilly at best.

Whidbey, Fidalgo, and Camano

These three large islands form a tight cluster running southward from the San Juans. They hug the eastern shore of Puget Sound so closely that bridges connect them to the mainland or to each other at three points, while ferries serve only at two (not counting the San Juan routes).

Though less isolated than the San Juans, all three are quite rural. Except for Whidbey Island Naval Air Station, adjoining Oak Harbor, and the city of Anacortes, the three islands are mostly wooded or cultivated as small farms.

Whidbey Island

Whidbey Island fills a great deal of what might otherwise be upper Puget Sound.

Most of it is peaceful and agricultural, a dawdler's escape from freeways and fast-moving crowds. It has 2½ fine state parks—each of distinct character—another of Puget Sound's colorful old shoreside villages, and several pokeabout roads.

At the south end, access is by ferry from Mukilteo on the mainland just south of Everett (Exit 189 from I-5). State 20 runs off the north end, across Fidalgo Island, and rejoins I-5 at Exit 230.

South Whidbey State Park, on the west shore about 10 miles from the ferry pier at Columbia Beach, is a 54-unit camping park with a shoal beach for swimmers, divers, clammers, and shore fishermen. A loop road branches off State 525 to the 85-acre park.

Not far north, the turnoff to the Keystone ferry terminal (connecting to Port Townsend on the Olympic Peninsula; see page 48) also leads to Fort Casey State Park.

Fort Casey was once a coastal defense post. The park preserves not only the huge old concrete emplacements of batteries Trevor, Vallew, Kingsbury, Moore, and Worth, but also four guns.

Also on the post, an old lighthouse has been turned into an interpretive display.

The rest of the 137-acre, 35-campsite park mixes woods, open meadows, a 2-mile swimming beach, and some short hiking trails. Part of the old fort is a satellite campus for Seattle Pacific College.

Coupeville, 3 miles north, has a new town straddling State 20. The quaint original community lies east, along the water. Several restaurants and art and craft shops occupy mid-1800s buildings.

Puget Sound Ferry Routes

Ferries of every size and shape ply the sheltered waters of Puget Sound on crossings as short as 7 minutes, as long as 4 hours.

While locals use the boats mostly as commuter vessels, they are transportation, restful interlude, and unusual experience all rolled into one for visitors from drier parts of the world.

The routes correspond to letters on the Puget Sound map.

Washington State ferries

A Anacortes–San Juan Islands, with stops at Lopez, Shaw, San Juan, and Orcas; length of trip varies according to number of stops.

B Mukilteo–Columbia Beach; 15 minutes.

C Edmonds–Kingston; 25 minutes.

D Seattle Ferry Terminal–Winslow; 25 minutes.

E Seattle Ferry Terminal–Bremerton; 60 minutes.

F Fauntleroy (West Seattle)–Vashon–Southworth; 30 minutes.

G Point Defiance (Tacoma)–Tahlequah; 15 minutes.

H Port Townsend–Keystone; 35 minutes.

Other ferry routes

I Anacortes–Guemes (Skagit County); 7 minutes.

J Port Angeles–Victoria, B.C. (Black Ball Transport, Inc.); 1 hour 25 minutes.

K Steilacoom–Ketron Island–Anderson Island (Pierce County); 30 minutes.

L Gooseberry Point (Bellingham)–Lummi Island (Whatcom County); 10 minutes.

M Seattle (Pier 64)–Victoria, B.C. (British Columbia Ferry System); 4 hours, May–September only.

About half of Deception Pass State Park occupies the northerly tip of Whidbey Island.

The salt-water beach is mostly for strolling. Up at a lake are swimming areas and a concessionaire with food and rental rowboats. In shady woods between the beach and the lake are more than half of the park's 254 campsites. Two large picnic areas round out this segment.

On the east side of the highway is a boat launch, but most of the area is preserved untouched as the Cornet Bay Environments—a complex of saltwater, freshwater, and forest ecologies for students. Hiking trails thread through the preserve.

Fidalgo Island

Fidalgo is most easily identifiable as the site of Anacortes, or as the gateway to the San Juans. It also holds the other half of Deception Pass State Park, the Swinomish Indian Reservation, and two major marine research stations.

The Fidalgo side of Deception Pass State Park has a wooded waterside picnic ground at Rosario Beach and a boat launch, campground, and picnic area on Bowman Bay. Between these two areas is Rosario Head, with a fine viewpoint from its top and a fine undersea garden at the bottom. Inshore, Pass Lake is stocked with trout.

Anacortes, the major community on Fidalgo, is part fishing village, part oil refinery town, and, not least, the departure point for ferries to the San Juan Islands.

The fact that the town harbors several refineries and still has wooded outskirts, miles of scenic beaches, and large marinas for pleasure boats hints at the unspoiled nature of this whole region.

The ferry terminal is well west of town. Further west, city-operated Washington Park has 66 campsites (22 trailer hookups), a long beach, and boat launching ramp.

For scenery watchers, Mt. Erie just south of town offers a 360° panorama of sound and mountains from its 1,200-foot summit, reached by road.

For collectors of curiosities, Causland Park, three blocks west of the main street by way of Eighth, has rock walls that call to mind Sabatino Rodia's Watts Towers or some of Antoni Gaudi's gaudier walls in Barcelona, Spain.

Landbound recreationists in town have three main choices. Similk Bay Golf Course (18 holes; 6,600 yards; par 72) is well groomed and plays as long as the yardage promises. It adjoins State 20, just on the island side of Swinomish Slough. Behind the red brick bulk of the junior high school, 6 blocks west of the main street via 22nd Street, are 6 much-used tennis courts. Next to them is an Olympic-size indoor swimming pool.

But it remains true that boating and fishing are the staple recreation hereabouts. Major charter services operate at marinas on either side of Cap Sante, a tall rock at the northeastern corner of both the island and the main business district. The local quarry include salmon, halibut, cod, and rockfish.

In addition to State 20, another bridge at La Conner gives access to the island some miles south. A county road runs from that cheering village (see page 39) to connect with State 20 on the outskirts of Anacortes.

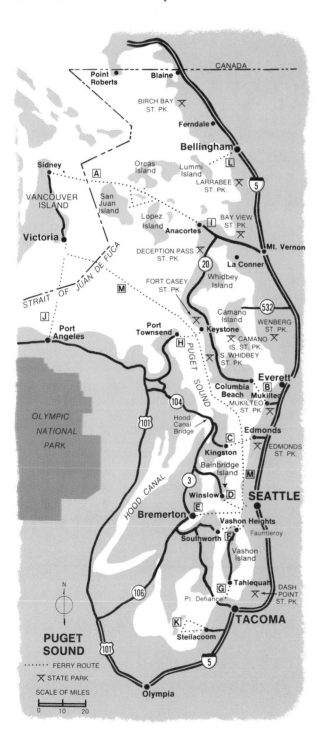

PUGET SOUND

FERRY ROUTE
STATE PARK
SCALE OF MILES
0   10   20

Shoreside diversity

Man and Mother Nature share the long shore of Puget Sound in easy harmony. La Conner (above) typifies the picturesque fishing village of this region from waterfront to inevitable mountain—in this case Baker—peering over one shoulder. Where towns are not, beaches (right) beckon to picnickers, clammers, sometimes even to swimmers.

Camano Island

Camano echoes the long, looping profile of Whidbey Island, but in miniature.

For years it has been a salt-water fisherman's retreat, with many private cottages, a few small shoreside resorts, and Camano Island State Park.

The park's 134 wooded acres shelter 86 campsites. Also at hand are covered kitchens, picnic sites, a boat launching ramp, and moorages. Only mad dogs and polar bears would think to swim in the cold, deep waters of Saratoga Passage, but scuba divers have a rich underwater garden.

The island is easily accessible from Exit 212 off I-5, via State 530 and State 532. A bridge takes the highway across a narrow arm of Puget Sound onto the island.

The Upper Puget Sound Shoreline

The mainland shore north of Everett is not quite as public as the island shores, but it does have a highly attractive shoreside town in La Conner, a beach resort in Birch Bay that is nearly perfect for families with small children, a superb scenic drive in the Chuckanut, and a picnic park with some camping on Point Roberts, a tiny peninsula that can be reached by car only through Canada.

La Conner

Old as a fishing village, new as a fun-junky source of arts, crafts, and antiques, La Conner is not without sophistication.

Creaking piers, plain buildings, and fancy Victorians house a mélange of canneries, bait shops, cafes, and galleries along slow-moving Swinomish Slough some 75 miles north of Seattle.

The place is an eclectic outgrowth of a local Indian population—the Swinomish—early English and American settlers, and a newly arrived assortment of writers, painters, potters, weavers, and antiquarians who have fled urban surroundings. With the new wave of artists and artisans have come a fine inn and several good restaurants.

Many of the local Indians are commercial fishermen. The Swinomish Indian Fish Co., on the reservation across the slough from downtown, retails both fresh and smoked fish.

La Conner also is home port to more than 100 pleasure craft. Adjacent to the big marina, a string of float piers is busy with fishermen in winter.

On summer weekends the sternwheeler *John Edward* runs excursions along the slough and through other local waters. Inquire about rides at the Lighthouse Restaurant on First Street.

A good bit of pioneer history lives on in La Conner. On First Street at Calhoun, Washington's oldest weekly newspaper, the *Puget Sound Mail*, still prints on the presses it started with in 1873. The imposing 3-story, 22-room Gaches Mansion towers above the other local Victorian houses. Nearby, the Volunteer Firemen Museum contains gear going back to the 1850s. On Fourth Street is the Skagit County Historical Museum.

Pioneer Park just south of town has playground equipment and picnic grounds.

From Anacortes, the area is accessible by local roads on either side of Swinomish Slough. The turns from State 20 are marked clearly. From Interstate 5, exit 221 for Conway leads to La Conner.

Chuckanut Drive

For sustained scenery, no other road in the Puget Sound basin equals Chuckanut Drive (State 11). For more than 10 of its 20 miles, the road clings to a high bluff overlooking Rosario Strait and the San Juan Islands. At the geographic midpoint and scenic high point, 1,965-acre Larrabee State Park runs from high hills down to the shore.

At the shore are a boat launch and a swimming beach. Waters are bone-chilling, though; scuba divers enjoy these waters more than recreational bathers. Inland are some agreeable hiking trails and 101 campsites (26 trailer hookups).

At its south end, the Chuckanut joins I-5 at Exit 231. At the north, it runs into the Fairhaven district of Bellingham. From there, drivers can poke on into town on city streets or slip back onto I-5 at Exit 250.

Birch Bay

Birch Bay, a few miles north of Bellingham, is the kind of resort community where all the juke boxes ought to have Ted Weems' "Heartaches" at the top of the play list because the overwhelming flavor is an old time one, even by the strict standards of this cautious, conservative region. It has a small permanent carnival, a roller arena, a bike rental outfit that offers one-gear, balloon-tire models, and a host of resorts with rough-hewn, immune-to-tracked-sand housekeeping cabins named Seagull, Marigold, and so forth.

Nostalgia aside, Birch Bay is an almost flawless place for families with small children. Moppets can entertain themselves safely for hours on end.

The bay floor is so flat that a modest tide goes out half a mile and a minus tide a mile or more, exposing a vast tract of clean, hard-packed sand and hundreds of shallow pools. The sand is good for digging horse clams (also called "gapers") and cockles, great for sandcastling, and eccentric as a softball field. The pools hold schools of tiny fish (mostly stickleback and baby flounder) and some legal-size Dungeness crab.

At high tide the shoals produce the warmest swimming water anywhere in the sound. Even moderately sunny days heat up the waters enough.

Rangers at Birch Bay State Park, at the south end of the resort, can explain much about the bay and its sea life. The park also has 179 campsites (53 trailer hookups) and some short walking trails through woods and alongside salt marshes.

In addition to the bay and the nostalgia noted before, a rolling and pretty, but not demanding, Birch Bay Golf Course (18 holes; 5,092 yards; par 68) lies right along the shore.

Those whose tastes run away from aging cottages can find some modern motels, rentable condominiums, and commercial camping parks in Birch Bay.

On Interstate 5 North of Seattle

Because Interstate 5 feeds Vancouver, the North Cascades, the San Juans, and other islands, it draws heavy visitor traffic along its last 100 miles to the United States–Canada border.

The roadside attractions are noncommercial and, considering their sparse numbers, surprisingly diverse.

Everett

Long a lumber port and mill town, Everett has such visitor attractions as the 747 assembly plant of Boeing Airplane Company, an arboretum and children's park, and a pair of fine golf courses.

The Boeing assembly plant puts together pieces of 747s gathered from fabrication plants elsewhere around the U.S. Tours usually show the gigantic planes in varying stages of production. The plant is at Paine Field, west of I-5 via Exit 189, the same exit leading to the Mukilteo ferry pier. Tours take place only on weekdays.

Of the two local public courses, Everett Municipal (18 holes; 6,114 yards; par 72) is the old-timer, a well-groomed, gently rolling layout with mature trees in tight rows. From I-5, Exit 195 east on Grand Avenue leads to the course. The newer course is Walter Hall Golf Course (18 holes; 6,200 yards; par 72), a mile east via Exit 189.

Kayak Point, north of Everett, has a 470-acre shoreside picnic and camping park and a golf course, both operated by the Snohomish County Park Department. From I-5, Kayak Point Park and Kayak Point Golf Course (18 holes; 6,210 yards; par 71) are reached by Exit 206.

Bellingham

Although Bellingham faces Puget Sound with its wide-mouthed bay, most of its appeal to visitors comes from the landward sides. The old village of Fairhaven has been restored as a shoppers' delight. The pleasing Whatcom Museum of History and Art now occupies the toweringly overdone old city hall. And the community has developed some of the finest municipal parks in the whole region.

Accommodations. In spite of its position in the narrow space between Seattle and Vancouver, B.C., Bellingham has 15 hotels and motels in or near town. The greatest concentration is south of the main business district and west of the freeway, on Samish Way between exits 252 and 253.

Attractions. Fairhaven, at the head of Chuckanut Drive, acquired several ambitious brick buildings toward the end of the 19th century when locals thought it would become a major railroad terminal. Long idle, these structures have now become the heart of a fanciful collection of shops offering cookware, books, ice cream, fine Mexican dresses, fine wines, and 23 other kinds of goods. Fairhaven also has several restaurants.

For ornate excesses, Bellingham's former City Hall outdoes every public building in western Washington, with the possible exception of the courthouse at Port Townsend. Inside, however, the Whatcom Museum of History and Art is both stately and attractive.

The main floor is devoted to art, with Northwest painters dominating the permanent exhibits. Works by Mark Tobey and Kenneth Callahan are included.

The top floor gives a small but lucid history of local logging in the form of hand tool displays and dioramas, as well as an Indian display explaining the relationship of environment to clothing for a wide range of northern coastal tribes.

Parks and recreation. Bellingham has three remarkable city parks.

Cornwall, north of the downtown by way of Broadway and then Meridian, is a wooded oasis of calm in the city. Its spacious confines hold excellent picnic areas, children's play areas, and—in a part of the world daft for the sport—a long row of horseshoe pits.

Whatcom Falls Park, on the east side of town on Lakeway Avenue (Exit 252 from the freeway), offers the same range of activities plus a fishing pond for children and some pleasant short hikes along Whatcom Creek and Falls. Nearby, small Bloedel-Donovan Park fronts on Lake Whatcom. It has a fine swimming beach.

The third local park is Lake Padden, the newest, largest (with 1,008 acres), and most diverse. The park holds ball fields, a 3-mile walking trail around the lake (much of it in woods), picnic sites, bank fishing, two well-kept tennis courts, a swimming beach, and a municipal golf course. Lake Padden Golf Course (18 holes; 6,716 yards; par 72) plays fairly level and fairly tight.

The park is accessible from I-5 via Samish Way, which passes by both west and east gates of the park. Exits are 246 and 252.

At the south end of Lake Whatcom, Sudden Valley Golf Course (18 holes; 6,497 yards; par 72) allows some visitor play with reservations.

Roadside Attractions along Interstate 5

Several parks relieve the freeway tedium of I-5 between Everett and the British Columbia border. They are noted from south to north.

Wenberg State Park, 18 miles northwest of Everett, adjoins Lake Goodwin. The 46-acre park has 75 campsites (10 trailer hookups), freshwater fishing, a boat launch, and a swimming beach. Picnic shelters are available. Exit 206 from the freeway leads directly to the park.

Near the town of Ferndale, Hovander County Park does a fine job of preserving a typical family farm of this region. The house is open to tour; most of its rooms are furnished in livable fashion, with some turned into display areas of memorabilia. The big red barn houses old farm equipment and a collection of animals city kids can pet and get acquainted with. One of the hayfields has been turned into a large picnic area with stoves, ball fields, and some fine views of Mt. Baker. Exit 262 from I-5 leads west on Axton Road. A mile from the freeway, signs point the way to Hovander County Park.

Peace Arch State Park is half in the United States, half in Canada. The big white arch straddles the border, as do formal gardens, picnic areas, and children's play areas. The park adjoins the U.S. Customs station; use exit 276.

Tacoma and Environs

Flanking Seattle to the south, Tacoma and its hinterland form a pleasing extension of that curious mixture of urban, rural, and wild that characterizes the whole Puget Sound region. Sometimes the passage from one area to another is so swift as to bewilder, but for the most part changes are gradual.

In general, the Tacoma area places more emphasis on the urban and less on the wild than the region north of Seattle, so the visitor attractions tend toward parks, museums, shopping districts, and the like.

The City of Tacoma

A mill town, deep-water port, neighbor to Fort Lewis and McChord Air Force Base, gateway to Mt. Rainier on one side and the Olympic Peninsula on the other, Tacoma reaches north to touch the Seattle metropolitan area and stretches south much of the way to Olympia.

Within Tacoma's long sprawl a renascent downtown offers some specialty shopping, while on the west side Point Defiance municipal park is the only challenger in the Pacific Northwest to Vancouver's splendid Stanley Park. Small museums, a botanical garden, and some good golf courses add other flavors.

Accommodations. Tacoma has several large motels, nearly all of them on or near I-5 between the city center and Fort Lewis to the south. There is one major downtown motor hotel.

Attractions. Tacoma's old city hall, modeled after Renaissance hill castles in Italy, has been remodeled recently into a collection of shops and restaurants, even including a nightclub.

Aside from the shops and some excellent interior design details, what makes this restoration notable is its lofty clock tower, open to the public on weekends. Free guided tours to the 2½-ton clockworks begin hourly on weekend afternoons from Daley's Jewelry on the fourth floor. The building is at South Seventh and Commerce streets.

Nearby, specialty shopping and local events make the pedestrian mall, on Broadway between South Ninth and South 15th streets, another focal point of the downtown for shoppers.

Still within a close distance, the Tacoma Art Museum is at South 12th Street and Pacific Avenue, and the Washington State Historical Society at 315 North Stadium Way.

Plant lovers may wish to visit the botanical conservatory in Wright Park, still close to downtown at South Sixth and South G streets. Orchids and other tropicals make up the principal permanent collection.

Parks and recreation. Well north of the downtown, Point Defiance Park occupies a big part of the peninsula between the Narrows and Commencement Bay.

Within the confines of this park are a Never Never Land for small children, Fort Nisqually, the Camp Six logging museum, and a zoo and aquarium. The park also contains swimming beaches, a boat launch, play equipment, picnic sites, and some excellent wooded walking trails. Last, it has on one edge the ferry dock serving southern Vashon Island.

Fort Nisqually is an honest-to-goodness pioneer fort made out of peeled upright logs with pointed tips. Originally a Hudson's Bay Company trading post, it now serves as a fantasy come true for kids who always wanted to go west with Davy Crockett.

Camp Six includes a replica of an old-time logging camp complete with most of the working gear, a museum, and a steam-powered Shea locomotive that runs on weekends on a 1½-mile track. The cost of a ride is nominal.

The aquarium is noted for its collections of octopi, sea otters, and penguins.

Across Commencement Bay from Point Defiance, Dash Point State Park has another swimming beach and some agreeable picnic grounds. The park has 138 campsites (28 trailer hookups). It is most easily reached via State 509, an extension of South 11th Street from downtown. From I-5, Exit 137, Taylor Way, connects with State 509.

Tacomans support a diverse collection of public golf courses in and near town. Elks-Allenmore Golf Club (18 holes; 6,355 yards; par 71) is handy to I-5 via Exit 132 onto State 16, the route to the Tacoma Narrows Bridge. Meadow Park Golf Course (18 holes; 6,000 yards; par 72) is in the same quarter of town. Brookdale Golf Club (18 holes; 6,100 yards; par 71) is east of I-5 near Mc-Chord Air Force Base; it is accessible from the freeway on State 512. Spanaway Lake Golf Course (18 holes; 7,000 yards; par 72) adjoins a lakeside county park in the same district. North of town, Northshore Golf Course (9 holes; 3,450 yards; par 36) is in the Dash Point district.

The Countryside

Yet another of Puget Sound's peaceful islands, a game farm, and several historical museums are close to Tacoma.

Vashon Island has few formal parks or other specific attractions. However, quiet roads through forested heights make it most agreeable for Sunday drives or bicycle excursions. The ferry from Point Defiance docks at the south end of the island. Another ferry runs from the north end of Vashon to West Seattle, making a loop trip possible. Along the way, stub roads lead to quiet beaches, most of them on the west side. The only park is on the west side of Maury Island (actually a peninsula of Vashon). Dockton Park has children's play equipment, picnic tables, and stoves. A boat moorage is here as well, in the deeply sheltered waters of Quartermaster Harbor.

At Steilacoom, a village on the Puget Sound shoreline south of Tacoma, the South Tacoma State Game Farm raises pheasants, steelhead, and rainbow trout. The grounds are also a refuge for local animals and migratory birds. Visitors may take a self-guided tour. The farm is open from 8 A.M. to 8 P.M. daily. To get to it, head west from I-5 at Exit 125, Bridgeport Way. Continue on Bridgeport to South 75th Street. Signs mark the way from there.

East of Tacoma, in the daffodil and berry farming town of Puyallup, the home of pioneer Ezra Meeker is a memorial both to him and to the Oregon Trail, which Meeker did much to preserve in the national memory. The 17-room mansion is open Sundays, 1 to 5 P.M., for tours. It is at 321 East Pioneer Avenue.

East of I-5 between Tacoma and Seattle is the small town of Auburn. The White River Valley Historical Society Museum demonstrates how people got along the Oregon and other early trails. The museum's one great hall is filled with pioneer memorabilia, tools, buggies, and the like. It is two blocks east of Auburn Way on Ninth Street. It is open Thursday and Sunday, 2 to 4:30 P.M.

Light air to spare
The lofty Olympic Mountains shelter endless miles . . . but not all . . . of the sailor's paradise that is Puget Sound.

In untamable wilderness, land and sea compete to yield the richer rewards

The Olympic

It is hard to think of another place in North America where such mountains as the Olympics are so close to seawater on so many sides, with such dramatic results. On this smallish peninsula—75 miles north to south and 85 miles west to east—are the largest temperate-zone rain forests in the world, and an irrigated plain. Here are dangerously rocky, storm-swept ocean waters and an inland sea so sheltered that people water-ski on much of it. Here are ancient glaciers at 7,000 feet elevation and sea-level gardens that do not see frost from March until January.

In sunny July and August, the peninsula looks—and is—paradisiacal. Its waters teem with fish and shellfish. Along roadsides, veritable encyclopedias of wild berries hang waiting for pickers.

How the west side of the peninsula could remain so lightly populated staggers the imagination of a summer visitor. The problem is winter. Endless successions of cold, gray, wet days have robbed a century's worth of settlers of their will to wait for spring, let alone to struggle. Only hardy loggers and fisherfolk have stayed.

Even on the east side, with more arable land and far less rain, population scarcely presses on available space.

So the Olympic Peninsula offers itself to visitors with astonishing generosity. The 1,400 square miles of Olympic National Park preserve the entire Olympic Mountain range and a 50-mile strip of coastline. The Olympic National Forest flanks the park all along its east and south sides and on its northwest corner, adding greatly to recreational opportunities. State and county parks amplify the choices still more. And private resorts take up where public lands leave off.

Driving around the edge of the peninsula is an easy weekend's work. Indeed, "making the loop" on U.S. 101 is one of the rites of passage for Washingtonians. But once the numbing sense of awe wears off, recreation here can be a lengthy, even lifetime occupation for campers, high-country hikers, fresh and salt-water fishermen, oysterers, crabbers, boaters, naturalists, and collectors of panoramic scenery.

Weather. Exceptions in local weather patterns are so numerous that few rules are left to prove. The lofty barrier of the Olympic Mountains tears to shreds weather coming in from the Pacific.

On the Pacific coast, most stations report annual average rainfall of more than 100 inches. At Quinault, the average is 134 inches; monthly totals break into double figures in October and stay there through March. In July and August, the averages are 2.6 and 2.8 inches. Snow is rare, as is summer heat.

On the east side of the peninsula, Bremerton receives 38 inches of rain a year, Port Angeles 24.6, Port Townsend only 18.3. Sequim, just 17 miles east of Port Angeles, gets a mere 16.8 inches of rain a year. In compensation for moderated rainfall, temperatures vary more widely than on the ocean side. Olympia has daily maximums in the 90° range on half a dozen days a year, and on rare occasion suffers at 100°. In winter, snow is rare near Puget Sound but likely in the foothills.

Up toward the tree line, the Olympic Mountains catch phenomenal volumes of precipitation. Rough estimates for the west side are the equivalent of 190 inches of rainfall. Winter snow packs to a depth estimated at 500 inches. But nobody knows the precise figure.

Highways. One highway, U.S. 101, loops around the Olympic Peninsula, beginning at Aberdeen on Grays Harbor (see page 58) and ending at Olympia, at the southern tip of Puget Sound. On the west and north, a handful of stub roads lead away from the highway to beaches or mountains. On the east, Kitsap Peninsula adds a plentiful choice of roads, almost all of them two-laners. Most Olympic Peninsula roads are paved, though some of the stubs leading to extraordinary wilderness are graveled at best and muddy at worst.

Logging trucks and trailer or camper rigs are abundant. Traffic moves slowly.

Except for a short piece of U.S. 101 north of Olympia and a brief stretch of State 3 between Bremerton and Silverdale, the only freeway is U.S. 12/State 8 across the base of the peninsula between Aberdeen and Olympia.

See additional maps on pages 52 and 57.

Peninsula

The Sheltered Side

The sheltered side of the Olympic Peninsula is the most human and diverse, offering every kind of salt and fresh-water recreation, high mountains, and a sprinkling of colorful shoreside towns.

Two quite different ways to travel the territory present themselves. U.S. 101 along Hood Canal is direct and scenic, with a minimum of towns, maximum access to the mountains, and good exposure to tidewater. The other route, east of that, wanders through a maze of islands, peninsulas, and bays on the Kitsap Peninsula, providing many opportunities to explore beaches.

Hood Canal Shoreline along U.S. 101

The Hood Canal shoreline invites a dawdling exploration of a long series of excellent parks, an intertidal zone rich with clams and native oysters, and fine scenery.

Though Hoodsport is the only community between Shelton and Sequim large enough to be called a town, restaurants, motels, and other comforts appear often along the 75-mile route.

Shoreside parks begin where the highway joins the canal for northbound motorists.

Potlatch State Park is a small camping unit—35 sites, 18 trailer hookups—but a major day use area. Mobs come at low tides to pick oysters, dig clams, and catch crabs at one of the richest public beaches.

Less than a mile north, Cushman Beach—the outflow from Tacoma Power Company's hydroelectric plant—also has oysters and clams.

The town of Hoodsport lies not far north of Cushman Beach. At the highwayside local cafe, the less adventurous need climb only six steps to taste the best of local oysters. For boaters, the public dock has a boat moorage across the road.

Some 4 miles north, Lilliwaup Recreational Tidelands offers more oyster and clam beds.

There is not much announcement—just pullouts north of the low bridge across Lilliwaup Creek.

Neighboring Eagle Creek Recreational Tidelands adds crabs to the roster of edible quarry.

Beyond Eagle Creek comes a long dry spell for all save the locally knowledgeable. Pleasant Harbor State Park breaks the drought. The park is principally a boat moorage, but its short beach does have both clams and oysters. Dosewallips State Park, less than 2 miles north, is the principal park on the upper canal. Its 425 acres of meadows and woodlands straddle U.S. 101. Dosewallips has 150 campsites (40 trailer hookups), hiking trails, and some sketchy tennis courts to go with beaches on both sides of the Dosewallips River mouth. Clams, oysters, and crabs can all be gotten here.

Only a few hundred yards farther north is the U.S. Forest Service's Seal Rock Campground, with 14 tent camps and 20 trailer sites, 10 picnic sites, and a long beach with clams and oysters.

Seal Rock also has a rhododendron nursery in this native habitat for the showy shrub. May or early June is peak blooming time.

Just beyond Seal Rock, U.S. 101 runs inland for some miles to the turnoff for Port Townsend at Discovery Bay, then inland until Sequim Bay.

Mountain Side of U.S. 101

The North Fork of the Skokomish River above Lake Cushman is the great gateway into the high Olympics from their easterly side. Close by, the Hamma Hamma and Dosewallips River watersheds offer other routes into the mountains.

Both backpackers and fishermen use the country all summer; in winter are steelhead runs.

Staircase Campground is the National Park Service base point for both day hikers and high-country campers. In woods alongside a dramatic sequence of rapids on the North Fork of the Skokomish are 59 fine campsites.

A 5-mile nature walk loops around the river valley from the campsite. Several other trails along the west side of the river offer fine day hikes.

Challenges in variety

On the Olympic Peninsula, the high country (above) of the national park has goats that think any lunch is theirs to share. Down along the shores, man has mainly himself to contend with. Port Townsend (right), as its buildings demonstrate, tried to challenge San Francisco in the 1880s. It missed the big money, but saved a good deal of peace and quiet.

The confirmed high-country hiker will find this a prime access point to most of the park's 600 miles of trails and can travel cross-country to either the north or west entrances to the park or retrace steps to the starting point.

Staircase Road departs from U.S. 101 in downtown Hoodsport. A ranger is on duty during the summers.

Lake Cushman State Park is on Staircase Road 10 miles closer to Hoodsport. With 80 campsites (30 trailer hookups) and two boat ramps, the 581-acre park caters to fishermen pursuing cutthroat trout. However, the isolated, woodsy site also is popular with hikers who prefer gentle foothills.

A resort at the south end of the lake, where the road from Hoodsport first reaches the shore, has accommodations and rental boats.

Another 22 lowland lakes in the region have public fishing access, mostly for trout but also for kokanee (sockeye salmon). In this era of scientific fish management, quality of each lake varies from year to year. Inquire at local sporting goods stores.

Some of these smaller lakes have Washington State Department of Natural Resources campgrounds on their shores.

Hamma Hamma Recreation Area, north of Hoodsport with access from U.S. 101, reaches from lowlands through foothills and on into the high country of the national park. Most of the development was done by the U.S. Forest Service within the Olympic National Forest. National Forest Service campgrounds are Hamma Hamma (12 trailer sites) at 600 feet elevation, Lena Creek (7 trailer, 7 tent sites) at 700 feet, and the walk-in Lena Lake (10 tent sites) at 1,800 feet.

One of the most popular day hikes on all the peninsula is the Lena Lakes trail, connecting Lena Creek and Lena Lake campgrounds. Another 3-mile hike up to Jefferson Ridge rewards the walker on a clear day with views to Seattle.

The Dosewallips River course has—in addition to Dosewallips State Park and Seal Rock Campground on Hood Canal—three foothill campgrounds. Elkhorn (4 trailer, 18 tent sites) and Steelhead (5 tent sites) are both at 600 feet elevation. Dosewallips Campground (33 tent sites) is higher.

A day hiker of sturdy stuff can make the Tunnel Creek trail in one day. It is only 3 miles long, but the elevation runs from 390 feet up to 5,200. (In an additional quarter mile, the route drops down to Harrison Lake at 4,750 feet.)

The Dosewallips, Skokomish (the main stream, not the north fork), Satsop, and Duckabush are the most productive winter steelhead streams on the east side of the peninsula.

The district Forest Service ranger station at Hoodsport, a few yards off U.S. 101 on Staircase Road, has maps and trail information.

Shelton, an old forest products town some miles south of the Hood Canal, is another rich source of information about fishing, hiking, and camping in this part of the world. The local chamber of commerce is a storehouse of published information on outdoor recreation along the canal and in other nearby districts.

Kitsap Peninsula

Of all the untidy sculpture left over from the last ice age in the Pacific Northwest, the Kitsap Peninsula is least orderly. In truth it is hard to think of Kitsap as one peninsula, since it is an endless collection of bays and points bounded on one side by Hood Canal and on the other by the main body of Puget Sound. However, the whole collection anchors to the mass of the Olympic Peninsula near Shelton, and it really is one peninsula.

A great many western Washingtonians and visitors make use of Kitsap's scroll-sawn edges for boating, fishing, shellfishing, and scenic weekend drives.

State 3 up Kitsap's spine serves as a diverting alternative to U.S. 101 for those Olympic Peninsula visitors whose tastes run more to picturesque small towns than to mountains. The peninsula can also be reached by ferry from Seattle or by way of the Narrows Bridge from Tacoma.

Bremerton. A major U.S. Navy shipyard and the ferry terminal connecting with Seattle are located here. Several sizable motels near State 3 in the northwest portion of town can make Bremerton a useful anchor point for visitors.

The U.S.S. *Missouri,* on which General Douglas McArthur received the surrender of Japan to end World War II, is open to visitors in the Naval Shipyard, along State 3 at the southwest corner of town. A plaque secured to the deck of the great old battleship marks the exact spot where the peace treaty was signed. Summer visiting hours are 10 A.M. to 8 P.M. daily; during the rest of the year they are noon to 4 P.M. weekdays and 10 A.M. to 4 P.M. weekends and holidays.

The remainder of the shipyard and the other ships in the moth-ball fleet are not open to visitors, but those wishing a close look can ride the Bremerton–Port Orchard foot passenger ferry from the First Street pier right past the taffrails of the big ships. The main ferry terminal houses a navy museum on its upper floor.

Tourable towns. Gig Harbor, Poulsbo, and Port Gamble reflect the diverse quality of life along Puget Sound. All court visitors.

Gig Harbor began as a small harbor for fishermen. It is still that, but around the core has grown a tourist village of art and craft shops, shoreside restaurants, and pleasure boat marinas.

The town is just off State 16, 4 miles north of the Narrows Bridge from Tacoma or 21 miles south of Bremerton.

Poulsbo, roughly halfway between Bremerton and Port Gamble, is just off State 3 on a spur road leading to Bainbridge Island. Until recently the town was an enclave of Norwegians. Recent additions have brought new ethnic groups to town without changing its Scandinavian character. Local shops play the Norse heritage to its fullest.

Port Gamble, 23 miles north of Bremerton via State 3, is a one-time company mill town that is now turning itself into a museumlike village.

The old general store on Main Street houses two museums. On the lower floor is a historic exhibit tracing the logging industry in a region now harvesting its third crop of trees. The upper floor houses an astounding 4,000-piece collection of shells and marine fossils from around the world. Both museums are open weekends all year.

Besides connecting directly to Bremerton by road, Port Gamble is 8 miles from the Kingston ferry terminal (connecting to Edmonds) and 1 mile from the Hood Canal Floating Bridge that leads onto the rest of the Olympic Peninsula.

Still farther north on a county road, the salmon resort village of Hansville is near the tip of the Kitsap Peninsula. Two camper park–resorts here rent 16-foot open boats (known regionally as "kickers"), motors, and gear for fishermen after both sea-run salmon and late-released hatchery fish that swim out their lives within Puget Sound.

Waterside parks. State and county parks with every degree of development dot the shorelines of Kitsap Peninsula and the islands alongside it. Many of the beaches can be reached only by boat, but more than enough are accessible by car.

Twanoh, Belfair, Scenic Beach, and Kitsap Memorial State Parks are on Hood Canal.

Twanoh, 25 miles west of Bremerton on State 106 (a connector to U.S. 101) is highly civilized. It has 101 campsites, 10 trailer hookups, food and grocery concessions, tennis courts, a sandy beach, boat launch, and moorage. The park interrupts a long row of vacation homes.

At this point, Hood Canal angles east-west instead of north-south. Its waters are calm and shallow, fine for swimming and water-skiing.

Belfair State Park, on a stub road leading west from the town of Belfair, is much more rustic. Its pebbly shoal beach is a favorite with oyster pickers. The park has 194 campsites, 47 trailer hookups, and abundant picnic tables; many are shaded by conifers but some are open. The park sits at the inner tip of Hood Canal.

Scenic Beach State Park, west of Silverdale on a county road, has 50 campsites within its 71 acres. There is a boat launch and a good beach.

Northernmost of the state parks is Kitsap Memorial, a 58-acre, 43-campsite beach park with picnic facilites and a boat moorage (but no ramp). It's just south of the Hood Canal Bridge on State 3.

In addition to these state parks, the Kitsap side of Hood Canal has a county park and several public beaches maintained by the Washington Department of Natural Resources. Most of the DNR beaches are accessible only by boat.

On the Puget Sound side of the peninsula are three more beach parks. Kopachuk is off State 16 west of Gig Harbor. It has 41 campsites, picnic tables, and a swimming beach. Illahee, 3 miles northeast of Bremerton by State 306, has 25 campsites, picnic tables, beach, and boat launch. Fay Bainbridge State Park, at the northern tip of Bainbridge Island, is accessible from the Winslow ferry from Seattle or by State 305 from Poulsbo. The 17-acre beach park has 30 campsites, a boat launch and moorage, and picnic sites.

Port Townsend

Port Townsend did not quite live up to the gaudy ambitions of its early days. It never became a major seaport or the state capital, but it made an exciting attempt before falling back to become a mill town and a military outpost guarding the mouth of Puget Sound against seaborne invasion.

The legacy of the town's early plans includes some fine Victorian architectural eccentricities and three state parks—attractions that have drawn a community of artists and craftsmen.

The town sits at the tip of its own peninsula, due north of the Kitsap Peninsula; it faces east across Puget Sound toward Whidbey Island. It can be reached by ferry from Whidbey, over the Hood Canal Floating Bridge from the Kitsap Peninsula, or by State 20 from U.S. 101.

A small business district runs along a narrow shelf next to the waterfront. A variety of art and craft shops are here, many in restored brick buildings. The residential community perches on a tall bluff above that shelf. As befits a one-time rival to San Francisco, Port Townsend's houses include a good many gingerbread Victorians. The old courthouse is a masterwork of overstatement.

Accommodations. Several comfortable motels are located on State 20 just west of the main business district. In addition to these there are two uncommon possibilities. Manresa Castle, near State 20 but up on the bluff, is an elegantly restored mansion with turrets, mansard roof, and other Charles Addams-ish externals. And duplexes in the officers' row of Fort Worden—now a state park—have been spruced up for rental by the day or week from May through September. Reservations are required.

Attractions. Aside from shopping, the principal attractions in town are old buildings. The local visitor information center provides brochures outlining a complete walking tour. One of the houses, Rothschild House, is a state parks heritage site.

Jefferson County Historical Museum is in city hall.

Parks and recreation. Port Townsend's ring of forts has turned into a ring of remarkably diverse state parks.

Fort Worden, immediately adjacent to town, now serves as an art center and conference ground as well as a regular state park. Its beaches, lawns, and picnic sites are open to day use. Visitors can watch artists in residence and look at two interpretive centers, the first built upon one of the old coastal gun emplacements and the second in Point Wilson Lighthouse. Sometimes casual visitors can find campsites or rooms in one of the refurbished officers' row houses, but for these they must compete with conference participants.

Fort Flagler State Park, some miles south of town on State 20, then east on a county road, is the park for fishermen and outdoorsmen. Another old coastal artillery post, it now holds 90 campsites, some hiking trails, and kitchens and picnic sites on its 783 acres. Beaches are its prime assets. Clams are abundant within the park and at four other nearby beach accesses. The park has a boat launch for salmon fishing or pot fishing for crab.

Though the park is isolated, a concessionaire rents boats and sells fishing tackle and groceries.

Flagler sits on Marrowstone Island. Two narrow bays between it and the peninsula holding Port Townsend are rich in sea life. One of those bays is an underwater park and learning center.

Between Fort Flagler and Port Townsend, old Fort Townsend State Park offers a spacious lawn and a serene stand of woods on a bluff looking east. Its beach has both clams and crabs. Secluded picnic sites round out the facilities for day visitors; there is a small group campground.

Port Ludlow, another old-time mill town just downsound from Port Townsend, now has a condominium resort with tennis courts; an 18-hole, par 72 golf course stretching out 6,907 yards from the back tees; rental boats; and swimming.

Also in the region is Port Townsend–Chevy Chase Golf Club (9 holes with 18 tees; 5,926 yards; par 72), 8 miles west of Port Townsend.

The Strait Side

If Puget Sound is sheltered and civilized, and if the Pacific beaches are stormy and wild, seldom touched by humanity, then the Strait of Juan de Fuca side of the Olympic Peninsula is a graceful bridge between the extremes.

Port Angeles and Sequim are the only sizable municipalities. The rest of the strait side is all coast, forest, and mountains, with just enough development to make a stay in the region snug for fishermen, hikers, and skiers who come to it.

Port Angeles proper is a working mill town as well as a gateway to other attractions. To the east 17 miles, Sequim and Dungeness form a low-key resort area appealing to beachcombers and golfers. To the west are the salmon ports of Sekiu, Clallam Bay, and Neah Bay. Behind Port Angeles looms some of the most accessible mountain scenery in the Olympic National Park.

Port Angeles

As a natural stopover point, Port Angeles has built a substantial collection of motels, restaurants, and other services for visitors. Otherwise, it serves as gateway to shore and mountains—and to Victoria, B.C., a 1½-hour ferry ride away.

The National Park Service maintains a visitor center and historical museum in town at 600 East Park Avenue.

Inside Ediz Hook, marinas offer rental kickers and charter boats to fishermen. (Even nonfishermen should ride out onto the hook for the view back across town to the mountains.)

Sequim-Dungeness

The folk of Sequim make much of the unlikely fact that local farms and gardens must be irrigated for lack of rainfall. The Olympics cast their strongest rain shadow across this small valley, leaving it with as few as 10 inches of precipitation a year, and seldom more than 18. This mild, dry weather has made the town a popular retirement haven, complete with parks and golf courses.

Accommodations. They're not plentiful. Two motels flank U.S. 101 near Sequim. Dungeness has two cottage resorts along its bay front. At Sequim Bay is another resort and camper park.

Attractions. A working oyster farm, open to visitors, nestles below the bluffs at Dungeness. More unusual, the Olympic Game Farm between Sequim and Dungeness breeds Siberian tigers and other endangered species. The farm is also home to several four-footed movie stars when they are not working. From April through October, visitors may drive through or attend a lecture tour for modest fees.

Parks and recreation. Sequim Bay State Park, on the bay east of town, has 119 campsites (26 trailer hookups) in its 92 wooded, shoreside acres. There are sheltered picnic sites, a swimming beach that also harbors clams, and a boat launch.

Dungeness Recreation Area, a Clallam County park occupying the base of Dungeness Spit, has several picnic areas and 67 campsites in mixed scrub and woods. A walking trail through the Dungeness National Wildlife Refuge leads out onto sandy Dungeness Spit itself. Its seaward beach, 7½ miles long, is laden with driftwood. Shore fishing there is productive. On the inner side, both clams and crabs can be caught by waders, though boats and pots make the task easier. A state park boat launching ramp is at Cline Spit, accessible from the village of Dungeness.

Two challenging golf courses flank Sequim. Dungeness Golf Course (18 holes; 6,900 yards; par 72), north of U.S. 101 via Kitchen Road, is fairly open but persistently rolling and heavily trapped. On the road to Dungeness, SunLand (18 holes; 6,475 yards; par 72) is more level.

Finally, the floor of Dungeness Valley makes for easy bicycling on alternate roads north of U.S. 101. The county has maps of recommended routes, available at the Sequim visitor information office.

The Salmon Ports

State 112 is a road for salmon and halibut fishermen. Beginning at Port Angeles and running almost to the northwest tip of the Olympic Peninsula, the route is dotted with towns and resorts catering to fishermen.

In addition to the Port Angeles marinas inside Ediz Hook, a camper park at Agate and Crescent beaches offers both charter and rental boats.

Clallam Bay and Sekiu lie close together some 50 miles west of Port Angeles. Half a dozen resorts and camper parks offer rental boats or charters.

Neah Bay, in the Makah Indian Reservation, is the farthest west and busiest of the sport-fishing towns. Three large resorts operated by the Makah tribe offer both charters and boat launching.

The beaches at and near all these resorts are also popular sources of driftwood and agates.

Beaches near the town of Joyce, between Port Angeles and Clallam Bay, have smelt runs.

Inland from the Strait

Within a few miles of the beaches, the north side of the Olympic Peninsula offers a startling range of lowland lakes and towering alpine peaks. With them come fine fishing streams.

Heart of the Hills–Hurricane Ridge. State Highway 111, running south out of Port Angeles, begins its twisting climb before it gets to Heart of the Hills Campground, then keeps on climbing up to Hurricane Ridge.

Heart of the Hills, with 105 sites, is one of the largest summer camping units in Olympic National Park. It is also a launch point for hikes up to Hurricane Ridge.

Hurricane Ridge itself is a picnic area and a showcase viewpoint from late spring until fall. It offers about as fine a closeup of alpine peaks as can be seen from a road. The lodge and parking area is a launch point for hiking trails high and deep into the park.

At the expense of a modest stroll, visitors have a good chance of seeing wildlife ranging from mountain goats and bears down to marmots and chipmunks. In July, the meadowlands come alight with wildflowers.

The Olympics are not much in the way of winter mountains. Sea-girt, they collect snow too wet and heavy for snowshoers, cross-country skiers, or even snowmobilers. The lone exception is Hurricane Ridge, which is high enough to get drier snow and sheltered enough to keep the depths within reason. In winter the lodge becomes headquarters for a day-use ski area with 500 vertical feet of runs, one poma, and two rope tows.

Elwha River. About 10 miles west of Port Angeles, Elwha Road slips south from U.S. 101 up the Elwha River drainage. Along its lower course, this waterway is one of the most productive steelhead streams on the peninsula. The National Park Service has a 41-site campground just below Lake Mills. The road continues up tributary Boulder Creek to a higher campground with 20 tent sites. In addition to fishing access, the campgrounds are trailheads for high-country hikers.

Lake Crescent. Cradled among gentle hills more than mountains, long Lake Crescent is a tranquil haven in otherwise tumultuous country. Entirely within the national park boundary, the lake supports a diverse population of trout, which can be caught without a state license.

Concessionaire resorts at each end of the lake have launching ramps and rental boats. A national park visitor center at Storm King on U.S. 101 and several picnic grounds round out the facilities.

At the east end of Crescent is small, shallow Lake Sutherland, which is warm enough for swimming and yet cool enough for cutthroat trout.

From Fairholm at the west end of Crescent, a road runs up alongside the Soleduck River to an 84-site national park campground and high-country trailhead.

Pointblank mountains
From Hurricane Ridge in Olympic National Park, auto tourists get a close look at glaciated peaks.

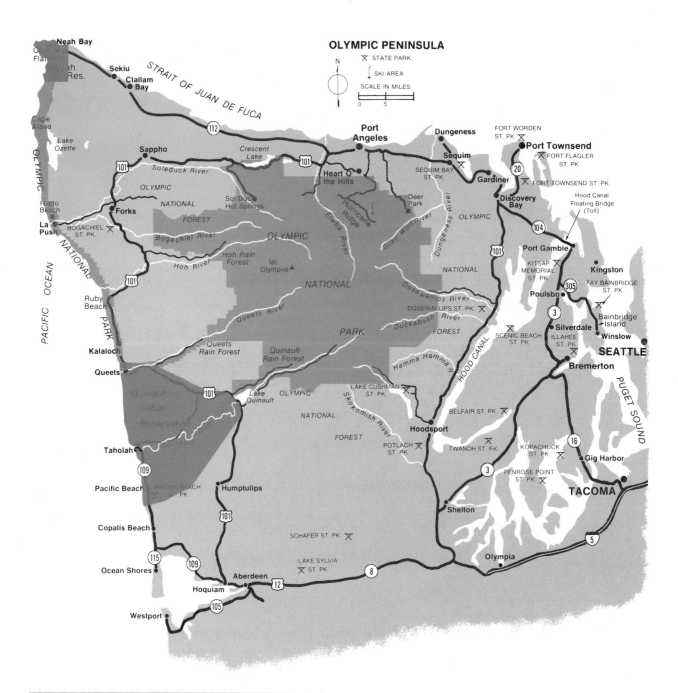

The Peninsula's Ocean Side

From the peninsula's northwesternmost tip down to Ruby Beach, the Pacific shoreline is rocky, stormswept, and remote. Four roads lead out to the shore, but no road runs along it for a shade more than 50 miles. Here is the ultimate opportunity for hikers on wild beaches. Inland from this shore is quite an opposite world: deep rain forests that fill river valleys with a serene, often silent sort of wilderness. For about 15 miles northward from the mouth of Grays Harbor, civilization rules along broad, sandy beaches famous for their hordes of razor clams—and hordes of diggers.

Wild Beaches

Most of the wild beaches toward the northern tip of the peninsula are for hikers. At Rialto and La Push, however, stub roads come to the backshore; then at Kalaloch U.S. 101 sticks close to the beaches for several miles, opening up the region.

Cape Flattery and Shi-Shi Beach. Cape Flattery is wondrously rugged and hard to use even though it adjoins comfortable Neah Bay within the Makah

Indian Reservation, some 66 miles west of Port Angeles. However, the makeshift road and the walk beyond it repay the effort in full. The steep, wave-wracked cliffs and offshore rocks provide scenery unique in the region.

Shi-Shi Beach is reached by the next best thing to no road at all. The road, such as it is, branches away from the road to Cape Flattery not far west of Neah Bay. An abandoned school bus marks the end for all cars of normal manufacture. From there the hike wanders through scrub to a serene 3-mile crescent of sand between Portage Head and Point of the Arches. The latter, a dramatic array of wave-tunneled rocks, closes off any access to the south.

The south end of Shi-Shi, Point of the Arches, and the beaches running south to the Ozette River were acquired in 1977 as an addition to the coastal strip of Olympic National Park.

Cape Alava and Lake Ozette. The only access to the shore in the 30 miles of coast between road's end at Neah Bay and road's end at Rialto is by trail from Lake Ozette.

The lake itself is among the largest in the state. Its east shore is being logged, while its west shore is safe within the park—giving the impression of a half-shaved head.

A resort with a campground is in the park at the northern tip of the lake, where the 22-mile road from Sekiu ends. From here, one trail wends out to Cape Alava; another goes out to Sand Point. The trails and the shore make a rough equilateral triangle, 3 miles to a leg. Hiking this is a fine introduction to the area. The hardy can do it in a day; most hikers camp or do only one leg.

Cape Alava, westernmost point in the 48 connected states, lies at the end of the more northerly trail, 3.3 miles from the resort. The trail is typical of shoreward paths in the region—muddy but easy walking through moss-festooned forest carpeted with ferns, salal, bunchberry dogwood, and young trees sprouting from the remains of fallen giants. Small meadows change the pace. Surf is audible for a long time, but the Pacific remains hidden until a walker steps onto the beach's back edge.

After reaching this picturesque point, site of an abandoned Indian village (now a Washington State University archaeological dig), hikers can head either south toward Sand Point or north toward an uncommon island and marine garden.

North a mile is Cannonball Island, named for large spherical concretions that wash out of its steep side. The island (also called Indian Island) lends itself to exploration at low tide, but getting trapped on it means sitting out a 12-hour tide.

About a mile north of the island, Carson Sea Cave forms an impressive garden of intertidal plants and animals. It can be explored only at low tide. Just beyond, the mouth of the Ozette River closes off any further push to the north.

Between Cannonball and Carson, hikers may come across bits and pieces from the bark *Austria*, wrecked here in 1887. Her anchor is the most noticeable remnant, but some pieces of hull, a bollard, and some chain also remain. She was a seaworthy vessel, 18 years old, 1,300 tons, and in able hands when a gale blew her ashore.

Sand Point is at the end of the trail that wends southwest from the Lake Ozette road.

This trail is usually the first leg for hikers making the 9-mile Ozette–Sand Point–Cape Alava triangle. Heading south from Sand Point turns the venture into a stouter hike. Though no walk for a novice, it is not hazardous to go all the way to Rialto Beach, at the mouth of the Quillayute River some 16 miles south.

The dedicated beach hiker will find the shore memorable for scenery, tidepools, and the guaranteed exertion of scrambling up and over one or more of the narrow headlands along the shore. A lucky traveler may spot a wild animal scouting the water's edge for food.

The hike is punctuated by memorials to three shipwrecks. The first of these, the Norwegian Memorial, is roughly west of the southern tip of Lake Ozette, about 8 miles south of Sand Point. (The easy way to reach the monument is by a boat taxi from the resort to the south end of the lake, where a 2-mile trail drops to the shore in exactly the right place.) The memorial marks the common grave of 18 men who perished in the wreck of the three-masted bark *Prince Arthur*, which mistook a cabin's light for that of Tatoosh Island and turned onto the rocks one January night in 1903.

The Chilean Memorial is 5 miles south of the Norwegian, just around the tip of Cape Johnson, and 3 miles north of Rialto Beach. It does double duty. The schooner *W. J. Pirrie* ran aground in November 1920, with 20 of 22 aboard drowning. Another Chilean vessel, the bark *Lenore*, grounded with lives lost 37 years earlier.

La Push and Rialto Beach. A paved road turns west from U.S. 101 about a mile north of the town of Forks and pursues a scenic way to the sea. Six miles inland the road divides. The north branch goes through Mora campgrounds to Rialto Beach on the north side of the Quillayute River; the south branch goes to the resort town of La Push.

Rialto Beach is the center of national park activity in this part of the coastal strip. A good-size picnic ground is at the backshore. A particularly good smelt run takes place on the broad, sandy beach, which is also the roadhead for hikes north.

The National Park Service campground, Mora, has 91 sites well inland in sheltering woods. Motels flank the campground.

La Push is a commercial and sport salmon harbor in the Quillayute (or Quileute) Indian Reservation. A low-key resort, it offers fine beaches.

The Indian residents of the town have retained their traditional skill with the dugout canoe. They paddle nimbly through seas that give veteran coast guardsmen the shudders. However, visitors are not required to use canoes; they go out in larger rental craft or aboard charter boats.

La Push also has fine beaches and is one endpoint of a superior 16-mile hike along the coast south. First Beach, adjoining the south jetty of the river in town, has a parking lot behind a tremendous tangle of driftwood. The south end is marked by a small, easily accessible sea cave.

Second Beach can be reached along the shore at low tide but is handier by way of a trail that joins the road into town. A tall offshore rock (known regionally as a "sea stack") close inshore and rugged Teawhit Head to the south make this beach one of the most scenic in the region.

Tidepools along Teawhit are rich with sea life. Ruth Kirk noted that this is one of the world's best places to observe intertidal invertebrates, because the fog is sometimes so thick that animals do not notice that the tide has gone out and left them behind. (Mrs. Kirk's book *The Olympic Seashore* is an indispensable guide for serious explorers and a charming, literate companion for every visitor. It is available at park visitor centers.)

Third Beach is accessible only by a 1-mile trail from La Push Road. (Teawhit Head cannot be rounded or climbed from Second Beach.) From a point near the south end of this secluded beach begins the difficult trail to Oil City, 15 miles south. Hikers must climb over several lofty headlands, slither along on seaweed-slicked boulders, and keep going after fatigue sets in if they are to make the trip in 2 days.

The south end of the beach trail is at Oil City—a name on a map, no more. U.S. 101 is 12 gravel-road miles inland.

On this beach hike and the more northerly one between Rialto and Ozette, hikers must carry maps and tide tables, go around heads only at low tides, and go over them on marked trails when tides are high or rising. Wise hikers check in at a ranger station before departing on either hike.

Kalaloch and Ruby Beach. This short stretch of shore is the northernmost at which a road parallels the shore. Kalaloch offers a sandy beach, a roomy lodge, and a 195-site campground right at the shore. Seven numbered beaches flank it—the first two to the south, the others to the north. Ruby Beach is just north of Beach Seven. All within 6 miles, these beaches offer a gentle yet fairly complete introduction to wilderness beaches.

U.S. 101 stays just far enough inland to be out of sight and out of mind. Hikes from highwayside parking lots to shores run half a mile or less. Once on one beach, a wanderer can walk easily to the next. Surf fishing is productive at all beaches. Kalaloch itself has some razor clams; Beach Two has fine driftwood; Beach Four has smelt.

Rain Forests

On the inland side of U.S. 101 the world is almost as wet as on the beach side. In the deep river valleys—the Quinault, Queets, and Hoh—local rain is supplemented by water coming down from the high peaks. As the valleys flatten, the water slows enough to create true climax rain forests—places so dense with vegetation that only a few trails can be kept open. Sitka spruce and Douglas fir grow to 275 feet, with 8-foot trunk diameters; mosses and ferns dominate a diverse forest understory.

Roads poke into all three of the river valleys.

Lake Quinault and the river above it are the most developed areas, under a cooperative administration of the national park, the Olympic National Forest, and the Quinault Indian Reservation.

The National Park Service administers the north shore, including a ranger station and the 31-site July Creek campground (for tents only). On the south side, the Forest Service has three campgrounds—Olallie (10 tent sites), Willaby (7 tent, 12 trailer sites), and Falls Creek (21 tent, 5 trailer sites)—a ranger station, and a rain forest interpretive display. Willaby and Falls Creek have beaches and boat launching ramps. Concessionaire campgrounds and lodges ring the lake; Quinault Lodge on the south side is the oldest and most famous. Amanda Park, in the Quinault Reservation at the west end of the lake, offers stores, gas stations, and other commercial services. The Quinaults control all use of the lake itself.

The two roads leading from U.S. 101 along the north and south shores of the lake continue through the rain forest well into the high country. A crossroad ties the two together near their eastern ends. The northern road ends at North Fork Campground (10 tent sites); the southern one goes to Graves Creek Campground (45 sites, open to trailers). These are departure points for top-of-the-world hikes across the Olympics. A National Park Service ranger is stationed at each campground.

The Queets River rain forest, a few miles north, is much less heavily used. An unpaved stub road

---

The temperate jungle

Rain forests are common in the tropics, but only the Olympics have created a large one in a cool climate.

ambles along the river, ending at the 95-site Queets Campground of the national park. It, too, is a departure point for high-country hikes.

The Hoh River rain forest is the northernmost geographically, but falls in between the other two in terms of development. At the high end of a road on the north side of the river, the national park's 95-site Hoh Campground leads to high-country trails. Outside the park boundary, four commercial campgrounds dot the road. Two others are on another road on the river's south bank, and three more are right along U.S. 101 near the river.

Bogachiel State Park, 19 acres and 42 campsites, is a useful base point for exploring the Bogachiel River valley, a few miles north of the Hoh. This valley is transitional—lusher than a typical Pacific Northwest forest but less overgrown than the climax rain forests to the south. The river can produce fine catches, particularly of sea-run cutthroat in autumn. Along its bank relatively open, easy-going hiking trails penetrate high toward its headwaters within the national park.

The state park is just west of U.S. 101, 6 miles south of Forks. The principal trails run eastward from there, or from a stub road leading east from U.S. 101.

Though the Bogachiel has a special reputation for cutthroat trout, these coast-side rivers are legendary among winter steelheaders. At that season fishermen can not only harvest fish but also enjoy the rain forests when the lack of deciduous leaf makes them somewhat more open. Big wild animals come down to winter in the lowlands, and chances of seeing them are good.

Tame Beaches

For years the citizens of Grays Harbor had the sandy, razor clam–rich beaches north of the bay pretty much to themselves. In mobile modern times, however, visitors may outnumber locals 100 to 1 when a favorable tide brings 30,000 clammers running.

All those visitors have given rise to a substantial resort development north along the shore until the Quinault Reservation pinches off the possibility.

Ocean Shores, on the north spit of Grays Harbor, is both newest and largest of the resort communities. Up the coast, Ocean City, Copalis, and Pacific Beach are older and quieter.

To such natural attractions as razor clamming, surf fishing, and beachcombing, the resorts have added offshore salmon fishing, golf, art galleries, and even an occasional splash of night life.

The beach proper is one long park, but except for Ocean City State Park and state-operated beach accesses in each town, the backshore is privately owned.

An amble-gaited stub road, State 109, branches west from U.S. 101 at Hoquiam to serve the region.

Ocean Shores started out in the 1960s with Hollywood money and Hollywood airs. The approach did not pan out. With time, the atmosphere has come into harmony with the region, and the resort shows signs of prosperity. It has 600 rentable rooms, several restaurants, a nightclub-theatre, and a golf course as legacies of the original notion; it now has expanded outdoor opportunities aimed at fishermen, clammers, and beachcombers.

The municipally-owned golf course (18 holes; 6,021 yards; par 71) is flat and not heavily treed, but sneaky water makes it tougher than it looks.

A small fleet of charter boats is available for fishermen at the resort, and a water taxi gives access to the huge fleet across the bay at Westport (see page 63). A stable rents horses for beach rides; clammers can easily rent gear for digging.

Oyehut is a quieter, smaller extension of Ocean Shores, adjoining it on the north.

Ocean City State Park is on the local road that leads from State 109 into Ocean Shores; the park entrance is only a few hundred feet from the highway. The 112-acre park spreads out across low, rolling dunes. Most of its 179 campsites and 29 trailer hookups are sheltered in scrub trees well back from the shore. A road goes west to the beach. This access is supplemented by two public access spots in Ocean Shores, another at Oyehut, and a fourth just north at the town of Ocean City.

This park, the only formal one in the area, has the only picnic sites for miles around.

Ocean City, straddling the highway to the north, is primarily a sequence of vacation homes.

Copalis Beach, next in the line to the north, is the oldest and best known of the resort towns in the north beaches. It has a mixture of motels and beach cottage resorts, restaurants, and private trailer-camper parks. Though there is no park, two public accesses lead to the beach and its supply of razor clams and surf fish.

Pacific Beach, another 8 miles up the road, is more dramatically set than its neighbors to the south. Rocks begin to compete successfully with sand at this point. The town tucks under the lee of a bluff at the back of a deep cove. The south end of its beach pinches off at a forested headland. Around the corner to the north, a long, narrow ribbon of dark, fine sand stretches as far as Moclips on the southern boundary of the Quinault Indian Reservation. (The sand continues for a way. However, the Quinaults grew tired of non-Quinaults spray-painting graffiti on the beach rocks and littering the place and closed off their beaches to all outsiders.)

This is a razor clammer's beach in season and a drift hunter's beach all year, especially in winter.

At Pacific Beach a concessionaire operates a campground at state park standards, in cooperation with the State Parks Department. The 9-acre site has 105 campsites and 10 trailer hookups. The town also has several motels.

Closing the Loop

Most treks across the base of the Olympic Peninsula go fast. U.S. 12/State 8 encourages speedy travel with four-lane road all the way and freeway most of the distance.

For those with some time at hand, Olympia, at the foot of Puget Sound, has much to recommend it. Between Olympia and Grays Harbor, the southern edge of the Olympic Mountains offers the remotest, yet gentlest, side of the range.

Olympia, State Capital

Olympia attracts a great deal of attention from geography students and political figures because it is Washington's capital city. It attracts as much or more attention from gastronomes because incomparable oysters live in shoal bays north and west of town.

Large-scale renovation of a faded waterfront and downtown will keep parts of the city torn up for some years to come. Happily for visitors, construction will not affect the capitol grounds, the oysters, or any of several fine parks.

Accommodations. A brisk convention trade and political visitors have caused several large motels to be built in Olympia in recent years. The greatest cluster is along Capitol Way, off I-5 via Exit 105. The largest facility is right next to Exit 102.

Attractions. The capitol grounds downtown, oyster farms northwest of the city, and a brewery south of town lead the list of places to visit.

The great dome of the state legislature's Roman-Doric building dominates the city skyline. Under it—and beneath a massive brass Tiffany chandelier hanging 185 feet above marble floors—an organist plays weekday concerts. A narrated tour of the building is available most weekdays.

Just south of the legislative building, the State Library building houses sculpture, mosaics, and paintings by outstanding Northwest artists in addition to its large book collection.

Both buildings are set in 55 lavishly landscaped acres of grounds. Great banks of rhododendrons blossom on the heels of flowering cherries in spring, the showiest season. A replica of Denmark's Tivoli Fountain provides a dramatic display of changing colors throughout the year.

Capitol Way, the city's main street, runs along the east side of the grounds.

A block off Capitol Way at 211 West 21st Street, the State Capitol Museum has a permanent collection of Northwest art as well as rotating exhibits. The handsome old mansion also houses an illuminating geologic survey of the state and oddments of pioneer history. The museum is open weekdays.

The Olympia Brewing Company in the neighboring town of Tumwater is small by the standards of American brewers today, but its plant next to I-5 is impressively large all the same. Visitors are welcome to tour the spotless brewery and taste its end product. Tours run daily during normal business hours; Exit 104 gives direct access.

Northwest of the city along U.S. 101 headed toward the old logging and mill town of Shelton, the properly named Oyster Bay spreads out wide and shallow. The Olympia Oyster Co., largest of 15 producers in the bay, gives visitors a first-hand look at the tiny, richly flavored native Olympia oyster between 10 A.M. and 2 P.M. weekdays. To

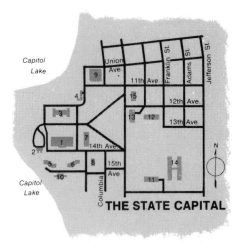

THE STATE CAPITAL

1 Legislative Building
2 Governor's Mansion
3 Temple of Justice
4 Greenhouse
5 Public Health Building
6 Public Lands Building
7 Insurance Building
8 Institutions Building
9 General Administration
10 State Library
11 Employment Security
12 Highways-Licenses
13 Archives and Records
14 Highway Building
15 Thurston County Courthouse

reach the shore, turn off U.S. 101 onto the old Shelton Highway just north of Kennedy Creek Bridge.

Parks and recreation. Olympia supports a sizable park system and offers excellent golf and tennis facilities.

Capitol Lake Park, just below the capitol grounds, is a salt-water swimming stadium all summer long and a spawning route for salmon in mid-August. On shore, picnic grounds and playground equipment make the park a pleasant family stopping point.

Priest Point Park, on Budd Inlet, is the city's largest picnic and recreation park. Reached on East Bay Drive, it has salt-water swimming beaches and nature trails as well as picnic areas.

Tumwater Falls Park, next to the Olympia Brewery, is also a handy picnic spot and playground.

A major recreational development just south of the Olympia brewery buildings includes a golf course and a tennis club with both indoor and outdoor courts. Tumwater Valley Golf Club (18 holes; 6,531 yards; par 72) ambles along the bottom of Tumwater Valley; it is long now, and getting tougher as its trees grow up. Tumwater Valley Racquet Club reserves three of its eight indoor courts for visitors, who must call a day ahead for reservations. Play is by hourly fee.

Besides the club and school courts, Woodruff Park at 1500 Harrison Avenue, a few blocks west of Capitol Lake, has four tennis courts.

Other golf courses in the region include Capitol City Golf Course (18 holes; 6,088 yards; par 72) in Lacey; Scott Lake Golf Club (18 holes; 5,451 yards; par 69), 8 miles south of Olympia via I-5; and Delphi Golf Course (9 holes; 2,400 yards; par 35), 6 miles west of town on Alpine Hills Road.

Between Olympia and the Coast

Between Olympia at the foot of Puget Sound and the side-by-side towns of Aberdeen and Hoquiam on Grays Harbor, several pleasant parks invite casual visits, and some fairly remote mountainous country invites people who like to get away from it all.

Lake Sylvia State Park, 235 acres with 35 campsites, attracts fishermen from afar, swimmers from nearby. It is just a mile north of Montesano.

Schafer State Park. Somewhat more remote than Lake Sylvia, Schafer hides away in foothills north of Satsop, on the Satsop River. The 119-acre park has 53 campsites (6 trailer hookups), fishing, and swimming. Facilities also include sheltered kitchens and picnic tables.

Lake Wynoochee requires a strong desire to fish or to get away from it all. The Corps of Engineers Visitor Center near Wynoochee Dam, well inside Olympic National Forest, is 30 winding miles from Montesano. A nine-site campground is even higher up, at Wynoochee Falls.

Aberdeen and Hoquiam. Business dominates this pair of hard-working towns. The deep-water port mostly handles local forest products. A strategic location, plus a sizable collection of motels, has made the area an important overnight stop for visitors to the Olympic Peninsula.

Useful Addresses on the Olympic Peninsula

- Olympic Peninsula Travel Association
  c/o Washington State Ferries
  Seattle Ferry Terminal, Pier 52
  Seattle, WA 98104
- Olympic National Park
  600 East Park Ave.
  Port Angeles, WA 98362
- Olympic National Forest
  Federal Building
  Olympia, WA 98501

Chambers of Commerce

- P.O. Box 229, Bremerton, WA 98310
- P.O. Box 1467, Forks, WA 98331
- Grays Harbor, P.O. Box 450,
  Aberdeen, WA 98520
- P.O. Box 382, Ocean Shores, WA 98569
- P.O. Box 1427, Olympia, WA 98507
- Olympic North Beach, P.O. Box 555,
  Copalis, WA 98535
- 1217 E. First, Port Angeles, WA 98362
- 2139 Sims Way,
  Port Townsend, WA 98368
- P.O. Box 1063, Poulsbo, WA 98370
- Sequim-Dungeness, P.O. Box 907,
  Sequim, WA 98382
- P.O. Box 666, Shelton, WA 98584

A shoreline for hikers

The roadless Olympic National Park shore—more than 30 miles of it—offers visitors afternoon strolls or rugged 3-day hikes.

Mighty salmon, fast-digging clams attract vacationers to a gentle coastline

Southwest

Southwest Washington is two places—or, if not that, then two states of mind.

The coast from Grays Harbor south to the Columbia River mouth caters to deep-sea fishermen, razor clammers, drift hunters, winter wave watchers, and everybody else with a taste for salt water. Westport and the North Beach Peninsula ask for—and get—crowds of visitors.

The inland valleys do no such thing; their excellent rivers and lakes are underpublicized and not at all crowded by fishermen, boaters, or campers. True, it takes a great deal of rain to keep all that greenery growing and all those rivers full. True, the woods are full of loggers and the fields of dairy and other farmers who do not favor frivolity. For both reasons, the region has considerable appeal for anyone seeking a day or two of calm outdoor relaxation.

Along Interstate 5, several tidy, attractive commercial centers offer civilized respite to the road-weary, along with some agreeably lively history.

Weather. The profile here follows that in the rest of western Washington, with not quite so many local quirks as areas farther north. The low hills of the coast ranges do not create dramatic rain forests or rain shadows as the Olympics do.

Average rainfall varies from 90 inches along the coast and the west-facing foothills down to 40 inches a year in the broad valleys. (Naselle, hard against the coast ranges on the Columbia River, is the regional champion with 114 inches.) Measurable precipitation comes on 160 to 180 days each year; about 50 days are cloudless. October through March is very gray and wet. July is the driest month—less than an inch of rain scattered over 5 days is typical.

Real heat is rare. In the warmest lowlands a typical year has only half a dozen days that reach the 90° range. Real cold is almost as rare. Some stations have never recorded a 0° reading, though inland frost comes 50 to 60 nights a year at lower elevations, more often at higher elevations.

Highways. The region has only two freeways. The principal one is Interstate Highway 5, relentlessly efficient carrier of north-south traffic. The other, U.S. 12, arcs west from I-5 from a junction near Centralia to Aberdeen on Grays Harbor. All other roads are two-lane. Most major roads are wide and asphalt paved, with occasional uphill passing lanes. Expect to share any route other than I-5 with logging trucks.

As elsewhere in Washington, all federal and state highways carry green mile markers. On I-5 the numbers increase from south to north. The same is true of U.S. 101 from Megler to Aberdeen. On U.S. 12, mile 0 is at Aberdeen. On State Routes 4 and 6, however, numbers go up east to west.

The Southwest Coast

As the crow flies, Westport, at the mouth of Grays Harbor, is but 50 miles from Ilwaco, at the mouth of the Columbia River. However, the vast, oyster-laden shoals of Willapa Bay complicate matters.

Without the bay, the region would be a single long sandy beach with rolling, forested hills behind it. The bay gives variety to beaches and to the resort towns along them.

In practical terms, Westport and its environs put salmon first and razor clams second, while the North Beach Peninsula reverses that order. Willapa Bay's contributions to the mix are oysters and sheltered water for small boats.

North Beach Peninsula

Except for Cape Disappointment and North Head, which loom up gloomily above the Columbia River mouth, the North Beach Peninsula barely shows on topographic maps. It is 28 miles long, but few spots on the sandy spit reach 40 feet above sea level.

Its nature makes the peninsula a perfect environment for cranberries and razor clams. The razor clams, in turn, make it an excellent environment for tourists. Local oyster beds in Willapa

Corner

See additional map on page 65.

Seattle Spokane

Harbor come as a bonus, as do huge schools of salmon in offshore waters.

Accommodations. For a long time Long Beach and its peninsula neighbors stood as the kind of old-fashioned resort towns that made a body want to play the local nine-hole golf course in tweed knickers and cap. During the Gay 90s this was a favored retreat of Portlanders. A good many of the accommodations still are clusters of shingled beach cottages patterned on the venerable model. However, with the mid-1970s have come several large new buildings that conform to current architectural fashions for oceanside resort hotels.

Most of the new and many of the old resorts are in Long Beach and neighboring Seaview. The smaller towns of Klipsan and Ocean Park several miles north have kept their old-timey flavors.

In late autumn and winter, only a few of these resorts stay open.

Overnight camper parks thread throughout the area.

Attractions. Two small oystering towns huddle on the bay side of the peninsula toward its north end. Both are worth a visit by observers of rare industries and by photographers and water colorists who think highly of aging and picturesque architecture, both residential and marine. The towns, Nahcotta and Oysterville, can be reached from Ilwaco by Peninsula Road or from Long Beach via State 103 to Ocean Park, then east.

The canneries and smokehouses of Nahcotta welcome visitors in late fall and early winter, their active time. In summer there is very little oyster harvesting, and therefore very little processing.

Just south of the oystermen's dock in Nahcotta, the Willapa Bay Shellfish Laboratory is open to visitors weekdays all year around. This is the place to learn about edible shellfish from the bay. Having learned, bay clammers and crabbers can return to the dock to rent skiffs (power to be provided by the renter) and crab rings. Oysters are not for public picking but can be bought.

Parks and recreation. After a fashion, the whole length of sandy beach from North Head to the tip of the spit is state park. At least it is all accessible through state-run access points—one at Seaview, one at Long Beach, one at Klipsan, three at Ocean Park, and one west of Oysterville.

This is the home of the razor clam in its season, as well as one of the richest beaches on the coast for winter combing in search of Japanese glass fishing floats.

Both may be found in or on 28 straight miles of basalt sand so fine that people can (and do) drive automobiles over it to get to the clam beds or the drift, or merely for the novelty. There is some excuse for cluttering up the beach with automobiles and crusting up the automobiles with salt: every time the jetties have been extended, the shore currents have retreated a corresponding distance, dumping their loads of sand that much sooner. Resorts that once were right next to the water (the hummocky ridge running all along the spit is the old backshore) now find themselves as much as half a mile away from it at high tide. But driving directly over the clam beds destroys them, so cars should drive as high on the beach as sand is packed.

The technique for hunting razors is noted on page 68. Tough as that chore might be, serious beachcombing is tougher. Though the peninsula catches huge amounts of drift from the Japanese current in winter, most of it is snaffled off the beach by professionals before it comes to rest. The trick is to get up and follow the incoming highest high tide of the day, working along the edge of the surf.

The peninsula does have two state parks; one is developed, the other is a natural preserve.

Fort Canby State Park occupies a dip between Cape Disappointment inside the Columbia River mouth and North Head just outside.

The park has 350 campsites tucked into a loosely set stand of birch just inside the main gate. Picnic sites for day users are up on North Head. To the east of the main gate is a boat launch.

Westward from the campsites, an asphalt road runs alongside the hulking stonework of the Columbia's north jetty. Toward the inner end of the

The bountiful Pacific

Near the Columbia River's mouth (above), deep basalt sands hold rich crops of razor clams. Offshore (left) are salmon, schooling for their spawning runs. If the prices for these prized catches of southwest Washington are hard work in tough conditions, the rewards to serious eaters are unbeatable.

jetty, a sandy beach encourages swimming in sun-warmed shoals, but the main event is another mile west. There a large parking lot gives access to a fishing platform on the jetty and to a beach good for both surf fishing and drift gathering. Veterans work the river side of the jetty for sea bass in winter and the ocean side for perch in summer. Surf fishermen work wave troughs north of the jetty for perch and other browsing species the year around.

This is also one of the fine vantage points in all the world for winter storm watching. On a blustery day, the Columbia bar is a seething mass of waves, the jetty a constant lash of spray.

Up on Cape Disappointment, students of Lewis and Clark can spend hours in a fine interpretive center considering the epic journey of the great explorers. Rising up from some old gun emplacements, the center offers a solid retreat from heavy weather.

The expedition of 1805 had no such comfort when it arrived in the dead of winter to be greeted by a typical day: "...at two o'clock," reads the journal, "the flood tide set in, accompanied by a high wind from the south, which, about four o'clock, shifted to the southwest, and blew almost a gale directly from the sea. The immense waves now broke over the place where we were encamped, and the large trees, some of them 5 or 6 feet thick, which had lodged at the point, were drifted over our camp. We remained in the water and drenched with rain during the rest of the day."

For those who would get out on the river, where Lewis and Clark hated to go, Ilwaco is home to many charter craft. This is a place for novices to leave the skippering to wise locals. Much as the Columbia bar has been tamed by dredges and jetties, it is still no place to get caught when the weather makes up. In the short history of navigation across the bar, more than 200 ships have been lost or damaged at a cost of more than 1,500 lives. The number of people lost in small boats runs a good many more. Ignorance of weather and wave conditions is doubtless the leading cause of tragedy. Besides, the locals can smell out schooling salmon quicker than a newcomer can stumble upon them.

Leadbetter State Park, clear at the other end of the peninsula from Fort Canby–Ilwaco, has a different appeal. A unit in the Willapa National Wildlife Refuge, the park starts out as sparse woods and slowly becomes open sand dunes. This is the place for long walks on unspoiled ocean or bay beaches, and maybe for a bit of dune sliding.

Peninsula Road (parallel to the more westerly State 103) runs north from Nahcotta to Oysterville, then turns west. From this leg, a bumpy dirt track leads north into Leadbetter State Park.

The principal section of the wildlife refuge is Long Island, 6 miles long and only 400 yards off the shore of Willapa Bay at its southern tip. On the island are seven marine campsites with picnic tables, 20 miles of woodsy trails, and—for company—otters, raccoons, and some of 200 species of waterfowl and shore birds. (March is the peak month for birdwatching.)

Before going to the island, check in at the refuge headquarters on U.S. 101, 12 miles northeast of Ilwaco. The headquarters itself is worth a visit for display ponds of Canada geese, a whistling swan, and other rare birds.

Westport and Environs

Until the late 1950s, Westport was a sleepy commercial fishing village just inside the south jetty of Grays Harbor. It had one pier with a packing shed, a Coast Guard station, and a main street with two combination saloons and restaurants.

When offshore sport fishing for salmon boomed, Westport boomed with it. Now the boat basin houses an astonishingly large collection of trim craft, and the waterfront street (formerly nonexistent) is a proportionately long collection of charter offices, restaurants, and motels.

The atmosphere then and now is rough-hewn and hardy, maybe boisterous. The trip across the Grays Harbor bar can—and often does—make an average roller-coaster ride seem as stately as a boardwalk tour in an English electric wheelchair. The Columbia bar is more savage, but if the seas at Westport come in straighter, they do not come much flatter. Hence the regulars here can eat pickles and drink beer on a deck that changes planes by 45° every minute or two, and they will. They will also sing and shout over dawn coffee as well as stronger drink, and will sleep as much like logs in one of the town's $7-a-night dormitory bunks as they might in plush surroundings.

Downcoast at Grayland and beyond, where razor clams are the main attraction, things go more quietly.

Accommodations. The waterfront street in Westport has a plethora of motels ranging from the faintly luxurious down to the aforementioned dormitory-style operations. The interior of town holds several clusters of cottages. Grayland also has a number of old-fashioned beach cottage resorts. Overnight parks for campers are plentiful.

Attractions. Fishing charters are the attraction. Salmon is king, and king salmon is the king of kings, but its spring-through-fall runs are short enough that the charter fleet runs off-season trips after halibut and other lesser fry. A typical day trip on one of the 190-plus boats in the fleet costs slightly less than $30 without rental gear, slightly more with it. The Westport Charter Association, Westport, WA 98595, provides a roster of members and other information on request.

Parks and recreation. Visitors have a choice of beach parks on this 12-mile stretch of coast.

Westhaven State Park runs from the jetty south to the old, deactivated Westport Light, where there is a second access road. This day-use area is a haunt for surf fishermen and drift hunters.

Twin Harbors State Park, straddling State 105 3 miles south of Westport, is the major camping park here. It has 319 sites and 49 trailer hookups tucked into a wooded area east of the highway. A picnic area, with kitchens and shelters, adjoins that and spills across to the beach side of the road.

Grayland State Park, another 3 miles south, is larger than Twin Harbors—210 acres compared to 168—but has only 60 campsites to supplement its older neighbor to the north. The park has beach frontage backed by the camp and picnic areas in scrub growth along the backshore.

In addition to these, the state park system maintains two other beach accesses: one between Grayland and Twin Harbors parks, the other 3 miles south of Grayland on State 105.

Willapa Harbor

Except for the sheltered side of the Long Beach Peninsula, Willapa Bay gets relatively little attention from visitors, and alas for those who miss a tranquil day in gentle beauty.

The less settled parts of the bay's backshore offer a chance to camp in handsome scenery and a good many chances to fish or picnic.

Along U.S. 101 between the south end of the bay and the oystering town of South Bend, one county camping park and one day-use state park are augmented by several state-operated public fishing access sites.

Bruceport County Park rolls down a slope from the highway to the bay's edge 7 miles south of South Bend. Tall conifers shade its campsites and picnic area.

The park, incidentally, marks the site of the first oyster farm on the bay, begun when the schooner *Robert Bruce* burned in 1851, leaving her crew with no way to make a living but harvesting shellfish for the Gold Rush trade in San Francisco.

Bush-Pacific Pioneer State Park and the adjoining village of Bay Center are another 5 miles south. Just south of the Palix River Bridge, a spur road cuts west from U.S. 101 across a swamp full of red-winged blackbirds. Bay Center comes first, an agreeable collection of piers and frame buildings surrounded by metal tubs, wire baskets, and other tools of the oystering trade. The business area lies

in the lee of a rounded hill. Up top are houses and the state park. Most of the park is an open-floored stand of tall trees, with picnic tables scattered in dappled shade atop a unique duff of fir needles and oyster shells.

Neither Bruceport nor Bush-Pacific has suitable beaches for swimming or fishing—the oyster beds are too near. In compensation, the views of working oystermen in spring and fall are both beautiful and instructive.

For those who would get onto the water, two clearly signed public fishing accesses are located between the Palix River and the Nemah.

North of Raymond one must go all the way to the bay mouth to find another access to shore. (Coming down from Westport is quicker, but not as beautiful a ride.) State 105 from Raymond to Tokeland stays right with an unspoiled shoreline.

Tokeland itself is a small sport fishing village. The place is so serene that the local bait shop rents crab rings so people can fish off the public dock if they are not of a mind to take a charter trip.

In addition to crabbing, Tokeland is a fine place for winter drift hunting. The road stops well short of the end of the spit, keeping all but the serious from collecting in the area.

As for the side-by-side but unidentical towns of Raymond and South Bend, they do not court visitors. Raymond tends to milling and shipping; South Bend devotes itself to oysters. Neither has many motel or hotel rooms. A small pioneer museum in South Bend is the lone attraction.

The Columbia River Mouth

State 4 slips west from Longview toward the mouth of the Columbia, 75 miles distant. Except for a hilly stretch in the middle, State 4, its branch State 401, and U.S. 101 hug the bank of this busiest stretch of the river all the way to Ilwaco.

The waterside routes have some pleasant low-key diversions.

Cathlamet, an early-day logging town, has arrived in the present with a distinct flavor, owing in one way to the complete absence of fast-food franchises and in another to the presence on Main Street of an elegantly restored old hotel.

Within walking distance of downtown is a traditional Pacific Northwest town park, a woodsy place with a sheltered cookhouse, horseshoe pits, a ball field, and—a modern addition—two excellent lighted tennis courts.

Near town the nine-hole, 2,641-yard, par 35 Skyline Golf Course threads through tall conifers.

Nearby the tiny community of Skamokawa (locally pronounced Ska-*mock*-away), though not

Venice, sits on a slough-crossed plain that makes getting around town in a boat as easy as using a car, or easier. Students of marine architecture will find all manner of quirky nautical designs.

Collectors of ferry rides can cross the Columbia on one of the two routes that still connect Washington and Oregon. From Cathlamet a bridge crosses to Puget Island; from the opposite side of the island, a small car ferry runs a quick course to Westport, Oregon.

Collectors of covered bridges can look up one of Washington's rare survivors at Grays River, on a local road just west of Skamokawa and just north of State 4.

But the Columbia itself is the principal source of local recreation. Fishermen and boaters make the most of it in a region where protected channels offer water smooth enough for water-skiing.

Countyline Park, a few miles east of Cathlamet, is the place for bank fishermen. In season its long sandy beach is stuck full of poles whose owners hope—with some reason—for salmon. (Sturgeon fanciers gather on a steeper shore a mile or so east, opposite large piers on an island.) The day-use park, administered jointly by Cowlitz and Wahkiakum counties, also has picnic tables.

Boaters can get onto the river from public launching ramps a mile east of Skamokawa and at the town on Brooks Slough.

After splitting away from State 4 well to the west, State 401 rejoins the river near the Washington end of the Astoria-Megler toll bridge, which carries U.S. 101 across the Columbia.

Fort Columbia State Park, within 2 miles, is now a serene picnic park and historic museum after a quiet career as a shore battery post protecting a river that was never invaded. The 591-acre park has virtually the only swimming beach on the Columbia below Vancouver, except for one right at the mouth.

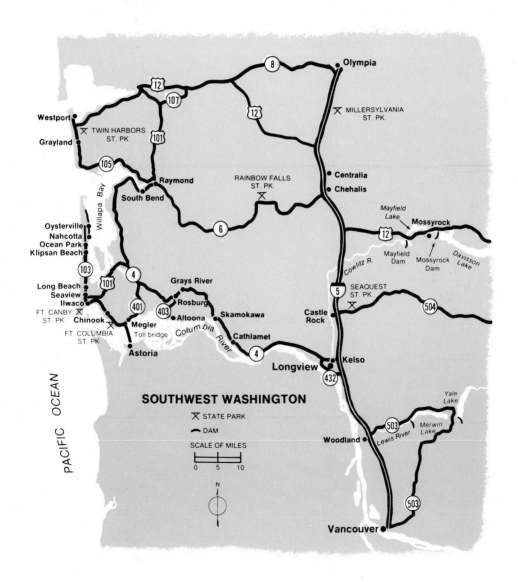

SOUTHWEST WASHINGTON

✕ STATE PARK

⌒ DAM

SCALE OF MILES
0 5 10

N

The nearby town of Chinook has a riverbank camping park used mostly by fishermen. An adjoining boat launch operated by the Port of Chinook charges a small fee. Several modest motels amplify the overnight possibilities.

Ilwaco at the river mouth has already been noted on page 63.

Cool Foothill Waters

Between Interstate 5 and the Cascade Mountains, southwestern Washington has some superior recreation for fishermen and boaters who prefer less size and bustle than the Columbia provides.

Lewis River

Only 60 miles separate Lewis River's tumbling headwaters on Mt. Adams from its placid union with the Columbia near Woodland.

Within that short span are whitewater for kayaking, three big pools behind as many dams, and finally, a slow floater's paradise.

A steelheader's river where it runs, the Lewis is voluminous enough for sailboaters where it has been stilled.

Merwin Lake is the downstream reservoir. Its west end is just 10 miles from Interstate 5; from Exit 21, State 503 leads straight to it. The state route continues up to the next pool, Yale Lake. From there the Lewis River Road pushes on up to the third reservoir, Swift, where the country begins to be high mountains.

In the lowlands, Merwin Park advertises itself as a picnic and swimming park with room for 2,000 people. Close to Merwin Dam, it has sheltered picnic stoves and other civilized comforts. Speelyai Bay Park, 11 miles uplake, also has picnic sites and swimming, but a boat ramp and service area have made it a favorite of power boaters.

Up on Yale Lake, on Lewis River Road, Yale and Cougar parks are picnic and swimming units. Yale has a boat launch. East of Cougar Park, Cougar Camp has 45 sites (tents only), a boat launch, and a swimming beach. Reservations are mandatory (from Pacific Power Recreation Department, Public Service Building, Portland, OR 97204; the same

address will provide a brochure with details on Lewis River parks). Toward the upper end of Yale, Beaver Bay campsite allows trailers and does not require reservations, but does levy a small overnight fee.

On Swift, topmost lake in the chain, Swift Camp has 101 camp or picnic sites and a boat launch. Eagle Cliff Park has a handful of amenities for bank fishermen, who crowd it.

All is not water.

Ape Cave is 2 miles of lava tube—the longest cave of its kind on the continent. Inside it is as dark and cold as most caves are, but no more than a good lantern and stout shoes are required to explore it. To get to it from Yale, go east 12 miles on Lewis River Road, then follow Forest Road N 90 to its junction with N 83. There, turn north (left) and continue 3 miles to the cave.

Cedar Creek grist mill, a classic example of a pioneer mill, is handier. The crude structure dating from 1876 is 9 miles east of Woodland via County Road 16, then left another mile along Grist Mill Road.

Another Lewis River, the east fork, adds two more parks to the regional possibilities. State 502 (Exit 9 from I-5) leads toward both. Alternatively, State 503 loops south from Merwin Lake into Battleground and the neighborhood of these parks.

Lewisville County Park is 3 miles north of Battleground and just east of State 503. A 640-acre woodland, it has a space for 9,000 picnickers and offers swimming beaches, playgrounds, and walking trails.

Battleground Lake State Park, cupped in the crater of a long-extinct volcano, has 50 campsites and several concessionaires to mitigate its isolation. The concessions include rental boats. The park's attractions are fishing and hiking.

Cowlitz River

Like the Lewis, the Cowlitz River in its free-running days was turbulent in the upper reaches, placid in the lower ones. With the coming of Mayfield and Mossyrock dams, it too has begun to be developed in its ballooned middle as a recreational resource.

U.S. 12 branches east from I-5 at Exit 68, 9 miles south of Chehalis. It provides ready access to Lake Mayfield and its neighbor, Davisson Lake.

Through 1977, Ike Kinswa State Park on Mayfield Lake was the only major waterside development. Tacoma City Light, builder of the dams, has several more parks on its drawing boards.

The 454-acre Kinswa park has 101 campsites and 41 trailer hookups tucked into fir woods. A

Salmon fleet at rest

Ilwaco, inside the Columbia River mouth, is—with Westport—a major harbor for salmon charter boats.

boat launching ramp accompanies them. The picnic grounds and a lawn-backed swimming beach are a separate unit some hundreds of yards west. Walking trails ramble all through the park.

The swimming beach, incidentally, is in a shallow lagoon fenced off from the main lake.

The park is reached by a loop road north of U.S. 12. Both ends of the loop are clearly posted on the highway.

Lower in the Cowlitz River Valley and well away from water, Lewis & Clark State Park is a 524-acre property devoted principally to picnickers, especially groups. It is on old U.S. Highway 99, the Jackson Highway, not far south of that road's junction with U.S. 12 and only 5 miles from I-5.

A mile nearer the freeway, also on the Jackson Highway, is Jackson Court House, a pioneer structure restored as a heritage site.

Digging Razor Clams

An unofficial spokesman for razor clammers once said that "digging for razor clams satisfies a man's basic urges to hunt, fish, and farm . . . all in one gloriously difficult operation."

If that overstates the case, it remains a fact that the razor (*Siliqua patula*) is the only clam with a sporting chance against any healthy shovel wielder.

The cold statistics are these: Razor clams can dig at a steady rate of as much as 9 inches a minute, to a depth of more than 3 feet. They live near the lower extreme of the intertidal zone, the hinged side of their long, slim shells faced out to sea. They inhabit only beaches where the surf sweeps in unchecked by offshore islands or other protection. The thickest concentrations for diggers seem to be on sand bars that retain an inch-deep glaze of water on the lowest tides of the year.

Above all other environments, the animals seem to prefer the basalt sands washed out to sea by the Columbia River. Washington's greatest razor beaches are along the sweep of shore from the Columbia mouth north as far as Pacific Beach, a few miles north of the Grays Harbor jetty. Lesser numbers inhabit beaches north of there.

Unless accompanied by some skill, no amount of industry will catch up with a plummeting razor. A new hand with some instruction can score about 50 percent of the time. A tyro on his own may go home skunked.

A proper shovel for razor digging has a blade that is long and thin (as the clam is) and tilted at about a 20° angle ahead of the handle. These shovels can be rented or bought at curio shops, bus depots, and most retail stores near the major beaches. They are provided free to clients by some resorts.

The advanced technique—which takes practice—calls for working in the wash area of the waves, in an inch or more of water. The digger, after spotting the tip of a clam's siphon, drives his shovel straight into the sand 6 inches on the seaward side of the "show" (as the dime-size dimple around the siphon is called), then pushes the handle away seaward. The pressure thus exerted keeps the clam from burrowing. The digger then reaches in alongside his shovel blade and gropes for the quarry, which he wiggles back and forth like a loose tooth to break the suction.

Dry digging is easier for beginners, who are less likely to keep a wary eye on the surf, and not as likely to recognize a show in the water as in dry sand. In dry digging, the trick is to balance speed with endurance. Teams of two usually do best, one starting with the shovel and the other, kneeling, taking over when the quarry can be grabbed.

Even dry digging must be done close enough to the wave line to make holes watery—hence the need to be quick before a cave-in fills the excavation.

The clam gun is a technological improvement on the shovel. It is a metal cylinder which is shoved downward into the sand around the clam. Placing a thumb over a hole on top of the cylinder maintains suction as the gunner pulls both clam and burrow above ground. The technique is legal and efficient, if not quite as sporting as a shovel.

A greatly increased population of clammers has forced Washington to shorten its season, to close some beaches altogether, and to reduce the daily bag limit. Check with the State Department of Fisheries or a local sporting goods shop before launching an expedition.

Eaters of razor clams usually grind the meat and fry it as patties, or they use it in chowders. It is a sweet and flavorful clam, but chewy at best and downright tough at worst.

For notes on other clams, see page 20.

Turning the other way off U.S. 12 onto the Jackson Highway leads directly to Matilda Jackson State Park, a 5-acre picnic park.

On Interstate 5

For whatever curious reason, cities along the major highway of southwest Washington tend to come in pairs: Portland-Vancouver (forgiving a state boundary), Longview-Kelso, and Centralia-Chehalis.

Some smaller single municipalities intersperse themselves along the freeway, but the paired towns generally offer the widest range of accommodations and diversions for anyone so wearied by the relentlessness of freeway driving that an hour's stop is the minimum.

Vancouver

Vancouver is Washington's oldest city. Its present role is as an extension of the sprawling Portland metropolitan area, but lively legacies of Hudson's Bay Company traders and U. S. Grant's tour as a U.S. Army officer lead the way in making this old town one of Washington's best for strolling with famous shades of the past.

Accommodations. Most of Vancouver's large, modern motels are in the downtown area west of I-5, from the riverfront north to 13th Street. Smaller clusters of motels are at NE 78th Street (Exit 4 from the freeway) and also along old U.S. 99 north of that road.

Attractions. In this oldest Washington city, the major points of interest come from the past. Vancouver has mapped out a walking tour of local history which is presently 5 miles long; it will be 20 miles in the future. A freewayside information center a few hundred feet north of the Interstate Bridge can give directions. The full walk is a pleasure, but it is possible to make quick visits to selected points. The major spots form a tight circle near downtown on both sides of the freeway.

Fort Vancouver, the beginning, was a Hudson's Bay Company trading post founded in 1824. It peaked in the 1840s on the site where its reconstruction now stands. Within that decade, colonial will prevailed over English attempts along the Columbia. A U.S. Army post came to occupy the same long, gentle slope facing down to the river.

The reconstructed trading post, an interpretive center explaining it, and the officers' row of the old army post form the nucleus of Vancouver's preserved early days. All may be reached from the Mill Plain Exit, 1C, from the freeway.

Officers' row, a fine demonstration that rank does have its privileges, comes highest on the slope. The oldest of its houses, dating to 1849, is a museum dedicated to Ulysses S. Grant, who kept office hours there as a rising young brevet major. The museum, containing Grant memorabilia, is open daily.

Not far downslope, a National Park Service interpretive center explains much about fur trading and other aspects of daily life in the Hudson's Bay Company stockade. The center is open daily. A children's playground and some picnic tables adjoin, all with an overview of the fort.

The fort proper is a painstaking restoration of the log stockade, corner blockhouse, and some of the interior buildings. Fans of western movies will recognize the architecture instantly, though serious fantasizing about 1846 comes hard because a busy airport is right next door.

On the other side of the freeway, in the present downtown, is the Clark County Historical Museum at 16th and Main. It has among its exhibits a painful re-creation of a pioneer doctor's office. The museum is open afternoons, Wednesday through Sunday.

Local pioneers of wealth are represented by the nearby Slocum House at Sixth and Esther. Now a theater, the magnificent building began as a private residence. It still points up the fact that a widow's walk could be as appropriate on the house of a Columbia River–based seafarer as on any New Englander's.

Parks and recreation. Several major units of the municipal park system weave themselves among the historic points of interest.

Esther Short Park, flanking Slocum House in the downtown, is a superior elaboration on the traditional plaza park. Mature trees shade most of its 5 acres of picnic tables and playground equipment. The park also has ample playfields for joggers, Frisbee fans, and others.

On the other side of the freeway near the Mill Plain Boulevard exit—the same one that leads to Fort Vancouver—are two versatile parks and some tennis courts.

The 11 acres of George C. Marshall Park, a long block north of Mill Plain on Fort Vancouver Way, form the major unit. The park contains a recreation center, an indoor swimming pool, and picnic tables on a shaded knoll.

Just across McLoughlin Boulevard to the north of Marshall Park, City College Park has a lengthy fitness course modeled after the European parcours.

Facing the fitness course across Fort Vancouver Way are some modest tennis courts that belong to Clark College. Four better-surfaced, lighted courts are at Hudson's Bay High School, back south of Mill Plain on Fort Vancouver Way.

Longview-Kelso

Longview and Kelso occupy the point where Interstate 5 and the Columbia River part company, the freeway continuing north while the river bends west to meet the Pacific Ocean.

Longview sprang into existence all of a piece in 1923 as one of the West's earliest planned cities. The founders of this logging and milling town chose a riverbank site that could—and does—provide a major deep-water port, and they took pains to design handsome residential neighborhoods well away from the mills.

Neighboring Kelso, older but smaller, serves as the Cowlitz County seat and as a retail center.

Accommodations. Kelso, split by Interstate 5, has several major motels clustered near Exit 39. Most of Longview's motels are near the hub formed by 15th and Washington, the west edge of the main business district. The area is accessible from I-5 exits 36 and 39.

Attractions. Mills, the beginning of Longview, are still much of its economic life. The Weyerhaeuser sawmill is open to tour Monday through Friday at 9:30 A.M. and 1:30 P.M. from mid-June to Labor Day, and by prearrangement on Fridays at 1:30 P.M. the rest of the year. A big mill such as this one will dazzle all five senses with its sheer power.

The Reynolds Metals Company offers tours of its aluminum reduction plant Thursdays at 1 P.M.

Tollycraft, the boat builder, gives tours of its Kelso plant by appointment.

The Cowlitz County Museum, near the county courthouse in Kelso, includes a reconstructed log cabin among its souvenirs of local pioneers and Indians. The building is just off State 4 in the middle of town. Exit 39 leads past it from I-5.

Parks and recreation. Lake Sacajawea Park in Longview stretches more than a mile, a narrow ribbon of water flanked on either side by tree-shaded rolling lawns. The lawns in their turn are flanked by private gardens lush with rhododendrons. Their bloom time, May, is dazzling.

Picnic tables dot the lawns and some lakeside terraces. Bicycle trails—joggers outnumber cyclists these days—wind all through. There is no swimming, but the water is perfect for lazy summer rowing in small rental boats.

Just to the north, John Null Park has four good lighted tennis courts, a kids' playground, and some tree-shaded picnic tables. It is just off Ocean Beach Highway (State 4) via Pacific Street.

Mint Valley Municipal Golf Course (18 holes; 6,017 yards; par 71) is fairly level but has enough sand and water to make a grown man cry. It is north of State 4 via 38th Street, well west of downtown Longview.

Centralia-Chehalis

The tidy, attractive town of Centralia is the major commercial center for timber and dairying communities in the broad, gently rolling Cowlitz Plain.

Chehalis, 2 miles south, is both the Lewis County seat and a manufacturing town.

In addition to Centralia's being a useful stopover point on Interstate 5, the twin towns are close to the watery pleasures of the Cowlitz River, noted on page 67.

Accommodations. A major concentration of motels flanks I-5 at the north side of Centralia, Exit 82. A smaller number are at Exit 81, southwest of the main business district.

Parks and recreation. Fort Borst Historic Park adjoins the freeway on the west, 2 blocks from Exit 82. It has a fortlike log blockhouse reconstructed so long ago it looks like the original, a kids-only fishing lake, playground equipment, cooking shelters, and an infinity of picnic tables under tall conifers. Just west of the woodsy community kitchen lies a complex of sports fields.

Useful Addresses in Southwest Washington

- Fort Vancouver National Historic Site Vancouver, WA 98661

Chambers of Commerce

- P.O. Box 366, Battle Ground, WA 98604
- 222 Railroad Ave., Centralia, WA 98531
- P.O. Box 666, Chehalis, WA 98532
- Columbia Pacific Visitor Bureau, P.O. Box 93, Ilwaco, WA 98624
- P.O. Box 58, Kelso, WA 98626
- 1563 Olympia Way, Longview, WA 98632
- 817 Washington St., Vancouver, WA 98660
- Wahkiakum Visitors Bureau, Cathlamet, WA 98612
- Westport-Twin Harbors, P.O. Box 306, Westport, WA 98595

Graveyard of the Pacific
North Head light looks into the Columbia River mouth, perilous for ships but pleasing to see.

In these mountains for all seasons, Rainier is but one peak among hundreds

The Cascade

The Cascades are mountains to behold in a dozen different lights.

Awesome products of volcanic fire and glacial ice, they come as towering single peaks and in steep-walled, glacier-scoured rows. The Cascades also come as soft, rolling foothills and huge alpine meadowlands.

It is a fair truth to say that eight seasons of weather sweep across the Cascades, so different are the climates on the east slopes from those on the west.

The uses of these singularly diverse mountains are almost without limit. Fishing can be a year-round occupation. Lowland hiking trails also stay open through the winter, although midsummer in the high country brings out hikers and campers in their greatest numbers. Summer is also the season for mountaineering on a remarkable variety of rock and ice—some of it among the most difficult technical terrain in North America, some within the reach of aging beginners. In winter, deep snows provide a base for downhill and cross-country skiers, snowshoers, and, not least, inner-tube riders.

Nearly all of the high Cascades country is federal parkland. So too is much of the foothill country. Mt. Rainier National Park is the star of the show, the most visible and most visited mountain park in the region. The rest of the roster includes North Cascades National Park, Pasayten Wilderness, Glacier Peak Wilderness, Goat Rocks Wilderness, Mt. Adams Wilderness, and dozens of smaller recreational developments in the five national forests that surround the formal parks.

A general progression from rounded contours and relatively low elevations in the south to fierce heights in the north marks the march of the Cascades through Washington. The great row of isolated volcanoes starts with Mt. Adams and Mt. St. Helens in the south, proceeding northward with Mt. Rainier (the highest of all at 14,410 feet), then Shuksan and Baker near the British Columbia border. Impressive as these giants are, they do not separate east and west in Washington. The great wall of granite making up the main range does

that, in both climate and economy.

All this tends to make the Cascades sound remote to any but dedicated outdoorsmen. However, the reverse is true. Five major mountain passes allow close looks at striking scenery to the most sedentary of auto tourists. Well-maintained paved highways also reach well into the two national parks. Strung out along the pass roads are some of the state's most picturesque small towns.

Weather. This great, unbroken ridgepole of mountains sharply divides the climate of Washington state into the wet west and the dry east. The slopes themselves make up two more climate regions. In general effect, the west side exaggerates what goes on in the lowlands below, while the east slopes show a somewhat moderated form of the drier basin beyond.

Stampede Pass (just south of Snoqualmie Pass, a few miles off Interstate Highway 90), at a 4,000-foot elevation, gives a fair hint at westside weather. On the average, it is cloudy 241 days a year; precipitation falls on 206, with 85 of those days snowy. The annual total precipitation averages 92 inches a year, although the accumulated snow can reach a depth of 450 inches. Only 70 days are clear. On 190 nights a year the minimum temperature is 32°F. or less; on 94 days the maximum is freezing or below. The highest temperature on record is 90°F., an event so rare it does not figure in the statistical average.

Ellensburg, a few miles east at 1,727 feet, has dramatically different weather: 156 cloudy days in a year, but 110 clear ones. The annual precipitation is 8.86 inches; snow depth runs to a total of 31 inches. On 21 summer days the temperature tops 90°F.; in winter, 155 overnight lows are at freezing or lower, while 27 daily highs fail to warm to 32°F.

A howling rainstorm can come along at any time, though July and August are more reliably fair than other months. The first lingering westside snows come at higher elevations in September, work down to 3,000 feet by the last of October, and reach the 1,500-foot mark by midwinter. Dates on the east slopes lag 2 weeks or

See additional maps on pages 76, 81, and 88.

Mountains

so behind this schedule. Maximum accumulated depths are usually in March at the 3,000-foot level and up. In typical years, snow does not clear off elevations of 5,000 feet and higher before mid-July.

Highways. Four Cascade pass highways make a rickety-looking ladder with I-5 and U.S. 97 as the north-south legs. Their characteristics are diverse indeed. From north to south the roads are:

• The North Cascades Highway, officially State 20, is the newcomer. Opened in 1972, the often narrow two-lane road connects the northern Puget Sound basin with the Methow and Okanogan Valleys between early spring and late fall. Heavy snows close it for the winter. Slow, noncommercial, beautifully scenic, it can be combined with the Stevens Pass Highway to make a loop.

• The Stevens Pass Highway, U.S. 2, joins Everett on the west with Wenatchee on the east. Most of the road is two wide lanes, but near the summit several sections of divided four-lane highway ease traffic a good deal. Pleasure drivers share the road with a considerable volume of commercial traffic, especially logging trucks on the west side. The scenery is almost as spectacular as that on the North Cascades route.

• The Snoqualmie Pass Highway, Interstate 90, is the workhorse road. The route has four lanes all the way from Seattle to Chicago. Much of it is divided, but a few spots in the higher reaches are not. Traffic is frequently intense. This is the main route for truckers, but it remains fast. In winter it is quickest to be plowed free of snow.

• The White Pass Highway, U.S. 12, is the southernmost mountain pass route, connecting the southwest corner of the state with Yakima. Except for some spectacular views of Mt. Rainier and one brief but glorious gorge, the up-close scenery is appealing more than awesome. A two-laner, its pace is leisurely.

The softened outlines of the Cascades toward the southern margin of Washington allow for some branch routes off White Pass Highway. A northward jog along State 123 to U.S. 410—the Chinook Pass Highway—offers a steeper, more scenic alternate route into the Yakima Valley. This route closes with the winter snows.

Mt. Rainier

People who have seen all the big mountains do not become blasé about Mt. Rainier. Rising almost 2 miles above surrounding foothills, this all-by-it-self mountain is a stunning sight. Rivers of ice pour from its dazzling summit. Wrinkled glaciers grind through immense amphitheaters. Waterfalls drop feathery plumes into shadowy canyons. Snowfields sweep down like great wings to a base more than 100 miles around.

In a region famous for snowy volcanoes, this colossus of fire and ice holds all the records: biggest single glacier and largest glacier system (almost 50 square miles) in the U.S. excluding Alaska, highest volcanic summit (14,410 feet) in the lower 48 states, greatest snowfall ever recorded anywhere in the world (93.5 feet at Paradise ranger station in 1972).

Rainier is so big it makes its own weather, is visible from almost every major Washington city, and, in a land rich with peaks, is known simply as The Mountain.

But statistics are a poor measure; this is a mountain to be seen and experienced first-hand. For any traveler who can get to the Puget Sound basin, there is no problem. Rainier's glaciers are the most accessible in the nation.

All of the soaring peak and much of the surrounding foothill country lie within well-developed Mt. Rainier National Park. Recreational developments in flanking sections of Snoqualmie and Gifford Pinchot national forests supplement the national park.

Mt. Rainier National Park

Mt. Rainier National Park offers itself equally to auto tourists, day hikers, back-country campers,

Mountain for all seasons

Mt. Rainier was not named to describe its weather. Still, on a scale of rainy, rainier, and rainiest, it approaches the high end even in midsummer. Veteran hikers know this and come prepared (left). However, July and August are months of frequent sunshine (above). Day hikers and campers flock to the national park's hundreds of miles of trails to revel in tonic air.

and ice climbers. Winter use is somewhat less intense, but the activities are attractive nonetheless.

The accessibility almost cannot be exaggerated. Fine roads nearly loop the park, but at the same time they are a reasonably direct alternate route to I-5. Seattle is but 70 miles away. The grand circle tour can be done from Seattle in 9 hours—a tour bus does it daily in summer—though most drivers spend more time than that.

Auto touring. U.S. 12—the White Pass Highway—cuts away from I-5 just south of Chehalis, at Exit 68. Its looping course almost touches the southeast corner of the park at its junction with State 123. State 123 works along the park's eastern boundary to a junction with State 410. The latter route continues northward beyond the park. Before U.S. 12 meets State 123, State Route 7 (then 706) branches away from it toward the southwest corner of the park. There, from the Nisqually entrance, national park roads loop east to a junction with State 123 near Ohanapecosh.

Along these roads are the park's major visitor centers, lodges, and campgrounds.

Longmire, in the southwest quarter, is park headquarters. At a 2,761-foot elevation, the area has a national park inn and a visitor center. It is also the head of a network of gentle hiking trails.

Paradise, 13 miles east and much higher at 5,400 feet, is the park's best-known visitor area and its only all-year attraction. It has wildflowers in abundance in July and August, a display of autumn color in September, and as much as 30 feet of accumulated snow in April. Several day hikes depart from the area around the old Paradise Inn (open through Labor Day), giving superior close-up views of Nisqually Glacier as one reward. This also is the launch point for the great climbs—to Camp Muir at 10,000 feet or to the summit.

In winter, Paradise stays open weekends only as a day-use ski and snow-play area.

Two of the park's five campgrounds are on the road between the Nisqually entrance and Paradise. Sunshine Point (22 sites) is at the entrance. Cougar Rock (200 sites) is about halfway between Longmire and Paradise.

Ohanapecosh, at a 1,900-foot elevation on State 123, is in deep forest alongside the Ohanapecosh River. Its particular allure is a population of native trout in a stretch of water open only to fly fishermen. Also of interest is the nearby Grove of Patriarchs, a forest 1,000 years old. A handful of gentle trails and a host of steep ones begin here in the southeast corner of the park.

Except for a 232-site National Park Service campground, Ohanapecosh has no overnight accommodations. Just outside the park are several National Forest Service campgrounds, and several motels and private campgrounds are in the village of Packwood (see page 78).

Sunrise, at 6,400 feet, is the highest point on park roads. On a 17-mile spur road off State 410, the area has a visitor center with displays explaining the volcanic history of Mt. Rainier. Located at the tree line, it is surrounded by alpine meadows rich with wildflowers.

The visitor center gives close views of Emmons Glacier and the snowy crest of Rainier. It is also an excellent vantage for watching climbers on difficult technical terrain. A skein of easy walks takes visitors closer to the major views.

Lower Sunrise Campground has 63 sites, the only accommodations there. Not far away as the crow flies, but several miles distant on a separate spur road, is the 125-site White River campground.

Both Sunrise and White River are open in summer only.

Rainier for day hikers. To appreciate Rainier's endless variety fully is to do some walking . . . on a high ridge where the roar of ice tumbling down from a glacier into a canyon can well up in engulfing waves . . . in an alpine garden as breezes ripple a sea of wildflowers . . . beside a glacier-fed stream clear and cold in the shade of trees 300 feet tall.

This park has hardly a corner that cannot be reached in a day hike. Partly this is because of the network of good roads, but the relatively small size of Rainier—378 square miles—is the key.

Along with the limited size there is the gigantic factor of the great snowy cone in the middle, which leaves the encircling band of forest and meadow only 5 miles wide on the average.

Within that band are 305 miles of marked trail. Some of those miles remain buried under snow for years on end. Many more are clear for only a short season, leaving limited opportunities in spring and fall. However, the summer possibilities are extensive.

The following is a roster of relatively short, easy hikes in each quarter of the park.

Four are in the northeast quarter.

Crystal Lakes trail runs east from State 410. A 3-mile hike gaining 2,300 feet of elevation, it ranges through forests into alpine meadows. Two lakes are on the route; elk and goats may be also.

Of the dozens of trails to choose from in the Sunrise area, one goes up 2,500 feet in 3¼ miles from the Sunrise parking lot to 7,800-foot Burroughs Mountain and dreamlike views of Winthrop and Emmons glaciers.

The 3-mile Glacier Basin trail starts at White River Campground and leads up 1,400 feet to spectacular flower fields; it offers probable encounters with marmots and mountaineers.

Summerland Trail starts from White River Road 3 miles back toward State 410 from the campground. It gains 1,500 feet over 4 miles en route to great views of Little Tahoma, an 11,700-foot side peak that was merely the main slope of a much

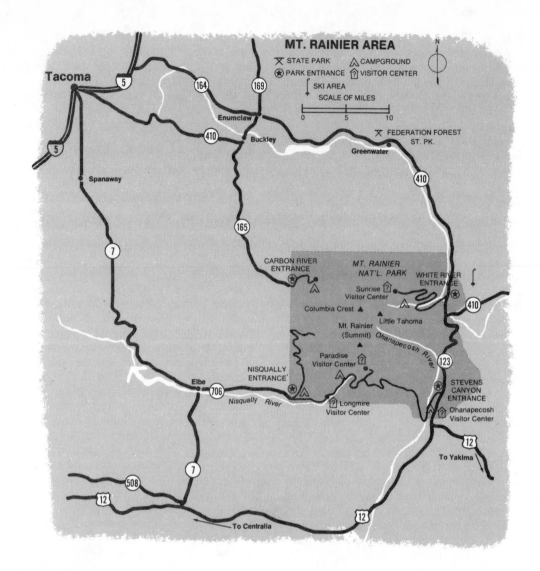

larger mountain until volcanic blasts blew the original lid off.

At Ohanapecosh in the southeast corner, the 3-mile Silver Falls Loop is a favorite hike, especially when storms sweep the exposed high country. The trail gains only 300 feet of elevation in its course through heavy forest. The trailhead is at the Ohanapecosh visitor center parking lot.

A few miles west via Stevens Canyon Road, Cowlitz Divide Trail climbs 2,000 feet in 3 miles. Most of the hike is on an open ridge much favored by elk. The trail starts at Box Canyon parking lot, 10 miles west of State 123.

Panorama Point is a 4½-mile loop trail from the parking lot at Paradise up through fine flower fields to some glorious views of glacier icefalls. The chances for solitude are much greater here than along the paved strollers' paths in the meadows surrounding Paradise.

Van Trump Park Trail climbs 1,900 feet in 2½ miles to Comet Falls, at 320 feet the highest waterfall in the park. Along the way are views of flow-

ers, falls, and often goats. The trail starts at Christine Falls parking lot, about midway up Paradise Road from the Nisqually entrance at the park's southwest corner.

Two hikes launch out from West Side Road, which branches off Paradise Road just inside the Nisqually entrance. Emerald Ridge Trail leads to a face-on view of Tahoma Glacier. The route gains 2,000 feet in 2½ miles. It goes through good goat country. The trailhead is 7½ miles north of Paradise Road. St. Andrews Park is an easy 3 miler that parallels the last 3 miles of West Side Road. Both hikes can be combined into a rugged 12-mile trip with a 3,000-foot change in elevation.

All these trails require maps available at park ranger stations.

Mt. Rainier National Park has a back door. The northwest corner is not connected to the net of park roads, but must be approached separately for its own charms. State 165 rambles through the old coal mining towns of Wilkeson and Carbonado, closely following the Carbon River. Some miles outside the park, State 165 becomes a gravel road leading to Mowich Lake in the park. The branch Carbon River Road is paved all the way to its end near Ipsut Creek Campground, also inside park boundaries.

Mowich Lake, popular with canoeists, is also the launch point for a pair of 3-mile hikes across gentle terrain. One trail leads to Spray Park, the other to Eunice Lake. There is a tents-only campground at Mowich. On the other fork, Ipsut Creek has trailer spaces. From the end of Carbon River Road, the Carbon Glacier Trail is a fine day hike of 3 miles. The walk can be extended 2 miles to a vast meadow of wildflowers and then stretched another 2 miles to Mystic Lake. The total gain in elevation is 3,500 feet.

The climbers' Rainier. With nearly 50 square miles of glaciers, some of the fiercest mountain weather in the world, and plenty of gnarled rock faces, Rainier presents nearly every climbing challenge imaginable. It remains an enduring fascination for mountaineers from near and far, and has been a training ground for expeditions headed for peaks from Alaska to the Himalayas.

But Rainier also offers routes gentle enough that anyone with a little determination and reasonably sound health can climb, under the supervision of the park-sanctioned guide service. Thousands do it every year on a 3-day outing (costing about $100) that combines a day's basic instruction with a 2-day summit ascent beginning from Paradise.

Scores of these climbers also descend with their guides into the summit ice caves for a brief tour. There is no extra charge.

The outfitter rents ice axes, boots, crampons, and backpack (about $17), but climbers must bring their own mountain clothing.

The guide service also offers ice and rock climbing courses. For reservations or information contact Rainier Mountaineering, Inc., Paradise, WA 98397.

Outside the Park

Near Mt. Rainier National Park and on the approaches to it are a wilderness zoo, a model forest, and one of Washington's finest ski areas—each an amplification of the park's attractions. The region also has some National Forest campgrounds.

Northwest Trek, the wilderness zoo, belongs to Tacoma's metropolitan park district. However, the 600-acre habitat lies in the Cascade foothills 27 miles south of Puyallup on State 161. From the perspective of visitors to Mt. Rainier, it is just off State 7 near Eatonville.

A forest-lined road leads into the park. In the core area a central building houses a restaurant, souvenir shop, and demonstration stage where attendants work with animals ranging from buffalo calves to ferrets. A nearby 3-acre enclosure holds bears and wolves. One display has beavers building behind a glass-front dam. But the highlight for most visitors is an hour-long tram ride through a 400-acre enclosure housing native northwest hoofed animals—deer, bison, mountain goats, woodland caribou, moose, and Roosevelt elk.

Five miles of trails outside the enclosure carry signs that identify local plants.

The zoo is open daily, June through October. The admission charge is modest.

Federation Forest State Park guards a virgin stand of timber on 612 acres along State 410 about halfway between Enumclaw and the northeast corner of Mt. Rainier National Park.

Poised on a bench above the White River, the park contains a striking range of plant life communities. Three can be seen on the short east loop of the park's interpretive trail. Five plant communities are contained within the 0.9-mile loop. There is an interpretive center in the park.

Crystal Mountain, most famous as a ski area, is in fact a year-round attraction for outdoorsmen.

In winter, the ski area runs five double chairlifts, a triple chairlift, nine rope tows, and a T-bar. The great bowl has 2,450 feet of vertical drop from a peak of 6,800 feet. Thirty miles of trails wind through 4,560 acres. More than a mile of runs are lighted for night skiers.

In addition to its deep snow and varied runs, the area has a wider range of accommodations and after-ski activities than most other ski areas in Washington.

In summertime, two of the chairlifts haul hikers up out of the bowl to trailheads for a short but strenuous day hike on Crystal Mountain Trail. Four other rugged day trails depart from parking lots at or near the ski area. Crystal Mountain is also a launch point for the Pacific Crest Trail and other long hikes. (The trails quickly ease into Mt. Rainier National Park; back-country permits are required for overnighters.)

The area is just off State 410, 76 miles from Seattle, about 2 miles short of the White River Entrance to Mt. Rainier National Park.

Another major ski area is only a few miles south and east of the park at White Pass (see page 78).

The Cascades South

In spite of towering Mt. Adams and Mt. St. Helens and in spite of craggy Goat Rocks Wilderness, the range south of Mt. Rainier is the gentlest part of the Cascades in Washington.

It is possible to make technically difficult rock and ice climbs here, but much of the region's attraction is more whimsical: huckleberry picking, mushroom hunting, and the like. Summer hiking is particularly agreeable, not only because there are many day hikes, but also because the weather tends to be warmer and drier than it is farther north. Not least, forest roads are plentiful, giving visitors better chances to drive close to a desired point than more rugged areas permit.

From an outdoorsman's point of view, to speak of the Cascade Mountains south of Mt. Rainier is to speak of Gifford Pinchot National Forest lands.

Within the forest are the two great peaks of the south state—Adams and St. Helens—as well as the White Pass Highway, major recreational waters of Packwood and Spirit lakes, and many other lakes and streams.

White Pass

The White Pass Highway, U.S. 12, connects Chehalis on Interstate 5 with the central Washington city of Yakima. The link provides its users with some excellent mountain scenery, a clear image of the difference between wet west and dry east, and—as all the passes do—access to recreation in variety.

The logging town of Morton marks the beginning of mountainous country on the west side, but it is Packwood, near the summit, that serves as headquarters for hikers, campers, horsemen, fishermen, and boaters. Road-free Packwood Lake is a short hike away. White Pass Ski Area and its resort are but a few miles east. A sketchy summer-only, four-wheel-drive road ambles southward from Packwood along one edge of Goat Rocks Wilderness, a mecca for hikers and equestrians. This road continues: one branch leads west to the Lewis River reservoirs, another to Carson on the banks of the Columbia, and yet a third to White Salmon-Bingen, also on the Columbia. But it is not a recommended route.

Several National Forest Service roadside campgrounds are in the region. La Wis Wis (107 sites) is near the junction of U.S. 12 and State 123 east of Packwood. White Pass (20 sites) and Dog Lake (17 sites) are on U.S. 12 at White Pass. Several smaller campgrounds are tucked back along forest roads.

Packwood proper has motels and commercial trailer parks along with stores, gas, and other services. It also is the site of a National Forest Service ranger station.

Packwood Lake. A 17-site National Forest Service campground and a resort with rental boats sit near the outlet dam of the lake. The only access to the area is via a 4.3-mile hike from the end of Forest Road 1320. (Inquire at Packwood ranger station for road directions.) At a 2,867-foot elevation, the lake occupies a forested alpine basin looking straight up to Goat Rocks. The serenity of the place is at least as appreciable as the supply of trout.

West of the lake is a network of hiking and horseback trails. To the east is Goat Rocks Wilderness Area.

Goat Rocks Wilderness Area. Much of the 82,680-acre wilderness soars above the tree line, a constantly shifting mixture of alpine meadow and bare rock. Within the area's boundaries, 95 miles of hiking trails reach most of the alpine areas. Indeed, perimeter trails put nearly all within reach of day hikers as well as back-country campers. All but 10 miles of the trail system are open to horses in a region generally well developed for both pack trips and short trail rides. (As in all wilderness areas, riders here must carry feed for their stock.)

The season is short. Most trails open to foot traffic by mid-July, but snow can remain on higher trails—especially the Cascade Crest section of the Pacific Crest Trail—into August. Even in summer, foul weather can brew up quickly, so adequate gear is necessary.

Most perimeter trails reach in from the western boundary of the wilderness area. Forest roads running south from Packwood lead to the trailheads. However, the Pacific Crest Trail, which crosses U.S. 12 at White Pass Campground, is hard to pick up anywhere but there. It runs 42½ miles southward through the wilderness area without touching another road. (When it finally does, it only touches a forest road midway between the Goat Rocks and Mt. Adams wilderness areas.) Only five other trails intersect.

White Pass Ski Area. White Pass has one of the most elaborate ski areas in the state—and some of the most elaborate accommodations to go with its runs. The vertical drop is 1,500 feet (from 6,000 down to 4,500). Three double chairs, a poma, and a rope tow serve the hill, which has a main bowl and several narrow runs cut through forests. Runs range from terrifying to bunny slope.

Village Inn, a 52-unit luxury condominium, faces the slopes from across U.S. 12. It has a restaurant, heated pool, and other after-ski amenities.

The incomparable garden
At Crystal Mountain and all through the Cascade foothills, August wildflowers enchant everyone.

Hints for High Country Hikers

Wilderness hiking, as all veterans know, wants more skill than merely putting one foot in front of the other for the required distance.

At least half (and sometimes all) of the pleasure comes with being prepared to deal with uncertain weather and all the other whims of nature.

The U.S. Forest Service and the National Park Service offer the following advice to wilderness hikers, and especially to campers:

1. Do not travel alone. Recommended minimum party size is four.

2. Have proper equipment, to include

- Sturdy boots with lug soles and ankle protection
- Loose-fitting, easy-on-easy-off clothing suitable for rain, wind, or cold
- Extra food and clothing
- Whistle (three blasts is the universal SOS)
- Map
- Compass
- Flashlight
- Fire starter (candle)
- First-aid kit
- Pocket knife
- Sunburn protection
- Waterproof matches

3. Plan your trip, tell family or friends of the plan, then follow it. (One experienced hiker says, "Tell everybody—hotel clerks, cab drivers, newspaper boys, maids, garage attendants, and anybody else you can find.") Vacationers, especially, need extra people aware of their plans. Checking in at a ranger station is the best bet of all.

4. Familiarize yourself with the trail and general area from a map and from any other sources. (The Mountaineers publish trail guides to all of mountainous Washington. These are widely available in bookstores and are quite reliable.)

5. Be in good physical condition. Do not over-extend yourself.

6. Be weather-wise. Both wetness and wind increase body heat loss.

7. Make camp (emergency or otherwise) before dark. Travel only in daylight hours.

Make camp near water, if possible. Water is more important than food. (Some sources of drinking water may be impure. It is generally wise to disinfect pond or stream water through 10 minutes' boiling, or with water purification tablets.)

Veteran backpackers know to carry everything they need into wilderness and other protected areas, where the only permitted use of resources is taking downed wood for fires. The trick is to limit pack weight to 35 pounds, maximum for comfortable uphill hiking.

Fire, not incidentally, requires careful use. The Forest Service recommends that hikers do not smoke on the trail, only during stops in safe places. Camp and cooking fires must be on bare earth and must be doused with water. (Burying live coals is risky; they may smoulder for hours, then break out anew.)

As courtesy to those who follow, all litter should be packed out.

Where trails are marked, it is in the interest of preserving delicate ecological communities to stay on them. Where trails switchback, shortcutting leads to erosion at least, and may cause rockfalls onto hikers below.

Packwood to the west and Rimrock to the east are nearby sources of supplementary accommodations, but Yakima, 50 miles east, has become a base camp for White Pass skiers.

All is not downhill. The main chairlift at White Pass also serves both cross-country skiers and snowshoers, who launch out from the top toward Hogback Mountain in Goat Rocks Wilderness. (In essence, this is the Pacific Crest Trail with the worst of the climb taken out.) The round trip runs about 5 miles.

Rimrock Lake and Tieton River. U.S. 12 slips along one shore of Rimrock Lake, then stays with the Tieton River for mile after scenic mile on the route to Yakima. This is fishing country. Along the lake are commercial resorts, summer homes, marinas, public boat launches, and a campground (Indian Creek, with 45 sites).

East on the river come—in order, between mileposts 167 and 171—four National Forest Service campgrounds called Hause Creek (49 sites), River Bend (6), Wild Rose (11), and Willows (16). All adjoin a cold, clear stream limited to fly fishermen. These miles of alternating riffles and pools, with tree-lined banks and snowy mountains in the background, are the stuff of calendar photographs, to say nothing of joyous fishing for the pure sport of it.

Mt. St. Helens and Spirit Lake

Eternally snow-covered Mt. St. Helens is one of the most symmetrical volcanic cones in the Cascades. Spirit Lake, nestled into forests on one shoulder, serves as the nucleus of a sprawling recreation area.

Spirit Lake. At a surface elevation of 3,200 feet, the lake lies in an amphitheater of high, timbered cliffs open to the mountain on the south.

Roughly 2½ miles long, the lake is the legacy of a glacial outwash that dammed the Toutle River. Its shoreline alternates between cliffs and gentle banks. Most development is along the southern shore. Here, at the end of State 504, are a resort, a ranger station, a Forest Service campground (114 tent, 29 trailer sites), and a public boat launch.

North and east, a maze of hiking trails leads to half a dozen primitive campgrounds.

State 504 ties to I-5 at Exit 49, near Castle Rock.

Mt. St. Helens. A paved road leads up from Spirit Lake to a viewpoint at the timber line, elevation 4,200 feet. From the parking lot here, the scene is up across vast expanses of gray white pumice and narrower ridges of black basalt to snowy glaciers high on the 9,677-foot volcanic cone. Those with sturdy legs can gain another 1,000 feet elevation by walking in the loose, shifting pumice. Higher climbs require ice equipment and modest technical climbing skill. From parking lot to peak, the trip up takes 7 hours, the return about 4.

At the timber line is a 10-site tent camping area; four picnic sites are there also.

Just around on the other side of the mountain is Swift Reservoir, topmost lake in the Lewis River hydroelectric development (see page 67).

Just north of Swift Dam via a forest road is Ape Cave, a lava tube that is the eeriest souvenir of Mt. St. Helens' volcanic origin. Two miles long, the cave is accessible by Forest Service roads N90 and N83. N90 turns north off the Lewis River Road.

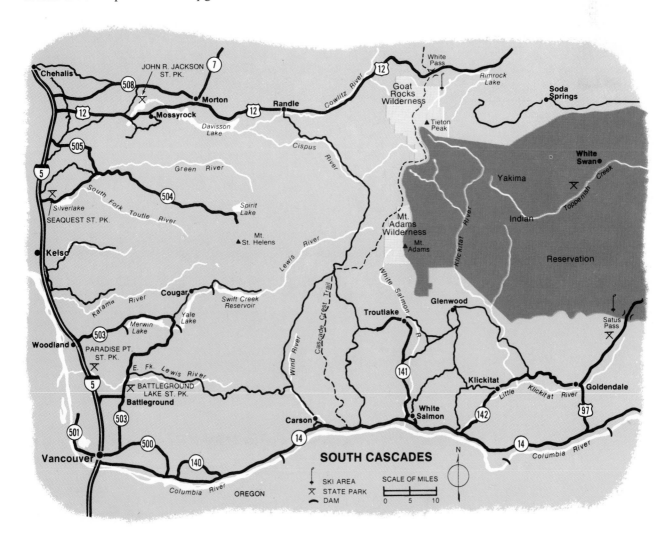

SOUTH CASCADES

SKI AREA
STATE PARK
DAM

SCALE OF MILES
0   5   10

The Columbia Side

Great, snowy Mt. Adams and some fine alpine meadowlands rise up from the banks of the Columbia, generously open to those who prefer to stay with the car, infinitely welcoming to hikers and backpackers.

Mt. Adams Wilderness Area. This roadless wilderness area encompasses the snowy peak and a considerable expanse of wooded flanks below.

The woodlands are notable for supporting an exceptional variety of trees, shrubs, and flowers. Here, all together, are species otherwise found on both sides of the Cascades and in the Rockies and Sierra Nevada.

The Pacific Crest Trail runs through the wilderness area, staying principally in meadowlands on the west side of the mountain. Three well-established routes to the summit are not difficult technical climbs, but they do require ice equipment and fair technique. The ascent takes about 10 hours.

The Mt. Adams ranger station is at Troutlake, the end of State 141 from White Salmon.

Several small National Forest Service campgrounds lie along forest roads N80 and N81 just outside the wilderness area's southern boundary. The names are Morrison Creek (9 sites), Cold Springs (2 sites), and Timberline (3 sites).

Bird Creek Meadows. Once a part of Gifford Pinchot National Forest, Bird Creek Meadows on the southeastern flank of Mt. Adams reverted to the Yakima Indians a few years ago. The Yakimas have maintained the old campgrounds at Bench, Bird, and Mirror Lakes, offering hiking, swimming, canoeing, and fishing on their lands for nominal overnight fees.

Both here and at Cold Creek, the mountain views are glorious, and the closer looks at meadows are full of the more intimate beauty of alpine wildflowers from July into September.

The road to the Bird Creek area begins at Troutlake and runs 18 miles under the numbers N700, N70, and N80, all slow and hard to drive.

Wind River. From Carson, a side road pokes up into the Wind River drainage, one of the most fully developed hiking and camping districts in Gifford Pinchot National Forest.

In a tight cluster at Wind River are a ranger station, a nursery forest, an arboretum, and a trout hatchery. Campgrounds loosely ring this core area.

Land of eternal snow

Camping in the snowy Cascades is high adventure in every sense. Strong updrafts produce lens-shaped cloud.

At Whiskey Creek, a branch road heads toward Goose Lake and Red Mountain lookout. From Red Mountain, a 1½-mile trail leads to the Indian Racetrack, a straight-line race course 10 feet wide and 1,000 feet long, in ancient times the testing ground of Indian horsemen of the region.

It is possible, although taxing, to continue eastward on forest roads to Troutlake, or to push north into the Lewis River drainage (see page 67).

The Central Cascades

Two great passes—Snoqualmie and Stevens—open wide the central Cascades to human exploration.

Both routes—but especially Snoqualmie—have been developed by human hands into reliable all-year passes with no few creature comforts along the roadways. Aside from their businesslike function of getting people somewhere else, both highways run in close contact with outdoor recreation: summer hiking, camping, and fishing, and snow sports in winter.

As for back country, no great volcanic peaks punctuate the range at its midsection. Rather, a freak of geological chance created hundreds of lakes in a topsy-turvy terrain. These lakes range from tiny tarns well above the tree line to sizable reservoirs down in heavily wooded foothills. A great number of these lakes lie between the two passes in a region widely known as the Alpine Lakes. For some time it has stood on the verge of official recognition as a wilderness area within the Snoqualmie, Mt. Baker, and Wenatchee national forests; it is currently treated much like one, pending de facto recognition.

Snoqualmie Pass

Low, wide Snoqualmie is Washington's best pass for people in a hurry, be they on business or in search of quick respite from urban cares. From Seattle all the way to Ellensburg, I-90 is four lanes. Nearly all of it is freeway. In winter, snowplows are almost as thick as passenger cars.

For Seattleites, the countryside around the pass has become a sort of "woods at the edge of town." In summer, hikers flock to gentle, well-groomed trails and fishermen crowd well-stocked lakes and streams virtually at roadside. In winter, a row of pass-top resorts makes Snoqualmie the state's focal point for skiers.

Because the road is so reliable and the recreation so accessible, this is the best place for a visitor who has time for only a sampler of mountains. On the other hand, Snoqualmie is not Washington's most rewarding pass for autobound collectors of dramatic mountain scenery or picturesque villages. (Combined with Stevens as a day-long loop drive, though, it becomes the quick leg of a richer exploration.)

The towns. Beyond the urban sphere of Seattle, North Bend is the only highway town of any size west of the pass. There is no failing to notice it for the time being. It has the only remaining stoplights on Interstate 90 in the state. At North Bend is a ranger station for Mt. Baker–Snoqualmie National Forest. Near town, just north of the freeway, is Snoqualmie Falls, a thundering cataract during the spring snowmelts. A short distance farther along the spur road, at the town of Snoqualmie, is a railroad museum with enough track to run short excursions of old steam trains.

To the east, side-by-side Cle Elum and Roslyn are the only sizable towns near the freeway between the pass and Ellensburg.

Cle Elum has, as a particular point of interest, a telephone museum at 221 East First Street; here is housed the sort of gear otherwise found only in French hotels. Neighboring Roslyn has a museum of old coal mining equipment. Both museums are open afternoons during the summer, or by appointment.

Hiking and camping. Snoqualmie Pass Highway runs through gentle enough terrain to allow easy outdoor recreation along the highway or on spur roads leading away from it. Several large lakes adjoin the road; the wilderness Alpine Lakes hide away in hikers' country to the north.

Curiously, the big lakes are on the east side of the pass. Some westside hikes reach small lakes.

Denny Creek Campground, with 20 tent and 12 trailer sites, flanks the freeway just west of the pass. This National Forest Service development is the head of a complex network of day hike and longer trails. The longer routes lead into the proposed Alpine Lakes wilderness.

East of the summit, Keechelus, Kachess, and Cle Elum lakes parallel each other only a few miles apart. Keechelus, flanking Interstate 90 to the south, is stocked with fish but otherwise not developed. Kachess is well developed as a lake for fishermen and boaters. A Forest Service road runs along the west shore of Kachess to a 178-site Forest Service campground and Box Canyon boat launch. Beyond this point, Little Kachess beckons paddleboaters with informal lakeside campsites, an annual restocking of trout, and an absolute absence of powerboats. Back on the opposite side of the highway, Lake Easton State Park has 100 developed campsites on a small impoundment of water just below the main body of Lake Kachess. From I-90, Exit 63 leads to Kachess; Exit 70 runs into Lake Easton.

Cle Elum Lake has private resorts catering to fishermen. State 903 is the exit from I-90. The state road pushes along the eastern shore of the lake, continuing to a resort and campground at Salmon LaSac.

Although more access routes to Alpine Lakes are along U.S. 2, the Stevens Pass Highway, there are three routes from I-90—two easy, one tougher.

The Pratt Lake group can be reached from Denny Creek over a ranging net of trails.

A formal trail leads 4 miles from the Alpental Ski Area at the pass to Snow Lake, largest of several lakes in the Snow Lake group. Less formal trails lead to the others.

Ingalls Lake is the main event among day hikes in the region, especially during its show of fall color. A 3½-mile trail climbs 2,600 feet. The rewards for making the steep, rocky climb include a striking display of alpine opposites—jagged spires and gentle basins, snowfields and parklands, gnarled pines rooted in ice-polished granite slabs, and—in season—fat cutthroat trout in the depths of Ingalls and the golden light of Lyall's larch in fall dress.

To get to the Ingalls Lake trailhead, leave I-90 at Cle Elum (Exit 85) and drive 6 miles east on State 970 to Teanaway Road. Take this road north 23 miles, following signs to North Fork Teanaway at all junctions. The parking area is the trailhead. A trail map available at the ranger's office in North Bend is required.

Winter sports. Snoqualmie Pass—accessible and reliably snowy—was Washington's earliest developed ski area. It still has more groomed slopes than any other pass in the state. Once exclusively a day-use area, it has developed a substantial number of overnight accommodations, restaurants, and other amenities for those who would stay for a time.

Four ski areas form a tight cluster.

Alpental's slopes range from 6,000 feet down to 3,200. They are served by four double chairlifts, a poma, and four rope tows. The area has five condominiums with rentals, a restaurant and bierstube, and a day lodge.

Hyak, with slopes from 4,125 feet down to 2,800, has four double chairlifts and seven rope tows. It also has a cross-country area. Facilities include a condominium development, day lodge, bierstube, and nursery.

Ski Acres has six double chairlifts and 14 rope tows on its main slopes, which range in elevation from 3,900 feet to 2,900. Again, there is a condominium with rentals. The area also has a day lodge, cafeteria, and bierstube.

Snoqualmie Summit's slopes, ranging from 3,900 feet down to 3,000, are served by two triple chairlifts, six double chairs, two pomas, and seven rope tows. A lodge offers overnight facilities. The area also has several restaurants.

Indian History in Washington

The same variable climate that makes contemporary Washington such a diverse economic and recreational region also made it home to a richly varied range of Indian societies long before anybody thought of organizing the United States of America.

The coastal Indians lived very much with saltwater. Their prime transportation was by boat. Their principal foods were salmon and other fish and shellfish. In the bleak, wet climate, they lived in immense, permanent longhouses made of logs.

In the interior were tribes that lived much more in the fashion of the plains Indians. They were skilled horsemen and hunters of mammals. The easily portable tepee was a common shelter.

Even the rhythms of their languages differed. Toward the coast, tribal and other names are long and typically liquid: Snohomish, Humptulips, Duckabush. In the interior, names clock more dryly off the tongue: Yakima, Spokane, Cayuse.

People with a bent for history extending back beyond European colonizers can find rich resources in Washington.

In Seattle, the United Indians of All Tribes office (3602–3604 West Government Way Extension, Seattle 98199; telephone 285-4425) has an information desk for the public. It can offer advice on Indian art, festivals, and other matters of interest.

The Thomas Burke Museum on the University of Washington campus is a trove of artifacts (see page 16).

In Spokane, The Pacific Northwest Indian Center is both a museum and a source of information (see page 119).

The Anthropological Museum on the Washington State University campus at Pullman is also a fine resource (see page 124).

Many other local and regional museums throughout the state offer displays explaining Indian life. Most of these are noted in the text.

In addition to the cross-country area at Hyak, the hiking trails out of Denny Creek Campground are used in winter by both cross-country skiers and snowshoers.

Stevens Pass

Stevens Pass does not make much of a hole in the steep, high wall of the Cascades. Looking ahead, especially toward the great, rocky west wall, the pass promises little but a harrowing ride.

It is not so.

A rich recreational countryside spreads out on either side of the highway and on both sides of the pass. Fishermen haunt the roadside Skykomish and Wenatchee rivers and their tributaries for steelhead and trout. Campers and hikers come to this country in summer, followed by ski jumpers, downhill and cross-country skiers in winter. The mock-Bavarian village of Leavenworth is only the most advertised of several attractive towns.

As for the road itself, it once turned bus drivers' hair prematurely gray because it curled so tightly and so much. However, it always followed streambeds rather than hanging from cliffs. Now the route has been straightened and widened. In the steep stretches near the 4,061-foot pass, four-lane sections make the road fairly quick to drive even in snow season.

The Stevens Pass Highway, U.S. 2, cuts away from I-5 at Everett. It runs straight and fairly level through farm country all the way to the village of Startup, some 30 miles east. From there the terrain is earnestly mountainous across the pass to Leavenworth and beyond. Fall color and rushing water make Tumwater Canyon, above Leavenworth, the most scenic part of a scenic route.

Towns en route. As befits an old mountain pass, towns here come at closer intervals than modern freeway travelers have learned to expect. What is more, the mixture of farms in the lowlands and logging country up higher has yielded picturesque combinations. The three towns most likely to invite close inspection are Snohomish, Skykomish, and Leavenworth.

Snohomish, on fertile farmland, is an old-line dairy town. The original main street along the Skykomish riverfront has spruced itself up in recent years with restaurants and a few specialty shops. Connoisseurs of Victorian architecture will find several admirable examples in the hilltop residential blocks across U.S. 2 from the riverfront area.

Fertile river bottom and dairy herds extend east beyond Monroe, almost to Sultan, where foothills finally crowd right up to the river bank. Beginning at Monroe, the Washington State Department of Fish and Game maintains public fishing accesses for winter steelheaders.

Skykomish, an old logging town, is so mountainous that the local school never has found a big enough flat spot to lay out a quarter-mile running track. (Fierce weather makes the track question moot but has helped the tiny high school produce several state champion basketball teams.) Closest westside town to the Stevens Pass ski area, Skykomish has a range of visitor facilities.

Leavenworth, over on the east slopes, remains the tourist capital of the Stevens Pass country despite challenges. Once dusty and forgotten after the loggers had come and gone, it transformed itself into a prosperous Bavarian village.

The original inspiration to go alpine was the lofty ski-jumping hill west of town. By 1977 the whole main street had blossomed with domes, cupolas, gingerbreaded balconies, and other bits of alpish architecture. The Chumstick Grange Hall has a half-timbered facade. Scroll-sawn eaves adorn the Forest Service ranger station. Even the phone company calls itself *Telefonzentrale.*

Linguistic purists must forgive a good deal, but the atmosphere in bakeries, confectioners, souvenir shops, and restaurants is *gemütlich.*

Not all is Germanic shops. A handsome riverfront park lies just behind the main street. The town also supports the scenic but tough Leavenworth Golf Club (18 holes; 5,500 yards; par 71) on a hillside above the river, as well as a ski area, and enough nearby fishing and hiking to keep anybody busy for a month. Accommodations are relatively abundant (Wenatchee, 19 miles east, is a reliable source for more accommodations).

Hiking and camping. The available hiking and camping country·in the region approaches an embarrassment of riches. The major areas are the Alpine Lakes on the west side and Wenatchee Lake on the east.

The Alpine Lakes area already has been noted in the section on Snoqualmie Pass, its other access. The following are day or weekend hikes, not outrageously strenuous.

Dorothy Lakes group. This 9-mile trail touching four big subalpine lakes (Dorothy, Bear, Deer, and Snoqualmie) is especially popular with families. Leave U.S. 2 about 3 miles west of Skykomish at Miller River Road (watch for the Money Creek campground sign). Drive it south about 10 miles to the road end and trail number 1072. Island-dotted Lake Dorothy is only 1½ miles away. The trail continues to the other lakes.

Foss Lakes. A 6-mile trail passes five lakes. The first, Foss, is only 1½ miles distant. Fishermen's paths and cross-country routes lead to several other lakes at higher elevations. Leave U.S. 2 at the Foss River Road, about 2 miles east of Skykomish. Follow signs south about 6½ miles to the road end and West Fork Foss River Trail.

Lake Wenatchee. This popular lake is outside the proposed Alpine Lakes Wilderness by a whisker in ground distance, and by a larger margin because it is well developed for tourists. A fine fishing lake, it nestles into a basin that also attracts hikers, cross-country skiers, and snowshoers.

A state park is at the lower tip, about 15 miles northwest of Leavenworth via U.S. 2 and a short local road. The park has 197 campsites and a boat launch. Another launching ramp is well up the east side of the lake. National Forest campgrounds flank the lake and dot the Wenatchee River above it. Nearly all are accessible on forest roads.

Winter sports. Stevens Pass offers at least one of every sort of winter sport area.

Sno Country is the big groomed ski bowl right at the pass. It has 1,700 feet of vertical drop from a peak elevation of 5,700 feet. The bowl is served by five double chairlifts, a triple chair, and two rope tows. The main face of the bowl is lighted for night skiing. The area has no accommodations, but motels in Skykomish and Leavenworth are much used by skiers who stay in the region for more than a day.

At Leavenworth, the primary attractions are the A–1, B–1, and C–1 jumps. The area also has two rope tows serving a small bowl with 500 feet of vertical drop. The area is north of town.

The big lodge at Lake Wenatchee is the hub of a superior network of logging roads and trails. This is probably the most popular spot in the Stevens Pass area for cross-country skiers and snowshoers, because snow tends to be lighter and drier east of the pass than on the west, and yet this area is not far past the summit.

In addition to these areas on the pass, one more is within easy reach of U.S. 2. Mission Ridge is but 13 miles from Wenatchee on a local dead-end road. The area has four double chairlifts and three rope tows serving a bowl with 1,150 feet of vertical drop. The slope is impressive enough that this area has become the site of a coaching clinic.

The North Cascades

The North Cascades are not the highest mountains in the world. They just look like contenders: craggy walls of granite looming nearly vertical for miles

---

Downhill skiers' delight
Snoqualmie and other Cascade passes have steep bowls for downhillers, gentler terrain for cross-country.

at a stretch, especially near the British Columbia border in the area called The Pickets.

In this forbidding terrain the sparse signs of civilization huddle along stream courses. Indeed, the first road across the north of the state opened only in 1972, a major feat of engineering even though the Skagit River on the west and Methow River on the east come very close together, providing natural routes for the highway for all but a few miles. State 20 will doubtless remain the only cross-state route in its part of the world.

For all the nearly impassable miles, the area is also a superior playground—a prime goal for fishermen, hikers, and campers, as well as high-country roamers and rock climbers. Theirs is a brief season, July through September in a typical year. Skiers, on the other hand, can start in November most years and finish on the Fourth of July if they are daft enough to sign up for the Slush Cup on Mt. Baker. The Okanogan and Methow valleys give limitless chances to cross-country skiers and snowshoers.

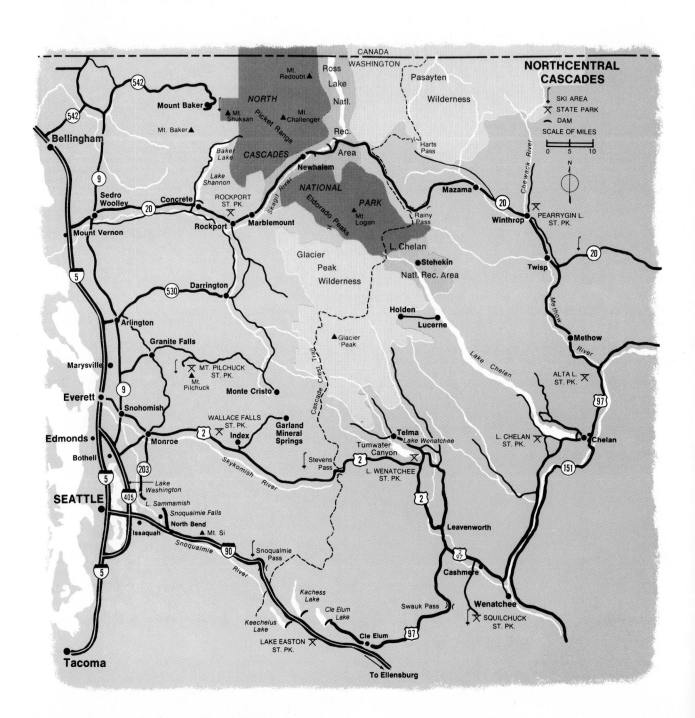

A whole welter of parklands eases the path for outdoorsmen. The two almost untouched units of North Cascades National Park occupy the heights. Separating them—and forming a corridor for the North Cascades Highway—is Ross Lake National Recreation Area. Flanking the southern unit of the national park is Lake Chelan National Recreation Area. Glacier Peak Wilderness Area flanks Chelan to the west, covering parts of Mt. Baker–Snoqualmie and Wenatchee national forests. Pasayten Wilderness, in Mt. Baker and Okanogan national forests, hugs the British Columbia border east of the national park. These areas approach 2,000 square miles, excluding other national forest lands.

Unlike regions farther south, the east slopes here are richer recreational resources than are the west. Except for Mount Baker and the lower tip of Ross Lake National Recreation Area, only a handful of westside parklands are available. The rest is either private land or too steep to cling to without climbing gear. Still, these westside parks are easily accessible from the Puget Sound basin, so they come first in this description.

Mt. Baker

There are two approaches to the Mt. Baker region—one from the north, the other from the south. State 542 from Bellingham is the northerly route, running along the Nooksack River, then turning up to Mt. Baker Lodge and Ski Area. The southerly approach branches away from State 20, the North Cascades Highway, at the town of Concrete. From there, a local road pokes along one shore of Baker Lake. All these areas are within Mt. Baker National Forest.

Mt. Baker Lodge is at Heather Meadows, an all-season anchor point. Summer weekends, the double chairlift hauls people up to Panorama Dome for top-of-the-world looks at Baker and Shuksan. A road winds up from the lodge to 4700-foot Austin Pass for those who would drive to their scenic highlight (and a 34-site picnic ground). For hikers, several trails begin at or near the lodge.

Camping in developed sites is available lower down, along the Nooksack River and State 542. There, five campgrounds offer a total of 63 tent and 37 trailer sites.

In winter, Mt. Baker Ski Area serves skiers with six double chairlifts and five rope tows. The main bowl has 1,200 feet of vertical drop from a peak elevation of 5,540 feet. Located on a north slope, the area has Washington's longest season, traditionally finishing on July 4 with the Slush Cup, a maniacal downhill course with a snow-melt lake as its outrun. A perfect run finishes with several yards of water-skiing to the farther bank. A less perfect run finishes slightly short of the bank.

Paul Bunyan Games

Timber carnivals throughout the wooded Pacific Northwest bring the strong-man skills of the logger out of the forests and into town where mere mortal folk can see how Paul Bunyan worked.

Some of these competitions are pure sport—ax throwing is a prime example. But most are workday skills honed to perfection. The sprint up and plunge back down a spar tree has its working counterpart. So does bucking, the cutting of a fallen tree into lengths, though the two-man saw widely known as a misery whip has long since disappeared from the commercial scene.

There is a professional circuit for which competitors have forsaken the working woods to chase big prize money and well-nigh unbelievable record times. Several of the major timber carnivals in Washington have both touring pro and local divisions, the latter for genuine loggers.

The following calendar lists durable timber carnivals with only approximate dates. Washington's Department of Commerce and Economic Development publishes an annual calendar of special events with precise fair dates.

MAY

Mason County Forest Festival, Shelton, 5 days, midmonth.

JUNE

Deming Logging Show, Deming, 2nd weekend. Timber Bowl Rodeo, Darrington, last weekend.

JULY

Loggerodeo, Sedro Woolley, 5 days, July 4 weekend.
Logging Show, Cathlamet, 3rd weekend.

AUGUST

Loggers Jubilee, Morton, 2nd weekend.

SEPTEMBER

Logger's Playday, Hoquiam, 2nd weekend.

Baker Lake, around on the south side of the mountain, has been developed for boaters, fishermen, campers, and hikers. Six boat launches dot the western shore. Shannon Creek Campground has 18 trailer sites; a Puget Power Company campground has more. Four other National Forest campgrounds have 56 tent sites.

In Cascades, alpine touches

The high Cascades are almost alpine in grandeur of scenery. In the foothill country, visitors find other notes reminiscent of the Alps. This hay field (above) for dairy cattle is near the town of Darrington. (The cattle are more likely to be Holsteins than Brown Swiss.) Leavenworth (right), on Stevens Pass Highway, has turned itself into a bit of Bavaria.

Stillaguamish River

Northeast of Everett, State 92 and a flurry of local roads poke into the Stillaguamish River basin. They lead, most particularly, to a small state park ski area, Mt. Pilchuck, and a pair of old mining towns, Silverton and Monte Cristo. More generally, they loop through abundant forest and up high enough to take in superior panoramas of snowy mountain peaks.

Although this is primarily conifer country, it yields massive autumn displays of golden alder, crimson vine maple, and the brown golds of big-leaf maple.

Informally known as the Monte Cristo back country, the area is well developed for camping, hiking, and stream fishing. Nearly all of 20 National Forest campgrounds border the Stillaguamish, the Sauk River, or tributary trout streams. Among them, the campgrounds have 94 tent sites and 123 trailer sites. Gold Basin is the largest unit, with 10 tent and 45 trailer sites. Most are 5 to 10-site units.

The 85-mile Mountain Loop Highway—all two lanes, most of it paved and none of it difficult—allows easy 1-day scenic drives. The southerly end of the route is at the town of Granite Falls a few miles east of Everett and I-5. The north end is on I-5 at Exit 208. Along the way, the loop passes through the towns of Darrington and Arlington.

In winter, Mt. Pilchuck Ski Area opens. Its 1,700-foot vertical drop, from a summit of 4,500 feet, is served by two double chairlifts and three rope tows. The area has two day lodges, a snack bar, and a bierstube.

North Cascades Highway—Ross Lake

Heading east from the Puget Sound basin, State Route 20 waits a long time to turn into a mountain road. But when it finally leaves the farmlands of the Skagit River Valley and begins to climb through forest toward the tree line, it becomes memorable for some sudden, stunning looks at spires of rock, at fjordlike lakes, and, here and there, across alpine meadowlands. On the east side of Rainy Pass, the road slopes down into the Methow Valley, which looks as unlike the Skagit as any valley could.

This is the easiest route for hikers and campers to take into the heart of the North Cascades. Several fine trails start along the highway. Three fair-size developed campgrounds lie along the route. These attractions beckon motorists out of their cars without demanding long physical exertion. As a bonus, one of the campgrounds is on fishable, boatable Diablo Lake.

The highway has a limited season. Once the snows grow heavy in November and early De-cember, the road closes down until the spring melt, possibly as late as April.

It is more accurate to say that only the high pass has a limited season. In fact, the western end of the road is popular in winter with Skagit River steelhead fishermen and eagle watchers. The stretch from Sedro Woolley up to Rockport attracts fisherfolk, including eagles. From Marblemount to Rockport the road passes through a 1,500-acre sanctuary for bald eagles, whose dwindling ranks do not look so thin here. Meanwhile, the eastern segment of the road carries a heavy traffic of skiers into the Methow Valley and Okanogan highlands (see page 112).

Returning to the summer road, the following is a quick summary of its principal attractions.

Concrete is the last town of any size on the west side. After it, stores and service stations are few and far between until Winthrop, at the other end of the mountainous road. A National Forest Service ranger station is at Concrete, principally to serve the Baker Lake area (see page 89).

Rockport is a small vacation center. Rockport State Park has 62 campsites (50 trailer hookups) in its 457 wooded acres. Alongside State 20 a mile west of Rockport proper, the park gives access to a public fishing area between itself and Concrete, to Steelhead Park on the river bank at Rockport, and to a riverbank rest area just east of the town.

Marblemount, just outside Ross Lake National Recreation Area, has a National Park Service ranger station (source of back-country camping permits and information about canoe trips on Ross Lake), a gas station, and a store.

Between Marblemount and Newhalem is the Goodell Creek National Park Service Campground, a 20-site unit.

Newhalem is Seattle City Light's headquarters for the Diablo and Ross Lake power projects. A large picnic area nestles betwixt road and river, looking toward the powerhouse. This is the departure point for tours of Diablo Dam; these must be arranged in advance through Seattle City Light's main office in Seattle (Skagit Tours Office, City Light Building, 1015 Third Avenue, Seattle 98104).

The tour takes in a powerhouse, an incline railway up to the dam, some antique generating equipment, and, not least, the awesome look from Diablo Lake Overlook up Thunder Creek to hanging glaciers on Colonial and Pyramid peaks.

A small resort is at the upper end of Diablo. It is a National Park Service concession and a mecca for trout fishermen. Reached by a spur road, this resort also is the gateway to Ross Lake.

Colonial Creek Campground flanks the Diablo shore on the lake's Thunder Creek arm, directly beneath the looming presence of Colonial Peak.

Freshwater Fishing

Lake and stream fishing in Washington does not seem to be as well known to outsiders as salt-water fishing for salmon, but it should be.

Steelhead is the prize catch of them all, but trout in variety may be had in every part of the state. In the regions east of the Cascade mountains, warm-water species—especially bass and crappie—are abundant. The Columbia River system supplements the list with shad and sturgeon.

A quick roster of freshwater fish includes the following:

Cutthroat. Also widely planted, the cutthroat is found more often in western than eastern Washington. Some Olympic Peninsula streams have sea-run populations much larger than those found in lakes. Though usually called a trout, it is a char.

Kokanee. A landlocked sockeye salmon, it is planted from hatcheries in many lowland lakes in western Washington and in some of the largest lakes of eastern Washington. The fish grows to several pounds but is prized more for its edibility than its ability to fight.

Smallmouth bass. The Snake River and the Columbia near its confluence with the Snake offer the most reliable fishing for this highly edible and hard-fighting species.

Steelhead. These are rainbow trout that spend part of each year in the sea, where abundant food allows them to grow to 20 pounds. They run in western Washington rivers for the most part, especially the Skagit and Skykomish on Puget Sound's east shore, and in most streams of the Olympic Peninsula. They also run in the Columbia as far up as a hatchery near Pasco.

It says something of the temperament of local fishermen that they prefer the winter run to the summer one, and do not think anyone is qualified to call himself a steelheader until he has watched ice form on his line.

Sturgeon. This fish, source of both caviar and delicious meat, ranges through the Columbia and Snake rivers. A big one weighs in at 1200 pounds (and cannot be kept).

Trout. Rainbow, eastern brook, and Dolly Varden all are available, especially in mountain lakes and streams. Generally, lakes are more productive than streams, though many heavily fished waters of both types are stocked annually. The Cascades are the focal point, but mountainous areas in both the northeast and southeast corners of the state have superior waters of their own.

Many Cascade streams are designated as "quality waters," which means they may be fished only with flies.

The Washington Game Department controls all fishing for gamefish, which is to say all but ocean-going food fish. The definition extends to include steelhead and cutthroat in saltwater as well as fresh.

The department requires licenses. The nonresident all-season license costs $24. There also is a 7-day license for $7.25. In addition, steelheaders must have a $3 permit card.

The summer season usually begins April 15 and extends until October 31. The winter season (mostly for steelhead) runs from December through March. However, many streams and lakes are subject to special closures.

Licenses and regulations booklets are available at most sporting goods shops.

A National Park Service campground, it has 149 campsites—some on each side of the road—a boat launch, showers, and other amenities. Several trails launch out from the area.

Ross Lake overlook adjoins the highway a few miles east of Colonial Creek. Once at the overlook, visitors have nothing to do but admire the view.

Only from Diablo Lake is Ross accessible. A boat travels from Diablo Dam to Ross Dam. The climb up from Diablo to Ross brings one to the floating resort on Ross. The narrow, 24-mile-long lake reaches north to the British Columbia border; it is a paradise for trout fishermen (the season opens late in June) and canoeists. Both make happy use of a rough dozen uplake boat-in camps.

Although the resort has rental boats, many canoeists bring their own. They paddle 3 miles up Diablo Gorge to the dam, having made advance arrangements through Ross Lake resort. The resort will ferry canoes up to Ross Lake on a stake-sided truck for a modest fee.

Diablo Lake Resort charges a parking fee and launch fee.

Ross and Diablo are both subject to sudden hard winds. Any newcomer who plans to canoe should seek advice and maps from the National Park Service ranger at Marblemount before setting out.

Not far beyond Ross Lake Overlook, the National Recreation Area boundary swings sharply northward, while State 20 continues its eastward way. This does not end the unspoiled scenery, however.

At Rainy Pass, the Pacific Crest National Scenic Trail crosses the highway. Terrain is tough both north and south. For those who would take a short stroll, a separate, gentle trail leads south from the pass 1.4 miles to Lake Ann.

Whistler Basin Viewpoint gives the road's closest view of a fragile alpine meadow. This one, like most, lights up with wildflowers in July or early August.

Washington Pass marks the beginning of a long, slow descent into the Methow Valley. Half a mile from the highway, a parking lot marks the beginning of an easy trail to an overlook that takes in Early Winters Creek, Snagtooth Ridge, Cooper Basin, Kangaroo Ridge, Liberty Bell Mountain, and more. Even a beat cop or a retired waiter would not resent the walk when sun shines on the view.

Early Winters, high up in the Methow Valley, marks the first return to civilization for eastbound motorists. An information office for the Okanogan National Forest is here, along with a six-unit tent campground. Between Washington Pass and Early Winters are two highwayside National Forest Service campgrounds, Lone Fir (26 sites) and Klipchuck (12 sites).

Harts Pass, at the end of a 23-mile road hewn out of rock in the 1880s for gold prospectors, is the northernmost road access in the U.S. to the Pacific Crest Trail.

A short but steep hike from Harts Pass campground along the crest trail to 7,300-foot Slate Peak rewards the hardy with a view even more grandiose than the one at Washington Pass overlook. This one reaches west to Mt. Baker and south to Glacier Peak. Just here, the trail touches the Pasayten Wilderness (see page 94). The road reaches up to Slate Peak, for those unable to walk it, but the flavor is not the same.

Heading south along the trail toward Rainy Pass and State 20 is a long walk with no nearby intermediate goals.

The road into Harts Pass will accommodate autos but not trailers. It branches away from State 20 at the Early Winters Information Station. Six small tents-only campgrounds line the way.

Winthrop was a town of sagging fortunes before the North Cascades Highway was completed. It has duded itself up with wooden sidewalks, false-front stores, and other good-as-the-movies westernisms as befits its new role as hub for travelers into the North Cascades National Park, the Pasayten Wilderness, and other parts of the Okanogan country.

The town is the commercial center of the Methow Valley, which in turn is a headquarters for pack-train operators during the summer and a haven for cross-country skiers and snowshoers in winter. Though not numerous, accommodations for travelers astonish with their diversity. The range is from modest hotel to refurbished stage-stop hotel to plush mountaintop lodge. The latter, Sun Mountain, caters particularly to cross-country skiers; it offers lessons and guided tours on 30 miles of maintained trails. Loners are welcome on the trail system.

A National Forest Service ranger station is located in Winthrop.

Four miles east, on eastside Methow Road, is the North Cascades Smokejumper Base, home of an airborne firefighting unit responsible for five national forests. Time a visit right, and training jumps will end well within hollering distance. The base is open daily during daylight hours.

Lake Chelan National Recreation Area

Lake Chelan cuts a long, deep slice into the eastern flank of the Cascades. At the head of the lake, far into the mountains and far beyond the last road to the outside, is the largest single development of the North Cascades National Park.

The old campers' and hikers' village of Stehekin was a base for forays into the Cascades long before the park was established. Now, as a park concession, three old resorts have been consolidated into one, North Cascades Lodge, which has both two-story alpine lodge buildings and separate cabin units.

A daily boat makes the 110-mile round trip between Chelan (see page 109) and Stehekin. A remarkable transition takes place along the way. At Chelan, low, lion-hide hills rim the lake. They hide the fjordlike nature of this mile-wide, 1,500-foot-deep souvenir of a great glacier.

It also is possible to fly in.

Then again, the willing can walk some of the distance. The daily boat stops at Moore, a trailhead roughly 6 miles south of Stehekin

Some visitors come to fish, mostly in deep trout holes along the Stehekin River. Some come just to relax. Most come to hike or set out on horseback for pack trips.

A 23-mile-long dirt road ambles yet deeper into the heart of the North Cascades from Stehekin. The lodge runs a shuttle bus along the road and rents cars.

Ten day hikes begin at Stehekin or along the road, as do eight well-maintained loops requiring 2 to 4 days. Finally, cross-Cascade hikes can begin or end in the region. (The other terminations are on the far boundary of Glacier Peak Wilderness near Darrington, and on State 20 at Colonial Creek in Ross Lake National Recreation Area.)

A local concessionaire runs the pack trips. The firm has an established, summer-only schedule for these. The lodge remains open the year around.

Detailed information is available from the Chelan Chamber of Commerce, the North Cascades National Park office at Chelan, and the National Forest Service ranger station at Chelan.

Glacier Peak Wilderness

Glacier Peak is the ridgepole of the Cascades between Lake Chelan to the east and the Suiattle River drainage above Darrington to the west.

It is purely the preserve of hikers and equestrians. No road pokes into it. Few day hikes reach inside its remote borders, although access roads come to its edges along the Suiattle River on the west and at Holden and Stehekin on the east. Holden is a religious retreat; a road leads to it from the Lake Chelan shore at Lucerne. Hikers are welcome to pass through.

Trails from these and a handful of other points reach up to join the Pacific Crest Trail, which winds through the wilderness.

Glacier Peak itself is a popular climb, not technically difficult by mountaineer's standards, but requiring first-rate equipment and reasonable technique on both rock and ice. The peak's elevation is 10,451 feet.

The season, predictably, is short. Passes along the trails open late in July or early August, then close again with the first heavy snows of October.

Pasayten Wilderness

Friendly as wildernesses go—because of both its gentle districts and its comparatively long season—the Pasayten Wilderness adjoins Ross Lake National Recreation Area on its east side, extending east into the Okanogan country from there. On the north it abuts British Columbia.

With the coming of the North Cascades Highway, several access routes became relatively easy. One is at Harts Pass, via a branch road from the highway at Early Winters (see page 93). Two more roads run north from Winthrop to the wilderness boundary, some miles east of Harts Pass but still in high country.

However, it is the Horseshoe Basin country in the Pasayten's northeast corner that is distinct for offering both gentler weather and gentler terrain.

By late June the relatively light local snowpack has melted away under an early sun. Snow-free routes run all the way to 8,000 feet.

The vast meadow of Horseshoe Basin is a superb example of what the Pasayten offers: miles of rolling tundra pocked with ponds and brooks, wildflower swales, groves of dwarf fir and whitebark pine, and a circle of rounded mountains that invite cross-country exploring.

To get to Horseshoe Basin, leave U.S. 97 at Tonasket, cross the Okanogan River, and follow signs 17 miles north and west to Loomis. Continue north 2 miles, then turn left on Forest Road 390. Follow this road 14 miles to its junction with a secondary road signed Iron Gate. Follow this very rough track about 5 miles to a parking area.

This territory is as popular with equestrians as with hikers. Pack-train operators are in both the Methow and Okanogan Valleys. The Forest Service can provide lists.

Useful Addresses in the Cascades

- Mt. Rainier National Park
  Longmire, WA 98397
- North Cascades National Park
  Sedro Wooley, WA 98284
- Mt. Baker-Snoqualmie National Forest
  1601 Second Avenue Bldg.
  Seattle, WA 98101
- Okanogan National Forest
  P.O. Box 950
  Okanogan, WA 98840
- Gifford Pinchot National Forest
  P.O. Box 449
  Vancouver, WA 98660
- Wenatchee National Forest
  P.O. Box 811
  Wenatchee, WA 98801

Chambers of Commerce

- P.O. Box 43, Cle Elum, WA 98922
- General Delivery, Darrington, WA 98241
- 436 N. Sprague St.,
  Ellensburg, WA 98926
- P.O. Box 313,
  Leavenworth, WA 98826
- P.O. Box 38, Monroe, WA 98272
- P.O. Box 32, Morton, WA 98356
- P.O. Box 357, North Bend, WA 98045
- P.O. Box 71, Winthrop, WA 98862

Where the Cascades meet the Columbia

From the Oregon side, looking across Crown Point, Beacon Rock is dim in the mists upstream (below). Once at Beacon Rock, hikers in the state park begin one trail 600 feet above the river and almost straight above the shore. They finish (left) 4 miles upstream and far back from the river's edge.

Columbia

In its powerful drive to the sea, the Columbia carved its own greatest monument

The Columbia River Gorge contains some of the great dramatic scenery in North America, yet manages to be memorable for manmade details as much as for its natural grandeur.

The gorge is a river-cut gap through the Cascade Mountain Range. Its scenic high point comes in the heart of the granite mountains near Bonneville Dam, where the north bank rises steadily toward snowy Mt. Adams while, on the Oregon side, Mt. Hood looms close, in clear view. Beyond the Cascades, the walls of the gorge are steep basalt cliffs as far as the mouth of the John Day River.

Unlike most vastnesses, which discourage use, the Columbia has been a scene of hectic commerce from earliest Indian history to the present. This is because its course through the gorge to the sea offers the most reliable year-round route between coastal ports and interior farms for both Washington and Oregon. As such, it is one of those rare boundaries that unifies more than it divides.

Unable to change the gorge much, humans have instead changed the river that quarried it. Four great hydroelectric dams slow the water's rush, making the Columbia much less apt to flood.

The Columbia drops 200 feet in the 143 nautical miles from Pasco to Portland. In its free-running days, Cascade and Celilo Falls and a few other spots gave riverboaters more drama than they wanted. Lewis and Clark reported in 1805 that the gorge was no fun. A sharper picture of the perils came in 1872, when a man named Ainsworth decided to take the 134-foot sternwheeler *Shoshone* down Cascade Falls during the spring floods. As the ship lined up for the run, currents swapped her end for end. Ainsworth rode her down stern first. He survived; so did *Shoshone*. But nobody else ever tried that particular run.

Locks and canals softened the falls around the turn of the century.

Between 1938 and 1955, dams drowned first one and then another of the old falls and rapids. Some parts of the old locks remain in view at Cascade, but all the other rough spots hide beneath deep, slow water; the Columbia up to Pasco is a safe route for commercial barges and pleasure boats.

Up on the banks, trucks and railroads augment the barge traffic and every kind of car and camper supplements pleasure boats.

It is no trick at all to wake up in the wet, woodsy world of Paul Bunyan and drive into hot, dry, sparsely settled cowboy country in time for lunch.

A great many people from the west side of the Cascades drive the gorge as a loop trip to cure the inner city blahs. No few continue east to frolic in sun-warmed water at the Tri-Cities of Pasco, Kennewick, and Richland. Some who have come to fish the river have never gone back home.

Weather. Nothing points out the corridor quality of the Columbia between Portland-Vancouver and the Tri-Cities so well as the weather.

At the Paul Bunyan end of the gorge, Vancouver collects 39 inches of rain a year. The average temperature in July is 67°, in January 38°. Up in cowboy country at Richland, the annual rainfall is 7.5 inches, the average July temperature 75°, and the average January reading 32°.

But averages take the sting out. Vancouver sees the thermometer at 90° or more on six summer days a year, while Richlanders see it at that level on 61 days.

Without mountains to cloud the issue, the progression from coastal maritime toward continental climate patterns is easy to see in changing vegetation with each passing mile, and likely to be felt.

Highways. On the Washington side, State 14 is it from Vancouver to Plymouth, where the road bends inland to shorten the trip to Kennewick. Except for a brief four-lane stretch from Vancouver through Washougal, the road is two lanes of asphalt. As far east as Bingen the going can be slow on hilly curves and through towns. East of Bingen the road becomes essentially level and straight, as fast as Interstate 80N, the freeway over on the Oregon side.

For those who need to swap sides, opportunity knocks often. There are bridges at Vancouver; just upstream from Bonneville Dam; at Bingen–Hood River; a short distance downstream from The Dalles Dam; just downstream from John Day Dam; and at Plymouth-Umatilla. Between John

River Gorge

See additional maps on pages 100 and 101.

Seattle Spokane

Day Dam and Umatilla, a barge ferry connects Roosevelt on the Washington side with Arlington on the Oregon.

For those who would stay with the cooling river after State 14 turns across country, the bridge from Plymouth to Umatilla leads to U.S. 395/730, which passes some fine scenery en route to Pasco.

For anybody with a boat, the river itself is an alternative highway. Each of the four dams has a free lock, so boaters can run all the way from the river mouth at Ilwaco to Tri-Cities without leaving the water. Shoreside facilities and accommodations are plentiful all along it.

Because of commercial navigation, traffic on the river stays tidy under Coast Guard control. Channels are marked clearly by buoys. On the odd occasion when wind roughens the waters too much, storm flags fly. (The pools are big enough for wind to generate real waves. Wallula pool, behind McNary Dam, is 61 miles long and as much as 4 miles wide, to cite one example. Sailboaters favor it, but a blowy day can chase all ashore.)

Bonneville Dam-the Granite Gorge

Eight miles east of Washougal, State 14 winds around the river side of a huge rock called Cape Horn. Here, hundreds of feet above the river, a three-car pullout offers an incomparable perspective on the granite gorge.

Almost straight down is an audaciously small farm, the scale-setter in the scene. Upstream, Beacon Rock, an even larger monolith than Cape Horn, reaching 848 feet above the river bank, hides Bonneville Dam behind it and still looks small in the panorama unfolding hill after hill to the east.

This is the heart—the part that keeps being re-elected a great scenic treasure.

Beacon Rock State Park provides intimate contact with the scenery. It encompasses the rock and a long piece of the gorge's wall.

Nobody climbed the rock until 1901. Now an infinity of ramps and steps makes the climb possible for any healthy soul who would gaze 20 miles downstream, farther upriver, or a few hundred feet across to the near wall of the gorge.

Straight across from the monolith, 50 campsites and several picnic sites are the anchor points for a net of trails along the gorge wall.

As summer warms, a swimming beach alongside Beacon Rock becomes a major park asset.

Bonneville Dam, first dam built on the navigable Columbia (in 1938), looks great from the Washington side and provides a close-up look at its locks. In the main, though, it is oriented toward the Oregon shore, where there is access to a trout and sturgeon hatchery, the powerhouse, and the other side of the locks.

Just upstream, a toll bridge permits a quick change to the Oregon side.

Stevenson, a mile east of the bridge, has much of the air of a Mark Twain river town. Tugs moor here. The river bank has a scattering of local boats, some functional, some sinking, some sunk. In summer, back streets are full of kids dressed for a remake of Huckleberry Finn.

For all of that, Stevenson is more logging town than river port.

A few miles upstream, ending at the Broughton Lumber Mill, is a genuine log flume—the most easterly one along the river, and a most engaging souvenir of the Paul Bunyan era of logging.

A log flume is nothing more or less than a sloping water trough set up on trestles. In the old days they were all over the rain-rich Pacific Northwest, a handy way to get logs out of the deep woods. Flumes also served as a sort of rapid transit system for camp loggers. Legend has it that they used to ride logs down the flumes for Saturday night dances, wearing caulked boots for the trip but carrying their dancing shoes in their hands. The legend is untrue—the loggers danced in their boots. But they did ride logs. Old photographs show agile types taking rides that would give surfers the shakes.

Bingen, 25 miles upstream, is the next riverside town beyond Stevenson. The main street and principal buildings are laid out to frame the Columbia just as roads and buildings frame the Rhine in the original Bingen in Germany. There the similarities used to end. However, just at the west end of town a small winery now draws its grapes from three local vineyards steep enough to satisfy any Rhinelander. Bingen Wine Cellars and its tasting room are housed in a big, Germanically ornamented building full of shops. The local hope is that this complex is a first step in revitalizing a logging town that was slipping into economic decline.

Not incidentally, roads here and just to the west make Bingen and neighboring White Salmon gateways into Gifford Pinchot National Forest and onto Mt. Adams (see page 83).

The Basalt Gorge to McNary Dam

Bingen is at the edge of the forests and at the end of the granite gorge. Very quickly to the east come basalt cliffs at the river's edge, with rolling grasslands above them.

For a few eastward miles roadside points of interest come close-packed; then they grow increasingly sparse. No accommodations and few eating places are to be found on State 14 between Bingen and the Tri-Cities. The Oregon side compensates, especially at The Dalles, Boardman, and Umatilla.

The Dalles Dam, some 17 miles upstream from Bingen, comes first in the line of roadside attractions. It is the only one of the lower Columbia's four great dams that visitors can use to cross from one state to the other. The sturdy may walk, but a free train carts most visitors from the locks on the Washington side to the powerhouse, then to the fish ladder on the Oregon side, and back. A picnic park is on the Oregon side.

U.S. 197 bridges the river just downstream for those who need to swap sides with a car.

Horsethief Lake State Park is just above the dam. The distinctive feature of this 338-acre riverside park is an Indian petroglyph incised into basalt, but Horsethief is popular for camping (30 sites), picnicking (open and sheltered tables), swimming, and fishing. A boat launching ramp and a moorage are here.

Maryhill Museum, 18 miles above Horsethief, changes the pace entirely. On a high cliff overlooking the river, the building is a far misplaced Flemish manor house built in the 1920s by a suitably eccentric Seattle lawyer named Sam Hill. Originally meant as a residence, it never served the purpose. Instead, Hill and friends slowly filled it with an odd gamut of fine materials: impressionist art (Manet, Cezanne, and others), Rodin sculptures, white elephants from the closets of Queen Marie of Rumania and Marshal Joffre of France, Indian artifacts from near and far, chess sets, amphorae. Maryhill is operated as a trust; there is a small admission fee.

Sometimes—when a plethora of amateurish snaps of Queen Marie is not on display—the lower gallery contains an excellent collection of photos of Celilo Falls back when the river still ran fast and free. The scenes are memorable, especially in contrast to the calm pool below the museum where those falls used to be.

Incidentally, weather governed the location of all of this. In the midst of a Seattle rainy spell, Hill decided that wet and dry must meet somewhere. He sent someone out to find that spot; Maryhill was the choice.

Not far east of the museum is another of Hill's whimsical contributions to mid-Columbian culture, a concrete model of Stonehenge. Hill meant it to be a replica of the original in Great Britain, but he was four decades ahead of the decoding of that great Druid astronomers' measuring device, so the one on the Columbia points nowhere in particular. Signs on State 14 lead to the model.

U.S. 97 crosses State 14 two miles east of Maryhill. It bridges the Columbia some hundreds of feet below the intersection. Just upstream of the bridge is 98-acre Maryhill State Park. Once a Corps of Engineers park, it has 50 trailer hookups, a boat launch and moorage, swimming beaches, and riverbank fishing spots.

John Day Dam, not far upstream, is the least visitable of the four great dams, but visitors can watch its locks in operation from the Washington side.

From this dam eastward, the amusements on Washington's bank come seldom.

Some 30 miles upstream, the Roosevelt-Arlington ferry offers the only opportunity to get a car across the river between U.S. 97 and Umatilla.

This and a ferry from Puget Island to Westport, Oregon, are the last two on the big Columbia. The 12-car tug-and-barge ferry runs on call from 7 A.M. to 10 P.M. Citizens' band radios on each shore put would-be passengers in touch with the skipper. The ride covers 5.5 miles.

Crow Butte State Park nestles into a quiet eddy of the river about midway between John Day and

---

The source of energy

Bonneville was the first great hydroelectric dam on the lower Columbia. It now has three bigger brothers generating electricity.

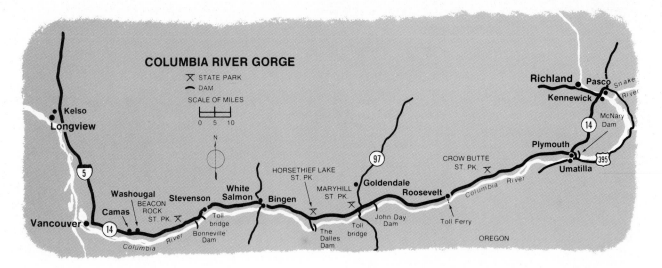

COLUMBIA RIVER GORGE

X STATE PARK
— DAM

SCALE OF MILES

0 5 10

McNary Dams. It has a fine, sheltered swimming beach in shoal water, a boat launch, and camp and picnic sites.

At Plymouth, a large municipal park comes in several sections. The major segment, on the river bank, has campsites, a boat launch, and swimming. The access to the bridge for Umatilla goes right past the entry. At this point, State 14 has already cut north across the Horse Heaven Hills toward Kennewick.

McNary Dam. A spur road past the Umatilla bridge leads to McNary Dam, farthest upstream of the dams on the navigable Columbia. Its locks, on the Washington side, have the highest lift of them all, 75 feet. Next to the locks on one side is a boat ramp and public dock, on the other a fish ladder and counting station. As usual, the larger visitor facilities are on the Oregon side. These include another fish ladder, a powerhouse tour, a picnic area and wildlife park below the dam, and a swimming beach and boat launch above it.

The Water-Cooled Tri-Cities

The Tri-Cities—Pasco, Kennewick, and Richland—have become a major weekend destination for sunseekers from west of the Cascades. Though almost no water falls from summer skies, dams and rivers provide so much of it underfoot that this sunny region ranks second only to Puget Sound as an aquatic playground.

The Snake joins the Columbia here. Riverbank parks flourish in profusion on both streams, beckoning swimmers, water-skiers, fishermen, and just plain float-around boaters. The high season runs from May through October, but fine weather may come earlier and stay later.

Although golf and tennis are not so highly developed as waterborne recreation, both can be pursued with pleasure through a long season. Golf courses, in fact, stay open the year around.

As a complement to the daylit outdoors, a modest night life is beginning at the convention motels, most of them in Richland.

Those who insist on serious contemplation amid frivolity can come here to ponder energy. The curious combination of running water and cloudless skies has made this a center of hydroelectric power generation and, more recently, solar studies. The historic happenstance of Hanford Atomic Energy Works next door to Richland adds nuclear energy to the mix. Telling exhibits on all three subjects invite public scrutiny.

The cities playing host to all of this share much, yet retain three distinct characters.

Richland grew out of Hanford, a closed government town built in the 1940s to nourish the Atomic Energy Works. Its rootlessness allowed it to become an uninhibited sprawl of contemporary shopping centers, motel rows, and residential neighborhoods.

Kennewick, its neighbor on the Columbia's west bank, connected by 7 miles of busy freeway, is a quiet retail and residential community and the pleasure boat capital of the region.

Pasco, across the Columbia from Kennewick, is the old-timer: a seat of agricultural industry, a major railyard, and the upper terminus of commercial barge traffic on the river. Low, plain-faced business buildings make its main street an archetypal western scene, especially when tumbleweeds race down it before stiff spring winds.

Accommodations. George Washington Way parallels the Columbia in Richland. Most of the major convention motels and many smaller ones are on this road. Pasco has one large motel north of town on the perimeter freeway, U.S. 12, and several smaller motels on Lewis, its main street.

Attractions. The curious coexistence of desert sun and abundant river water, plus the presence of the Hanford Atomic Energy Works, have made this region a veritable laboratory of energy.

Hanford Science Center, in Richland's Federal Building just off George Washington Way at Newton Street, is a complete museum–cum–learning center about all forms of energy, especially nuclear. Visitors can manipulate slave arms used for handling shielded radioactive materials, buy a glass ball of radioactive waste from a penny gum machine, and get answers to all manner of serious questions from oft-changed displays or knowledgeable staff.

The Hanford Science Center has some material on solar energy, but Columbia Engineering has the definitive display on that subject at 3070 George Washington Way in Richland. The firm has two buildings, one conventionally powered, the other solar powered. The solar unit is open to tour, from rooftop collectors to basement storage units. A lobby has a wide-ranging exhibit on solar energy, plus continuous monitoring gauges.

Finally, there are dam tours. The one at McNary, 25 miles down the Columbia, has already been noted (page 100). In addition there are tours at Wanapum Dam, 60 miles up the Columbia via State 240, the Vernita toll bridge, and State 243; at Ice Harbor Dam on the Snake, 12 miles east via State 124; and at Lower Monumental Dam, 60 miles east on the Snake near Kahlotus, en route to Colfax and the Palouse country. All explain the generation of hydroelectric power.

Long before any of these energy sources came to be tapped, this was rich agricultural country. Irrigation has made it still richer. Any drive east toward Dayton or Walla Walla gets into the heart of the farm country, but Pasco has two of the most visitable agricultural facilities.

Tomlinson's Dairy, on the Kahlotus Highway east of Pasco, shows dairying at its scientific peak. Free self-guided tours include both the milking parlor and a calf nursery. The dairy is open daily.

Preston Vineyards, 3 miles north of Pasco on U.S. 395, exemplifies a small, estatelike winery. The equipment is modern, the tasting room traditional. The latter is open daily at no charge. Family-owned vineyards surround the winery.

Finally, rail buffs can visit Burlington Northern's computerized rail switching yard 3 miles south of Pasco, off U.S. 12 via Oregon Street. Call ahead, (509) 547-6246. Best time to visit is 1 P.M.

Parks and recreation. Waterside parks fan out in every direction from downtown Kennewick, where Columbia Park serves as an admirable base point and/or measuring stick for all the rest.

Columbia Park, 434 acres strung out along 4½ miles of river bank, has a swimming lagoon at its south end, almost under the bridge carrying U.S. 12. At the north end is a concessionaire campground. In between are a short golf course, an island with a marina, several batches of kids' playground equipment, and a vast collection of picnic tables under mature shade trees.

Howard Amon Park in Richland is a smaller echo of Columbia for picnickers. It lacks a swimming area but does have boat launching ramps.

Two Rivers Park, 5 miles southeast of Kennewick and directly across the Columbia from the mouth of the Snake, is a 7-acre picnic and swimming park with a boat launch.

Hover Park, another 6 miles downriver, is 326 undeveloped acres for those who would fish or picnic in natural surroundings.

Two miles south of Pasco via U.S. 12/395, Sacajawea State Park occupies the tip of land where the Snake's north bank meets the east side of the Columbia. Ample picnic and play lawns roll gently under shading trees to a fine swimming beach, sheltered from boats by fences and patrolled by lifeguards. A boat moorage along the Snake side of the park caters to water-skiers.

Lewis and Clark camped on the spot in 1805; the park name commemorates their Indian guide. Her memory is further honored by an interpretive center. Before 1977 the center was a random collection of arrowheads and other Indian artifacts; an enlargement in that year added much explanatory material about the Lewis and Clark expedition and about American Indians.

A whole series of Corps of Engineers public parks dots the banks of the Snake. The first of them, going upstream, is Hood. On the south bank

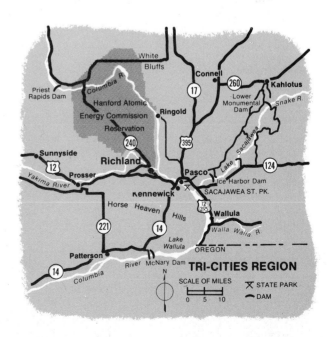

just upstream from U.S. 395/12 as it bridges the Snake, the picnic, swimming, and boating park is well shaded by mature trees. It has 60 campsites and 18 trailer hookups.

Charbonneau is next on the south bank, 16 miles east of Pasco. Young, quite open until its trees grow, it has 20 campsites next to its swimming beach and boat launch. (Charbonneau, incidentally, was Sacajawea's husband. His first name was Toussaint.)

Fishhook, 27 miles east of Pasco via State 124, then 4 miles north on a spur road, is much like Charbonneau except that the campground accommodates 100.

Over on the north bank is Levey Park, 14 miles east of Pasco via a county road along the river. Like the others it has fishing, swimming, a boat ramp, and camping (20 sites).

All of these are popular destinations for boaters from the Tri-Cities as well as land travelers.

For those who come without a boat, a large marina on manmade Clover Island at Kennewick has rentals in variety, but especially rigs for water-skiers.

Also on Clover Island are three cruise boats, available either for scheduled tours or as charters. Clover Island Charters runs its two vessels on scheduled tours as far upriver as Lewiston, Idaho, and as far down as The Dalles, Oregon. Beacon Charters runs its day boat, *Sun Princess,* on shorter tours.

• *Fishing* from boat or bank is diverse in these waters. In broad outline, steelheaders work the banks north of Pasco near a hatchery at Ringgold; bass fishermen stay along the riprap on the Pasco side of the river opposite Columbia Park; and sturgeoners head up the Snake looking for deep pockets. Fishermen after salmon and catfish distribute themselves widely.

• *Golf.* Six courses are open to public play within the three municipalities.

In Pasco, the well-groomed Pasco Municipal (18 holes; 6,524 yards; par 72) rolls steadily among loose plantings of mature trees, with just enough bunkers to keep a long hitter honest. It flanks U.S. 12 just north of town.

In Richland just off U.S. 12, the ambitiously designed Meadow Springs (18 holes; 6,980 yards from the back tees; par 72) flows through a small valley developed for homesites. In its youth it is open, but new trees are growing. Public play is limited, but visitors can frequently get a starting time. Richland Elks Golf Course (18 holes; 6,000 yards; par 69), just off State 224 in West Richland, is level and generally open but has some hazards. Sham-Na-Pum (18 holes; 6,458 yards; par 72) plays flat all the way and is quite open on the back nine. It adjoins George Washington Way on the south side of town.

In Kennewick, Tri-City Country Club (18 holes; 4,656 yards; par 65) is scenic and every bit as gentle as par promises. The course is on Underwood (State 14) west of downtown. Finally, Columbia Park Golf Course (18 holes; 3,100 yards; par 56) is dead level and wide open, a fine course for kids to get started on or for all hands on hot days when quicker is better. In Columbia Park, it is just far enough from the river bank to keep balls out of the water.

• *Tennis.* The Tri-Cities area was a hotbed of tennis long before the boom. The following public courts all have good surfaces and may produce a pickup game for a solo traveler.

In Richland, Howard Amon Park has four courts on Lee Street just off George Washington Way. Two are somewhat lighted.

In Pasco, Sylvester Park has four courts (three lighted) at Fifth and Sylvester. Not far away in Volunteer Park are another three courts. Volunteer is on Fourth (U.S. 395–Business) across from City Hall.

Richland, Pasco, and Kennewick high schools and Columbia Basin College add another 25 courts among them, all available when school is not in session.

Tri-City Court Club, with six indoor and four outdoor courts, allows visitors to play for hourly fees on a limited basis. The club is on the north side of Kennewick, near Richland's Columbia Shopping Center.

Amid the burning sands

At Tri-Cities, on the edge of a true desert, dams have made a vast watery playground rivaling Puget Sound.

Useful Addresses along the Columbia River Gorge

• Camas-Washougal Chamber of Commerce
  P.O. Box 915
  Camas, WA 98607

• Mid-Columbia Visitors Council
  Port-Marina Park
  Hood River, OR 97031

• Tri-Cities Visitor & Convention Bureau
  P.O. Box 2322
  Tri-Cities, WA 99302

A wide land that dams built,
this is home to the state's
cowboys, Indians . . . and farmers

Central

Grand Coulee Dam, along with Hoover on the Colorado River, is the granddaddy of giant hydroelectric dams in the West. On that count alone, it ranks year in and year out as Central Washington's premier visitor attraction.

However, having spawned many other hydroelectric and irrigation dams, Grand Coulee has also done much to turn Central Washington—the once inhospitable Columbia River Basin—into a summertime recreation ground in all the places where water has slowed and gathered.

"Basin" is the correct descriptive word in the sense that the Columbia River gathers water from every point of the compass before slipping through narrow Wallula Gap on the area's south boundary. But a basin it does not look to be. Only the Cascade Mountains to the west are close or high enough to look like a wall, and it is they that squeeze rain out of the clouds so that much of the land between rivers is parched and dry. What is more, the basin's floor is full of slow-wearing, sharp-edged basalt, much of it in the form of sheer walls.

Rugged terrain and vast size make this a loose sprawl of a place to get around in. Yakima, Wenatchee, and Moses Lake are the urban focal points. Most of the recreational opportunities are near them, save for the largest of them all—the great dam. It is way off by itself.

Weather. Yakima gives a fair impression of the regional climate: it averages 112 clear days a year, with another 87 partly cloudy. Measurable precipitation comes on 70 days in a typical season. Most of the annual 8 inches of precipitation arrives between November and March, much of it in the form of snow. Summers are warm, with 33 days at 90° F. and above (to a record 108°). First frosty nights come in mid-October. The last spring frost bites around April 20. In winter, the maximum temperature registers below 32° F. on 23 days; the minimum temperature sinks from there to –25° F. on 153 nights.

Farther north, in the Okanogan, summers are a shade cooler, winters a good deal sharper.

Another point to note is that a steady wind blows down the east slope of the Cascades in summer. At some places, such as Ellensburg, it never stops. In Yakima, Wenatchee, and Lake Chelan, the wind is typically an afternoon visitor. Farther from the mountains, it dwindles in both intensity and regularity.

Highways. Interstate 90—the major east-west route—is freeway all the way from Ellensburg through Moses Lake and beyond. To the north of I-90, two-lane U.S. 2 runs in more intimate contact with local farmlands. State 20, still farther north, tends to run in orchard and rangeland on the west side of the basin, then in forested mountain terrain on the east.

U.S. 97 runs north and south, sticking close to the Cascade foothills no matter where rivers might wander. Except for several short bits of freeway near Yakima and Wenatchee, it is all broad two-lane road, most of it straight and reasonably level. No other north-south route is so direct, but state highways farther east tend to be well-paved and wide, with a traffic tempo near the 55 mph speed limit.

Grand Coulee and Lesser Coulees

Grand Coulee Dam again plugs a narrow gap of the Columbia River course that was filled by ice during a great ice age. The ice dam forced a flooding river out into new channels, which are now known as Grand Coulee, Moses Coulee, Cheney Coulee, and others.

Today the river, back in its original channel, and the old alternate channels form a radiating web of streams and lakes rich in recreational development, all of them with Grand Coulee Dam as a sort of hub. Franklin D. Roosevelt Lake runs upstream behind the dam and far to the east of it (see page 124). Banks Lake occupies much of Grand Coulee; a chain of smaller lakes fills most of what is left. All of these waters have fish; most have campsites and boat launches.

See additional maps on pages 108, 109, and 112.

Washington

Grand Coulee Dam

Anyone who ever ran 2½ yards of concrete through a half-bag mixer to build a driveway will be interested to know that Grand Coulee Dam contains 11,975,521 cubic yards of the stuff.

The structure runs 5,233 feet long and stands 350 feet high from streambed to top.

The combined generating capacity of its three powerplants is rated at 6,180,000 kilowatts. A set of reversible pump-generators that pushes 1,600 cubic feet of water per second up to Banks Lake can add 100,000 kilowatts to the total.

(Most of the water pumped up to Banks does not come back down, though. Banks is at the head of a 500,000-acre irrigation system that extends down to the Oregon border.)

After a couple of off years, because of drought and the addition of the third powerhouse, Grand Coulee was expected to regain its form for visitors in 1978.

Self-guided tours cross the dam's top and burrow down inside amid awesome thrummings of generators and pumps. Evenings, colored lights play across torrents of water on the spillways, a sound-and-light show of overwhelming magnitude. An amphitheater faces the spillways, as do the two largest motels in the area. Relief maps and displays in a visitor center explain the scope of the river drainage and the dam's role in it.

Banks Lake

Grand Coulee Dam is pretty much a manmade wonder. Banks Lake is a remarkable cooperation of ancient natural history and contemporary human work. With a little help from two small dams, the irrigation reservoir fills 25 miles of Upper Grand Coulee. This coulee was originally scoured by the river, then left dry when melting ice allowed the stream to resume its usual course.

For visitors, the irrigation function plays a dim second to fishing and boating. A great many fishermen regard the oft-stocked lake as the state's most reliable source of trout.

Steamboat Rock State Park. A long, curving peninsula cuts away from the eastern shore of Banks Lake close to its midpoint, ending in a massive rock. Steamboat Rock State Park occupies most of that peninsula. The 900-acre park has 100 trailer hookups, a boat launch, and a sheltered moorage. From May through August or September, fishermen and boaters dominate. As bird hunting begins in the Pacific flyway, late-season fishermen compete with hunters for space.

Hiking trails wander from the green lawns of the campsite area up onto the rock after which the park is named. Incidentally, hallucinating under a midday sun is about the only way to see a steamboat in the long basalt outcrop.

Other access points. Electric City, at the north end of the lake near Grand Coulee Dam, also has a boat launch and marina.

At the south end of the lake, where U.S. 2 crosses an earth dam, the town of Coulee City has a camper park, boat launch, and moorage.

Dry Falls and Sun Lakes State Park

Just south of what is now Banks Lake, the ice age Columbia River, running 3 miles wide, used to plunge 400 feet over a falls before boiling on southward through the deep channel now called Lower Grand Coulee.

The old falls is now Dry Falls, a registered national landmark; in the old channel below lies a skein of trout-stocked small lakes. Much of this is packaged neatly as Sun Lakes State Park, the most visited single park in the Washington State system.

Dry Falls. Dry Falls ran out of water after the ice melted at the present site of Grand Coulee Dam, allowing the Columbia to regain its original, more westerly streambed. Now visitors at the lofty observation points along one rim can only dream at a falls 3½ miles wide and thrice as high as Niagara. A state park visitor center alongside State 17 explains in detail how this dramatic landscape was formed and reformed by the changing river.

A trail leads down one basalt wall to any of several small lakes, then south a mile to the main camping area of the state park.

Park Lake. The active center of Sun Lakes State Park runs along the shore of Park Lake, one of a dozen pools in the ancient riverbed. Here, nestled close together, are rental cabins; 216 campsites (18 trailer hookups); a stable with rental horses; the nine-hole, play-early (no shade) golf course; a swimming beach; rental boats; and even a fried chicken emporium.

All told the park covers 4,000 acres. Between Park Lake and Dry Falls, hiking and equestrian trails thread among four small lakes. Below Park Lake are the larger Blue, Alkali, and Lenore lakes.

The little strip of land separating Lenore and Alkali lakes carries a short road leading east from State 17 to Lake Lenore Caves, within the park. The caves, shallow cuts into a basalt bluff, apparently served as a rudimentary motel for Indians travelling through the area 11,000 to 4,000 years ago.

Summer Falls State Park. From May through October, irrigation water from Banks Lake is pumped over Summer Falls on its way to work. State park tables and a lawn at the base of the falls make a memorable picnic site when the falls are running.

This park is due east of Sun Lakes State Park on a local road that parallels State 17. From the north, Summer Falls can be reached directly from Coulee City. From Soap Lake on the south, head east on State 28 about 8 miles to the posted turn.

Soap Lake

Soap Lake had its heyday in the 1930s and 1940s, when mineral waters and mud baths were in greater vogue than now. Rather than change to suit more hectic times, the little resort community continues at its relaxed pace, waiting for the rest of the world to slow down.

The lake waters are extremely buoyant as well as mineralized, which makes them as popular with vacationing families in search of sun and safe swimming for kids as with seekers of spas.

Moses Lake

Moses Lake—town and body of water—sits at the bottom of the coulee country, 74 miles south of Grand Coulee Dam and 28 miles south of Sun Lakes State Park, but smack on freeway I-90.

The community grew from a sleepy hamlet to a sprawling small city when a U.S. Air Force Base (since decommissioned) was established there.

Agriculture has replaced airmen as the backbone of local economy. Amid fine lakes for boating, fishing, and bird hunting, Moses Lake also serves as headquarters for outdoorsmen. Not least, its freeway location has made it a useful overnight stopping point for east-west travelers.

Accommodations. Motels concentrate on Business Loop I-90, especially at the west edge of town near Exit 176. Restaurants are fairly plentiful near the motels.

Attractions. Adam East Museum, at the Moses Lake Civic Center just off Business I-90 at Balsam, houses paleontology from the coulee country and a large collection of Indian materials from the region. Admission is free Wednesday through Sunday. A picnic park adjoins.

Local settlement by European descendants is recorded in the Grant County Historical Museum at Ephrata, a spruce farm community 17 miles west and north of Moses Lake. The museum is open May through September; admission is free.

The old air base north of town, now Grant County Airport, is a principal training field for wide-body aircraft pilots. Every day, Boeing 747s practice touch-and-goes by the scores, accompanied by smaller numbers of DC-10s and other planes. For insatiable jumbo jet watchers, the field has an observation deck and a restaurant. The airport is accessible via State 17 to Ephrata.

At Ephrata, for contrast, a small field has become home to a considerable number of glider pilots.

Parks and recreation. McCosh Park, 3 blocks south of Business I-90 and the main shopping area via Cedar Street, has a fine municipal swimming pool, playground equipment for tots, four night-lighted tennis courts, picnic tables, and lawns enough for a jogger to work up a good sweat.

Moses Lake State Park faces town across the main body of the lake. On the west shore right next to the freeway, the day-use park has tree-shaded picnic sites, a swimming beach, and a boat launch.

Shallow, sun-warm Moses Lake supports a mixed population of water-skiers, swimmers, hydroplaners, and fishermen (the latter mostly after bass, perch, and crappie, and occasionally trout). Equipment for all these pursuits can be rented at several lakeshore motels, commercial camper parks, or marinas.

The unique Grand Coulee
Forty years after its debut, the key link in a vast power chain and 2-million-acre irrigation project is still growing in size.

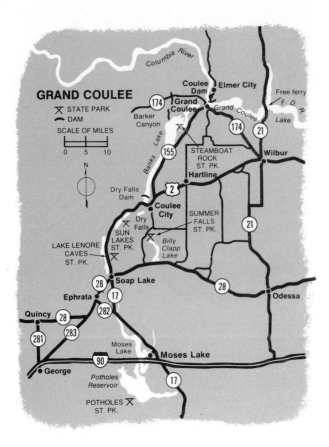

GRAND COULEE

✕ STATE PARK
⌒ DAM
SCALE OF MILES
0   5   10

Potholes State Park is the camper's nearest resource in a public park. Twenty miles south from I-90 Exit 179, the park has 126 campsites, a boat launch, and a marina. The shallow manmade lake is at its best for fishing and other recreation in spring. The heat of summer tends to shrink it.

In Ephrata, 17 miles north and west of Moses Lake, Oasis Park has usefully central campsites for all of the recreational and fishing waters from Potholes on the south to Banks Lake on the north.

Dozens of small lakes and streams offer excellent fishing in this region, and also to the north toward Banks Lake. Local sporting goods stores are invaluable sources of information about specialized requirements and seasons. Grant County maintains public access on 30 lakes and several connecting streams.

By the Riverside

As vast as it is, the Columbia River below Grand Coulee Dam becomes relatively elusive for recreationists all the way down to the Tri-Cities area. Only rarely do visitors have opportunities to get into or onto the river.

In spite of that, a mixture of towns, hydroelectric dams, and parks provides a surprisingly diverse set of ways to think about the river and to use it. In addition, the resort end of Lake Chelan—a kind of tributary to the Columbia—is a more than adequate replacement for watery recreation in the main river. Wenatchee serves most usefully as an urban focal point for all the rest.

Lake Chelan

Fjordlike, Lake Chelan snakes its way deep into the Cascade Mountains. The mountainous end is remote, nearly wilderness, but the end nearest the Columbia River supports a lively resort community devoted mostly to boating, both power and sail.

Several major motels line the north shore along the stub road, State 150. Several more motels fit between U.S. 97 and the south shore.

The town of Chelan maintains a large camping park at the edge of town on State 150. The park has picnic tables, a swimming beach, play lawns, and a pair of lighted tennis courts.

On a bluff high above, Lake Chelan Golf & Country Club (18 holes; 6,300 yards; par 72) bumps and rolls across a narrow bench, a fair test even when the scenery does not cause lapses of concentration.

Lake Chelan State Park, 9 miles west of Chelan via U.S. 97 and a spur road, tucks 201 campsites (21 trailer hookups) into 127 wooded lakeshore acres. The park has a boat launch and swimming beach, as well as a day-use picnic area.

Chelan's most famous attraction, though, is a day-long excursion trip by boat to Stehekin at the head of the lake. Many make the round trip just to savor scenery of a high order. Many more debark at Stehekin or one of the intermediate points to hike through that scenery. (See page 93 for further details on the upper lake.)

Although marinas at Chelan rent small boats, they recommend against up-lake trips. The long, narrow cut into the mountains gathers enough wind to produce very rough water in the upper reaches.

Wenatchee

Years ago, the local newspaper began referring to Wenatchee as the apple capital of the world and the buckle of the Pacific Northwest power belt. It is no poetic phrase, but, then, it takes no poetic license. It speaks the plain truth on both counts.

On the Columbia, the city is flanked by an impressive collection of hydroelectric dams both upstream and down. Down to tiny scraps, the region's arable lands bear orchards. Indeed, the intensity of local cultivation rivals that in mountainous Switzerland; some narrow benches in steep basalt cliffs hold only a few trees each.

Wenatchee has one other major function. At the crossroads of U.S. highways 97 and 2, it serves as gateway into the Cascades, the coulee country, and the Okanogan, and also as a stopover point for travelers on longer journeys to or from the coast, or north into British Columbia.

Accommodations. The main street north of the main shopping district holds an amazing number of motels, several of them large. East Wenatchee adds one large motel and several small ones to the roster.

Attractions. Wenatchee's two great attractions are a lush garden wrested out of one of the less hospitable basalt crags in the region, and a dam with a fine museum buried deep inside its concrete mass.

Ohme Gardens, a family enterprise since 1929, covers 9 acres of a lofty bluff with evergreens, heather, mosses, and several species of shrubs and alpine flowers. All these elements blend to approximate a high alpine meadow down in the hot, dry basin. Irrigation in the form of streams and pools is the key.

A spur road west off U.S. 97, 4 miles north of town, leads up to the parking lot. There is an admission fee.

Rocky Reach Dam, owned by the local utility district, is but a hop and skip up U.S. 97 from Ohme Gardens. A picnic ground and an eye-level look into the fish ladder are standard visitor fare. The welcome surprise is a three-part museum within the dam's main structure. One part is an agreeable look into local geology, and a second area offers some revealing displays of past Indian cultures. But the greatest space is given over to the Gallery of Electricity, where inventive displays explain the whole history of electricity from Ben Franklin's kite to some of the wizard microcircuitry of the space age. Along the way, to the great delight of kids, all kinds of obsolete electrical contrivances can be made to cheep, or growl, or give light.

Parks and recreation. One city and one county park provide excellent resources for picnics, playgrounds, and tennis. Pioneer Park, southwest of the downtown at Fuller and Russell, nestles under a dense, cooling grove of mature trees. Its picnic tables and barbecues are lighted for evening use, as are two tennis courts. (Two blocks away, Wenatchee High has eight more courts, unlighted.) Across the river in East Wenatchee, Eastmont County Park, at Grant Road and Georgia, is younger and more open. It has an imaginative playground, ample picnic tables, four lighted tennis courts, and an indoor swimming pool.

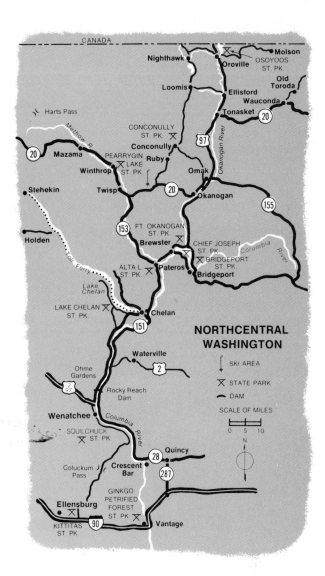

NORTHCENTRAL WASHINGTON

Five miles south of town on the west side of the river, Three Lakes Golf Course (18 holes; 5,269 yards; par 69) tucks into a serene little valley all its own. Nine miles south on the east side of the river, Rock Island Golf Course (9 holes, 18 tees; 5,841 yards; par 71) plays flatter, but with water close by. Other courses within reach are at Chelan (see page 108) and Crescent Bar (see page 111).

Cashmere

Cashmere perches just at the edge of the steep Cascade foothills, 13 miles west of Wenatchee on U.S. Highway 2.

Main Street in Cashmere is a picture book recreation of an old-fashioned Middle America Main Street—a stage set for a Booth Tarkington novel. (It's a little too clean and sunny for Mark Twain.)

The principal local industry is fruit growing and processing. The most famous form taken by local

Cowboys and Indians

In Central Washington, the range-riding cowboy still exists. In every part of the state are Indians, many of whom work as cowboys. Rodeos (below) are easy to find. Some Indian encampments (right) allow visitors (see page 85).

fruit is a jellied candy made in a trim little factory 1 block east of the north end of Main. It is open to visitors weekdays during business hours.

Cashmere's other specific attraction is the Willis Carey Museum, east of town on U.S. 2. The upstairs is a random gathering of pioneer and Indian artifacts. Downstairs is a series of thought-provoking habitats—a trapper's cabin, a farm kitchen—notable for their stark, comfortless reality. Behind the main building is an entire village of typical frontier structures.

Crescent Bar

At the foot of a 700-foot palisade a few miles west of Quincy on State 28, the road to Wenatchee, Crescent Bar is a commercial camper resort with great appeal to power boaters, water-skiers, and all who enjoy vacationing in recreational vehicles.

An oasis of lawns, trees, and beaches, it has 200 trailer hookups. Many are leased the year around, but overnighters can find space.

The development also has a 9-hole, 2,873-yard, par 35 golf course.

Vantage

Two state parks and Wanapum Dam make this once-dreary landscape one of the genuine oases along I-90's long, mostly dry run across eastern Washington.

Ginkgo Petrified Forest State Park, just north of the freeway on the Columbia's west bank, explores local geology, especially volcanic history and related petrified forests. A visitor center contains petrified wood from dozens of species the world around to compare with the local prehistoric forest of ginkgos. Outside the center, a grove of living ginkgos shades a pleasant picnic area.

The main body of the park and the petrified trees lie some hundreds of yards north of the visitor center. It is a preserve—no petrified wood or other material can be taken from it. But the opportunities to see a petrified forest are excellent.

Wanapum State Park sits south of the freeway, still on the west bank. This 451-acre park has 50 campsites (all with trailer hookups), a spacious riverside picnic lawn, and a swimming beach and boat launch.

Wanapum Dam is visible just downstream from the park, but access to it is on an east-shore road, State 243. It has the usual powerhouse and fish ladder tours, but, like Rocky Reach near Wenatchee, it is most notable for a fine museum. This one deals with humanity's long use of the Columbia River, beginning with Indians and running through the steamboat era into the present.

The Okanogan

Several river valleys in Central Washington are genuine cowboy country. Dry, rolling hills make good rangeland but not much else. The Okanogan River valley is the classic example. It also is the access route to fishing and hunting country.

This place should not be confused with the Okanagan, the northward extension of the valley into British Columbia. Much more changes at the border than the spelling of the name. On the B.C. side, three large lakes have been developed into dense resort areas, sunny escapes for Vancouverites. On Washington's side of the border, however, agriculture and cattle ranching remain the foremost activities, almost the only ones. Visitors come here in search of rugged wilderness, or dude ranching with far more emphasis on ranching than dude.

U.S. 97 burrows, straight and quick, from Brewster—where the Okanogan flows into the Columbia—north through Omak, Okanogan, and Oroville to the border. On either side of the route, camping parks make poking into the back country easy for fishermen, hunters, or seekers of ghost towns. Motels in the three towns are neither numerous nor large. Reservations are wise, especially at rodeo time (mid-August).

Parks in the Okanogan

A cluster of parks flanks the mouth of the Okanogan River.

Fort Okanogan State Park Museum sketches a quick history of the region through dioramas, photos, and small tools. It begins with Indian life before whites came and roams through time to the present, giving special attention to fur traders and riverboaters. Outside, sheltered picnic tables look down from a bluff to the riverbanks.

A few miles up the Columbia River from this site, Bridgeport State Park nestles into a shallow defile. Irrigation water from the nearby Chief Joseph Dam allows the park to maintain spreading lawns and shading trees all around its 28 campsites. The softness is a visual dessert in this hard, dry country.

Just outside the park gates, Lake Woods Golf Course (9 holes; 2,574 yards; par 34) extends the green carpet over another few acres.

An equal distance downstream from Fort Okanogan, Alta Lake State Park tucks into a narrow valley 2 miles up the Methow River from U.S. 97 at Pateros. The 200 campsites (16 trailer hookups) in this park shelter themselves under tall pines alongside the lake.

There is a swimming beach. Alta Lake Golf Course (9 holes; 3,400 yards; par 36) adjoins park.

In the Okanogan Valley proper, the city of Omak operates 73-acre East Side Park next to its rodeo grounds. The park, shaded by mature trees, has campsites, cooking shelters and picnic tables, a swimming pool, playground equipment, and even a pair of tennis courts.

Conconully State Park, several miles into the hills west of Omak, has 85 campsites in 43 acres. Between a lake and the ghost town of Ruby, it attracts swimmers and fishermen.

Almost at the Canadian border, Lake Osoyoos State Park, a mile north of Oroville on U.S. 97, comes closest to the resort character of British Columbia's share of the valley. In 41 acres it has 100 campsites, a spreading picnic ground, and boat launches (for water-skiers as much as fishermen), plus nearby stores and restaurants.

In addition to these major parks, the Okanogan hill country is dotted with state forest and national forest campgrounds (also see page 94).

Gold Country Ghost Towns

The Okanogan had a brief heyday as the site of a gold rush late in the 19th century. Scattered along tributary streams in the valley are a handful of ghost towns from that era.

Conconully once was the county seat; now it is only a scattering of rock walls from old courthouse vaults. It adjoins Conconully State Park.

Loomis is several miles north of Conconully via a rough road. It can be reached more easily from U.S. 97 at Ellisford.

A gravel road leads west from Oroville to Nighthawk. Actually, the road leads to the Similkameen River. A footbridge crosses the stream, giving access to abandoned buildings of the Ruby Mine and a leaky-seamed log cabin.

Molson is 13 miles east of Oroville. Developed more than most, with more surviving buildings, it most closely conforms to the movie image of a ghost town. It also has the richest collection of junk for kids to pick through.

The Space Age in Okanogan

Because the region was settled late and only sparsely, it has fewer radios than most of the U.S. For this reason a COMSAT earth station is located on a bluff north of Brewster.

A visitor center at the station explains in a lucid, friendly way how satellite communication works.

Brewster Flat Road leads to the station from the town of Brewster. Another road cuts west from U.S. 97 to it. The visitor center is open daily.

The Yakima Valley

The Yakima Valley is one of those improbably rich agricultural basins that crop up here and there in the world's temperate zones. This one is full of orchards, vineyards, hop fields, and more.

Although the district is not a classic vacation spot, lacking recreational waters and luxury resorts, it repays visitors with instructive looks at some specialized crops and with a benign summer climate.

The City of Yakima

Yakima, commercial center of the valley, means to bustle. It does. Most of its visitors come to do agricultural business. No few come for conven-

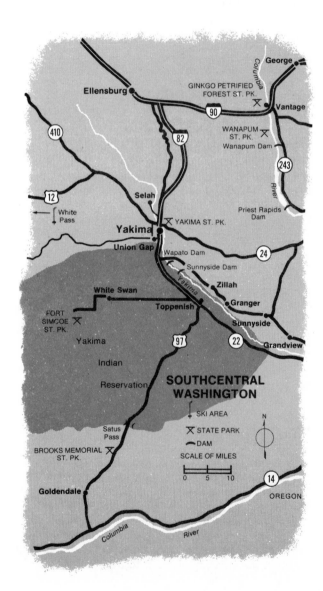

tions in a sparkling new center. Seattleites frequently use Yakima as a handy escape to sun.

Accommodations. Most of Yakima's plentiful motels run along North First, the connector between freeway U.S. 12 and downtown. The new convention center is downtown on Yakima Avenue, which crosses First to form the city's principal intersection. Restaurants are plentiful along both streets.

Attractions. The Yakima Valley Museum, at 21st and Tieton Drive in the southwest quarter of town, has uncommonly well-staged historical exhibits concerning both Yakima Indians and white settlers, but its crowning display is the Gannon Wagon collection. The diverse genius of horse-drawn vehicle designers has few better forums than this. A lumbering Conestoga stands a few feet and several light years away from a nimble trap, but not such a great distance from a charabanc. There is, of course, a surrey with fringe on top.

The museum, adjacent to an agreeable picnic park, is open Wednesday through Sunday.

Another era of transport rolls outside museum walls. As a gesture to the U.S. Bicentennial, Yakima retrieved a pair of ancient Brill electric trolleys from the city of Porto, Portugal. Spruced up and looking in their prime, they now run weekend rail excursions around town and out into nearby farm country. The season is April through October. For information, contact the Yakima Valley Visitor and Convention Bureau (see page 114).

Much of the 22 miles of electrified track serves agricultural processing and packing plants. Visitors who wish to see how farm goods get from field to table can arrange industrial tours of several of these plants through the Yakima Valley Visitor Bureau.

Parks and recreation. Yakima's excellent city park system is supplemented by a state camping park near town.

Franklin Park (adjacent to the Yakima Valley Museum, noted above) and Larson Park (next to the local community college at 16th and Arlington) both offer comfortable picnic facilities.

The same two parks have tennis courts—six at Franklin, a dozen at Larson. Six courts at Larson are lighted.

Public play golf courses are not abundant in a region where farmlands cannot be too large or too well watered, but there are two. Sun-Tides Golf Course (18 holes; 6,215 yards; par 70) is a level, young layout 4 miles northwest of downtown on U.S. 12. Westwood West Golf Course (9 holes; 2,626 yards; par 35) is older and rolls a bit. It is 5 miles west of town on Tieton Drive.

Yakima Sportsman State Park occupies 211 acres near the river a mile east of Yakima, just off Interstate 82, the freeway from Ellensburg. It

The Cowboy at His Best

Partly the rodeo is a joyous tribute to occupational skills. Partly it is a backward glance at the romance of the old west. But mostly it is a rip-roaring show.

Washington has plenty of working cowboys roaming its rangeland, most of it forming a long arc from the southeast corner up through the Columbia basin and farther north through the Okanogan country.

There are junior rodeos, an intercollegiate circuit, and—at the top of the prize-money heap—Rodeo Cowboys Association epics.

It is wise to write ahead to the local chamber of commerce for rodeo dates or to the Washington State Department of Commerce & Development for its annual calendar.

MAY

Washington State U. NIRA Rodeo, Pullman, 1st weekend.
49er Parade and Rodeo, Winthrop, 1st wknd.
Colorama Rodeo, Grand Coulee, 2nd weekend.
Tonasket Rodeo, Tonasket, 3rd weekend.
Winthrop Rodeo, Winthrop, last weekend.

JUNE

Roy Pioneer Rodeo, Roy, 1st weekend.
All Indian Rodeo, White Swan, 2nd week.
Little Britches Rodeo, Silverdale, 3rd weekend.
Colville Rodeo, Colville, 3rd weekend.
Toppenish PowWow Days, Toppenish, last weekend.

JULY

Loggerodeo, Sedro Woolley, 1st week.
Junior Rodeo, Everson, 2nd weekend.
Cheney Rodeo, Spokane, 2nd weekend.
Lake Chelan Rodeo, Chelan, 3rd weekend.
North Whidbey Stampede, Oak Harbor, last weekend.

AUGUST

PQHA Junior Rodeo, Colville, 1st weekend.
Omak Stampede and Suicide Race, Omak, 2nd weekend.
Saddle Club Rodeo, Long Beach, 2nd weekend.
Sun Downs RCA Rodeo, Kennewick, last wknd.

SEPTEMBER

Ellensburg Rodeo, Ellensburg, 1st weekend.
Rodeo, Winthrop, 1st weekend.
Roy Pioneer Rodeo, Roy, 1st weekend.

has 28 campsites, 36 trailer hookups, and a sizable picnic ground with kitchens and sheltered tables. The park also has a children's playground, a small zoo, and fishing ponds for children under 15.

The Lower Valley

Downstream from the city of Yakima, the dry hills spread farther apart and the irrigated valley floor grows green.

This is the heart of Washington's sprightly young table wine industry, and home of a hop industry with an international market among brewers who care. These specialized crops share space with a variety of tree fruit, melons, tomatoes, potatoes, sugar beets, and asparagus.

In harvest time, visitors can buy a bonanza at roadside.

Washington State University's Irrigated Agriculture Research and Extension Center at Prosser, 54 miles southeast of Yakima, offers an unparalleled opportunity for gardeners to find out all they wish to know about growing all the above, and roses and chrysanthemums as well. The center is open to visitors on weekdays. Signs show the way from downtown Prosser.

In Prosser, the Hinzerling Winery welcomes visitors, especially if they can call ahead. The family-owned cellar occupies a small building alongside U.S. 12, which skirts town along its north side. The winery's small annual production sells out quickly when released.

Prosser City Park, right downtown, is a useful picnic stop. The Benton County Historical Museum adjoins it. It is open daily, except Monday.

From Toppenish, on State 22 some 21 miles southeast of Yakima, a 20-mile spur road leads to Fort Simcoe in the Yakima Indian Reservation.

Fort Simcoe is a State Historic Park open May through October. It was originally a military outpost to suppress the Yakimas, through whose good graces it is open now. The park preserves a typical fort from the days of Indian wars.

The Yakimas fish the Yakima River with dip nets at the various irrigation dams. The two best observation points are 5 miles east of Yakima on U.S. 12 and at Horn Rapids just west of Richland, also on U.S. 12.

Yakima Canyon

The Yakima River rises high in the Cascades but does not carve its own valley until it gets to Yakima, the city. Between Ellensburg and Yakima, it reaches its scenic high point in the Yakima River Canyon.

The canyon used to be the main route between the two cities. Now a freeway up on the ridge top has freed the old canyon road from commercial duty, allowing pokeabouts to drive it for pleasure.

The river is quick but not rough. Each summer literally thousands of Washingtonians float down it on rafts, inner tubes, and other flexible craft.

The state has proposed the canyon as a park.

Ellensburg

This quiet, attractive old town is noted for three things in particular: it is home to the granddaddy of all Washington rodeos, on Labor Day weekend (see page 113); it is home to Central Washington State College; and it is the geographic center of the state. (The precise spot, at Fourth and Pine, is marked.)

Just outside town, the Olmstead Place is a Washington State Parks heritage site, a well-preserved example of a 19th-century farmstead including the original log cabin and some crude farm buildings.

The farm is 4 miles east of Ellensburg via the Kittitas Highway, which parallels I-90 along its north side.

Useful Addresses in Central Washington

- Coulee Dam National Recreation Area
  Coulee Dam, WA 99116

Chambers of Commerce

- P.O. Box 343, Cashmere, WA 98815

- P.O. Box 66, Coulee Dam, WA 99115

- P.O. Box 760, Grand Coulee, WA 99133

- Lake Chelan, P.O. Box 216
  Chelan, WA 98816

- P.O. Box 1093, Moses Lake, WA 98837

- P.O. Box 1125, Okanogan, WA 98840

- P.O. Box 87, Oroville, WA 98844

- P.O. Box 433, Soap Lake, WA 98851

- Wenatchee Visitor Bureau, P.O. Box 850,
  Wenatchee, WA 98801

- Yakima Valley Visitor Bureau,
  P.O. Box 124, Yakima, WA 98901

Basking in the sun

The southern tip of Lake Chelan is a thoroughly developed resort with fine beaches, boating, golf, and more. The city of Chelan's park (below) is one of four in the area. Otherwise, the district is one focal point of Central Washington's large, flourishing apple industry, famous for both Golden (left) and Red Delicious.

Washington's eastern edge—too little explored—holds surprises in rich variety

The Inland

Not many visitors from afar explore the eastern edge of Washington except for Spokane. Relentless Interstate Highway 90 invites drivers to stay on it with its combination of guaranteed speed and mediocre roadside scenery. Roads leading into the back country, meanwhile, promise dawdling speeds without promising any of the surefire attractions that make tempting reading in the adverts.

Despite lack of publicity, this rugged, little-tamed part of the state has some extraordinary natural and manmade scenery. Collectors of back roads must go a long way to find better or more diverse ones than these, which ramble through forests, along great rivers, and past small gold mines and farms of epic size. It is as farmland, incidentally, that the region calls itself the Inland Empire. Spokane is the hub of an agricultural realm that takes in much of eastern Washington and parts of Oregon and Idaho.

The Kettle Mountains, for example, may not be as famous as the Cascades, but the highest pass in Washington, at 5,575 feet, is in the Kettles near Republic. The Snake River may not be as voluminous as the Columbia, but it runs a dramatic 2,000 feet below the rim of its canyon not far west of Clarkston.

Also in the region one finds, more than elsewhere, lively evidence of the conflicts and cooperations between Indian and European cultures.

For all this country's fine points, a sparse population and an absence of resorts make it more to be driven through than used as a major vacation destination. Taking exception would be fishermen, backpackers, and other self-reliant outdoor types. For them the unspoiled countryside is so vast that many still have secret lakes or wooded campsites where no one else sets foot from year to year.

With all this, several agricultural and mining communities offer nearby town-type comfort. Spokane and Walla Walla offer urban respite.

Weather. Spokane has a genuine four-season climate. Summers are hot and dry. Winters are cold and fairly wet. Spring and fall lead up to the following seasons in traditional form. The rest of the region follows Spokane's pattern closely, except where high elevation tempers summer and exaggerates winter.

In summer, the city can expect 20 days at 90° F. or more (to an all-time record of 108°). Very little of the annual average 18 inches of precipitation falls between May and October.

Cold is more pervasive. Spokane experiences an average of 138 freezing nights a year, six of them reaching 0° F. or below. The record low is –20°. Snow is not uncommon but seldom gets deep.

In higher terrain to the north, summer is cooler and winter more bitter. South of Spokane, summers are as warm or warmer, but winters do not have quite so much bite.

Highways. Interstate 90 is the great flattened, straightened east-west corridor. Its exits are numbered to correspond to mileposts, which start at 1 in Seattle, reach 283 at Spokane, and finish at 296 just before the Idaho border.

U.S. 2, roughly parallel to and not far north of I-90, runs mostly in pleasant farm country from Grand Coulee to Spokane. Still farther north, State 20 is tough to drive but offers a rewarding east-west route through farm, timber, and mining country, all scenic.

U.S. 395 from Spokane to the Canadian border is the great north-south axis.

Going south from Spokane, U.S. 195 is the major route all the way to Clarkston. U.S. 12 runs east-west in the southeast quarter from Clarkston through Walla Walla to the Tri-Cities.

All these federal and state routes are two-laners. The federal routes are consistently wide, with wide shoulders. State roads may be narrower.

Spokane

Sedate Spokane, Washington's second largest city, did not go for flash before its world exposition of 1974 and has not gone for it since. Prosperous agricultural, lumber, and mining interests built a

See additional maps on page 124.

Empire

sober downtown between 1880 and 1940, using more red brick than anything else. Although some old buildings take fanciful turns, most are plain.

The physical drama in downtown Spokane comes from the Spokane River, which slips quietly into town from the east, but leaves the main shopping area as a thunderous series of falls. Some of the city's unifying bridges cross within awesomely close range.

For visitors, the city offers some fine preservations of its early wealth, a wide-ranging museum of Indian history, a tribute to native son Bing Crosby, concrete souvenirs of its spirited fair, and—typical of all Washington cities—abundant outdoor recreation in and near town.

Spokane, astride Interstate 90, also serves as a gateway to all the great outdoors of eastern Washington as well as Idaho's lake-filled panhandle.

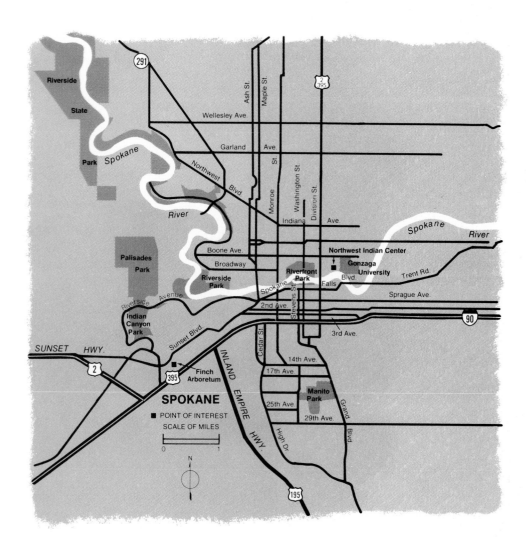

Spokane's special parks

In Spokane, formal garden in Manito Park (right) offers serenity, while circling carousel (below) in downtown park makes for glee.

Accommodations. One legacy of Expo'74 is a sizable collection of spanking new hotels and motels downtown, near the Spokane River as it sluices through the heart of the city. Most of these are on or near Division Street, accessible from the freeway at Exit 281. Another cluster of motels lies eastward along Sprague Avenue (parallel to the freeway and just north of it), handy to the Interstate Fairgrounds. A third grouping of motels flanks I-90 to the west, mostly along Sunset Boulevard.

Attractions. Early in 1977, downtown Riverfront Park, site of Expo '74, had gotten into a between time—no longer a fairground, but not yet recast into the major urban park it was planned to be. The rakishly tilted canvas cone of the United States pavilion was empty, save for contractors rebuilding it into an ice rink. Also still to come were attractions called Giant Games and Spokane Story, and a children's zoo.

The Washington State pavilion has been turned into a performing arts hall, home of the Spokane Symphony. For casual visitors the most usable elements are a summer-only aerial gondola ride across the thunderous face of Spokane Falls and Looff Carousel's hand-carved steeds, which spin within a glass-walled shelter. Spacious lawns and wandering pathways invite strollers and joggers.

Away from the Expo site, Cheney Cowles Memorial Museum at West 2316 First Avenue holds exhibits of local natural history and Indian and pioneer history. It also has fine arts galleries emphasizing northwest painters. Next door the English Tudor style Campbell House preserves a wealthy mode of living from the late 19th century. Mining magnate A. B. Campbell had his 20-room showplace built in 1898 at a price roughly equal to $250,000 today.

Both buildings are owned and operated by the Eastern Washington Historical Society; they are open daily except Monday.

Nearby at West 2208 Second Avenue, the privately owned Clark Mansion is open to tour for a fee daily except Monday in summer, Friday to Sunday in winter. An Italianate exterior hides an eclectic interior of French, Moorish, and Flemish as well as Italian motifs. Clark outdid Campbell, 26 rooms to 20.

Worlds away, the Pacific Northwest Indian Center looks into lives lived in vastly different circumstances. Inside a slab-sided, windowless cone, displays reveal the close human dependence upon nature in clothing, food, shelter, even weapons. Regional divisions emphasize differences between coastal and plains civilizations because of environment.

Located at East 200 Cataldo, between the Division Street bridge and Gonzaga University, the center is open daily. There is a nominal charge.

Over on the south side of the freeway, at 12th Avenue and Grand, the soaring Gothic spires of St. John the Evangelist provide a look at an entirely different relationship of man to nature. Built in 1927, the building is one of few truly Gothic style structures in the United States. Its walls lean toward each other, held apart only by lofty arches; its spires are medieval symbols of humanity's highest reach. The Episcopal cathedral is open to all visitors weekdays from 10 A.M. to 4 P.M.

In-town parks and recreation. Manito Park, a cool, green oasis of gardens and playgrounds unequaled in Eastern Washington, rambles across a high ridge south of the freeway in this surprisingly hilly city.

For gardeners the variety seems endless: formal Duncan Gardens, especially alive in May with the perfume of lilacs; Rose Hill, at its peak of bloom in June; a Japanese garden which surpasses seasons; and a greenhouse-conservatory sheltered from those seasons.

Out-of-towners can most readily get to the heart of these gardens, and also to picnic and play areas, by following Stevenson Street south from downtown. Stevenson bends to become Grand and straightens out just before reaching the 18th Avenue entrance to the park.

The 65-acre John A. Finch Arboretum holds 2,000 labeled trees and shrubs representing more than 120 genera, 600 species and varieties. Major groups include 75 varieties of crabapple and 65 of lilacs. (Spokane has an ongoing love affair with lilacs, for which it is an almost flawless environment.) Plantings date from 1949.

The arboretum tucks itself between I-90 and the Sunset Highway west of downtown, between freeway exits 277 and 279. It is open daily.

Two of Spokane's fine municipal golf courses are almost as much gardens as the city's other great parks. Indian Canyon Golf Course (18 holes; 6,256 yards; par 72) rolls along a heavily treed wall of the Latah Creek–Spokane River watercourse just a few blocks from Finch Arboretum. Downriver Golf Course (18 holes; 5,833 yards; par 71) looks directly into the Spokane River from its lofty bluff at the exact northwest corner of the city, right next to Riverside State Park.

A third municipal course on the east side of town is newer, flatter Esmerelda (18 holes; 6,077 yards; par 70). Other public courses in the region include Hangman Valley (18 holes; 6,500 yards; par 71) 5 miles south of the city on U.S. 195; Sun Dance Golf Course (18 holes; 6,000 yards; par 70) 3 miles north of Spokane on State 291; and Wandemere Golf Course (18 holes; 5,815 yards; par 69) 5 miles north of the city limits on U.S. 395.

For tennis players the most likely opportunity for a pickup game is at the six-court complex in Comstock Park, a few blocks southwest of Manito

Park at 29th Avenue and Howard. Manito has three courts just inside its 18th and Grand entrance. An under-the-freeway park has four lighted courts at 3rd Avenue and Bernard Street.

Suburban parks and recreation. Two huge state parks offer year-round recreation within easy reach of downtown Spokane. A zoo rounds out close-at-hand recreational opportunities.

Riverside State Park covers both banks of the Spokane River for several miles, beginning at the northwestern city limits and extending north beyond Nine Mile Falls. The 5,543-acre park has 110 campsites and abundant picnic sites in open groves of pine. There is a boat launch for river fishermen.

At the north end of the park, Spokane House Interpretive Center includes a model of the 1810 North West Company trading post, established as the first permanent white settlement in Washington by explorer-geographer David Thompson.

Trails all through the park draw heavy use from hikers in the dry season, snowmobilers in winter.

Mt. Spokane State Park, 35 miles north and east of town, snugs right up to the Idaho state line. It is a major park summer and winter. Summers, the cool air on higher slopes draws picnickers and hikers. In winter, four chair lifts and five rope tows serve groomed ski slopes with a total of 2,200 feet of vertical drop. Cross-country skiers take over the hiking trails.

State 206 leads north to the park. From I-90 Exit 289 the route is marked clearly.

The same Exit 289 leads to Spokane's Walk-In Wild Zoo, where a diverse collection of native animals and animals from similar environments lives without cages. Visitors stroll among them, able to touch the quieter species but kept at safe distances from the others by moats, gullies, and other natural-seeming barriers.

Southeast Corner

Washington's sparsely settled southeast corner offers a mixture of untamable wilderness, highly groomed farmland, and well-polished civility.

Far the greatest proportion of the space rests untamed. Hunters and fishermen flock to the region for big game, birds, and trout living in this wild region. Great, rolling expanses of farmland take up most of the rest. Civility cloaks the towns of Walla Walla and Pullman and their college campuses. Walla Walla in particular has a long history as an outpost of European civilization in a rugged land.

Two roads serve all three worlds.

Starting from the Columbia River near the Oregon border, U.S. 12 curves tight through hilly, ofttimes wild country en route to the town of Clarkston at the Idaho line. On either side of Walla Walla, wheat covers what land asparagus and sweet onions do not. Farther east, steep slopes leading up to the rugged Blue Mountains carry such thin plant cover that any grazing beast, cow or deer, must work hard for its dinner.

In 1806 Lewis and Clark returned, hungry, toward St. Louis along much the same route now traced by U.S. 12. Their journals testify to enduring hard times in hard country made of basalt.

The great explorers had come west a year earlier along the Snake River—rough then, tamed now into an agreeable boaters' route between the Tri-Cities on the Columbia and Clarkston (or Lewiston, just across the Idaho line).

From Clarkston-Lewiston, U.S. 195 scrambles up a prodigious canyon wall, 1800 vertical feet, without losing sight of the two towns. Then it scribes long, easy arcs across dry-farmed wheat lands past Pullman and on to Spokane.

Walla Walla

One of Washington's earliest settlements, Walla Walla began as the mission of Dr. Marcus Whitman. The contemporary town is a high-minded place widely known as the seat of Whitman College. An intervening period of frontier recklessness ended years ago, leaving hardly a trace. Hopeful history is the key attraction.

Whitman Mission. Poor Marcus Whitman was the kind of unyielding missionary whose would-be converts finally got mad enough to kill him. Cayuses massacred Whitman, his wife, and 11 other whites in 1847. Today the mission grounds have been restored to much their original form as a National Historic Site. A visitor center amplifies the details of a well-meaning but unhappy history. A picnic area set among trees on a green lawn offers current visitors a much kindlier welcome than the inhabitants of 1847 got.

The mission is 7 miles west of town, just off U.S. 12. It is open daily.

Fort Walla Walla Park. At the southwestern edge of town on the site of a military reservation established in 1858, Fort Walla Walla Park has campsites tucked into cool glens of cottonwood and birch alongside Garrison Creek.

Fort Walla Walla cemetery and the fort museum's reconstruction of a pioneer village face each other in the park. The cemetery is crowded with the graves of Nez Perce warriors and U.S. Cavalrymen from two encounters: the 1877 battle of Whitebird Cañon in Idaho, and the Battle of Boise fought by the legendary Chief Joseph. The pioneer

Child peeks *into painted buffalo hide tepee in Spokane's Pacific Northwest Indian Center.*

village uses log cabins, a one-room schoolhouse, and a smithy as the basis of an authentic pioneer atmosphere. The museum has related displays.

Other, less obvious points of historic interest in this architecturally distinctive old town can be found with the aid of a guide map available at the local chamber of commerce.

The Whitman campus can bring tears to the eyes of any nostalgic with a fondness for small New England colleges.

The region, incidentally, makes an easy change-of-pace day trip from Pasco-Kennewick-Richland, some 40 miles to the west. U.S. 12 and State 124 form a loop through constantly changing terrain and regularly changing crops. Walla Walla has ample accommodations for overnight stays.

Blue Mountains

The name rings true. As visitors approach from east, north, or west, the Blue Mountains rise up, hazy, smoky, and blue in the distance.

Up close, the hazy quality of the Blues evaporates. These mountains are craggy basalt. Fir and other forests cover bony ribs only part of the time.

The range is not awesomely high; only a handful of peaks top 6,000 feet. Yet this is isolated, nearly roadless country. Most of the range on Washington's side of the border lies within the Umatilla National Forest. A great part of the forest is set aside as the Wenaha Backcountry Area, in which 150 miles of trails are the preserve of backpackers and equestrians. (Most of the Blues and most of Umatilla National Forest are across the border in Oregon.)

Hunters come for deer. Fishermen come for rainbow and Dolly Varden trout, especially to the Tucannon River. Hikers come for trails free of racketing motors.

Access is intermittent. From Clarkston, State 129 drifts south to Fields Spring State Park, a 456-acre, 14-campsite gateway to the back country. Starting near the park, a dirt road winds up to the edge of the Wenaha Backcountry. A few miles west of

Pomeroy, the Tucannon River crosses U.S. 12. At that point another dirt road heads toward Wenaha, in company with the river. The riverside Tucannon Campground (11 tent, 5 trailer sites) caters to fishermen. It is the most developed and largest of a dozen Forest Service campgrounds in Washington's segment of Umatilla National Forest.

There are ranger stations at Walla Walla and Pomeroy.

The Snake River

Like several reaches of the Columbia, the Snake River has ample water in its stream bed and virtually none beyond the banks. Sometimes gently sloped, more often in towering walls, the countryside beyond the river seldom offers more than bare basalt to the wondering eye.

For the roadbound in summer, four dams and several parks give regular cooling access to the water at the expense of detours, mostly from U.S. 12. Boaters have the best of it, though, because the truly dramatic scenery belongs to them alone, and they can follow the heat-tempering river from Clarkston down to the Tri-Cities—or even to the mouth of the Columbia, for that matter.

In the 30 miles between Clarkston and Lower Granite Dam, the Snake burrows along at the bottom of the 2000-foot-deep, almost vertical-walled canyon it has carved in the several millennia since a great volcanic outpouring buried almost all of eastern Washington under a thick layer of basalt. No road goes near this awesome excavation. Several other scenic stretches, pale only in comparison, can also be seen only from the river.

From west to east the four dams on the Snake are Ice Harbor (10 miles upstream from the Columbia), Lower Monumental (60 miles from the Columbia), Little Goose (another 30 miles upstream), and Lower Granite (yet another 30 miles upstream, or 30 miles downriver from Clarkston). Each of the four has locks offering free passage to pleasure boats and commercial traffic. All four also have self-guided tours of powerhouses and fish ladders, and—perhaps most welcome—each has a riverside picnic park.

Several other riverside parks lighten the character of this austere region.

Boyer Park, just downstream from Lower Granite Dam, has both tent and trailer campsites and food service as well as boat launch, swimming beach, and picnic sites.

Central Ferry State Park, just off State 127 on the north bank of the river, has 60 trailer hookups and a boat launch, swimming beach, and picnic sites.

State 261 gives access to the settlement of Lyon's Ferry and to Lyon's Ferry State Park and Palouse Falls State Park. (Lyon's Ferry and Palouse Falls state parks are administered as a single 1,282-acre unit.) Both state parks have campsites—50 at Lyon's Ferry, 10 at the falls.

In springtime, when snow-melt waters feed the Palouse River, the detour to Palouse Falls is worth the time. From nowhere, from what seems to be dry rock, the roaring torrent of the falls plunges 198 feet in hasty descent toward the level of the Snake.

A hiking trail along the canyon wall connects the falls part of the park with the main recreation area at riverside. In cool weather the stroll is an amiable one, but in the heat of summer it becomes a burdensome effort. One-time Indian cave shelters now lie beneath waters backed up by Lower Granite Dam; they were the cause of the trail's construction.

For parks lower on the Snake, see page 101.

Fishermen work all the dammed pools of the Snake for bass, catfish, shad, salmon, steelhead, and sturgeon. Water-skiers travel miles to get to these ideally calm pools.

The Palouse

Any longtime sports fan reads "Palouse" and "Washington State University" as synonyms. WSU does pervade the region one way and another, but there is more to it.

Pullman and Washington State University. The town has almost the character of a neighborhood shopping district. (Nearby Moscow, Idaho, shares the duties as the regional commercial center.) WSU's campus, on a hill just east, dominates the scene. The school has several points of interest.

Conner Zoological Museum specializes in northwestern vertebrates, but represents animals of all the Americas. It is open from 8 A.M. to 5 P.M., Monday through Friday.

The Anthropological Museum constantly changes its exhibits, which focus on northwest Indians. The school is notably active in the field, maintaining archaeological digs at several points as well as living contacts. Hours are random at the museum.

The Museum of Art welcomes visitors from 10 A.M. to 4 P.M. weekdays during the school year. It displays local work and touring shows.

Not last there is Ferdinand's. WSU's Department of Food Sciences and Technology operates

Water in an unlikely place

The Palouse River is one of many that have carved courses deep into Eastern Washington's basalt plateau.

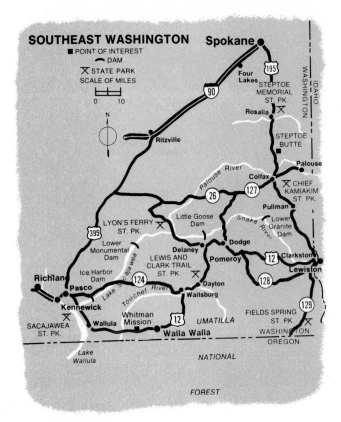

The Northeast Corner

In the northeast corner of Washington, population thins out to a minimum amidst great forests and seemingly uncountable lakes and streams. Economically, this is timber and mining country. For recreationists, it is hunting and fishing terrain.

The recreational resources are two, both huge. Coulee Dam National Recreation Area takes in both shores of Franklin D. Roosevelt Lake, alias the Columbia, for 120 miles upstream from Grand Coulee Dam. Colville National Forest takes in much of the high country.

The small town of Colville serves as anchor point for both. Situated at the junction of U.S. 395 and State 20, it is within easy reach of Spokane, 70 miles south. Two other towns are of some interest. Chewelah, between Spokane and Colville, has a fine pioneer museum and is also the gateway to the growing ski area called 49° North. Republic, well west of Colville via State 20, is an active gold mining town.

Coulee Dam National Recreation Area. Franklin D. Roosevelt Lake is the Columbia, stilled by

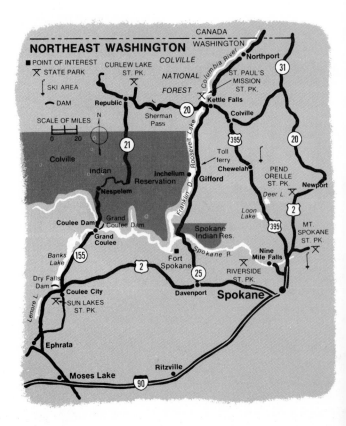

---

a creamery in Troy Hall. Ferdinand's is the retail store, which offers delicious ice creams, cheeses, and other dairy products made by the department.

Stadium Way turns north off the road to Moscow, leading into the heart of the campus. Parking stickers and a map of the campus are available at the Safety Building. Tours of the campus depart from French, the administration building, Monday through Friday at 1 P.M.

Kamiak and Steptoe buttes. Two buttes rise north of Pullman, one named for a Yakima war chief and the other for a U.S. Cavalry officer. Both buttes yield long, long views across rolling wheat country from parks at their summits.

Down on the roads, the overwhelming impression is that the plow has not missed a foot of land. Save for a rare small outcrop of rock, every slope has been moulded round and planted. From the tops of these buttes, the awesome scope of all this tilling becomes visible.

Kamiak Butte is some 8 miles from Pullman toward the town of Palouse, via State 27. Kamiak Butte County Park has a viewpoint up top and a tree-shaded picnic ground at the base.

Steptoe Butte is a short distance off U.S. 195, 25 miles north of Pullman. The 150-acre Steptoe Butte State Park atop it has picnic facilities and some short walking trails. (Another Steptoe park, Steptoe Memorial Battlefield, is 15 miles farther north at Rosalia. It commemorates one of Lt. Col.

Grand Coulee Dam. The lake reaches an impressive 120 miles above the dam, almost to Northport. The national recreation area administers the shores for that distance, and also runs a few miles up the Kettle River. It maintains 25 campgrounds (or, to be more precise, it maintains 19, while Colville and Spokane Indians administer the other 6). The sites range from small, primitive ones accessible only by boat up to sizable ones.

Toward the dam, campsites tend to be open, on gravelly beaches below basalt cliffs. The nearest towns are Grand Coulee and Coulee Dam. To the north, many sites nestle into riverside stands of conifers. Kettle Falls, Northport, and Colville are the most likely sources of supplies.

In general, the more accessible east shore draws a heavier visitor load than the west side. Bridges cross the lake at Northport and Kettle Falls. A toll ferry crosses between Gifford and Inchelium.

The lake's sheer length challenges boaters to make the whole journey over a span of days, camping along the way. Some even start upriver in Canada. But the majority of visitors come to fish a body of water which is home to walleye, mountain whitefish, kokanee, trout in variety, bass, and even sturgeon. The trout tend to concentrate in the cooler waters toward the north end of the lake and in the Kettle, Spokane, and other tributaries. Trolling from boats is the most successful system, but skillful bank fishermen can do well. The most productive months are September through November and May through June. A Washington State fishing license is required for all parts of the lake; Indian tribal licenses may be required.

Old Fort Spokane. The brief and unspectacular military life of old Fort Spokane left behind one of Washington's most elaborate souvenirs of the conflicts between settlers and Indians.

Four of 45 original buildings remain alongside a well-developed recreation park on the shore of Roosevelt Lake. The park is north of Davenport on State 25. A sign-guided tour rambles through the original quartermaster stable, powder magazine, storehouse, and reservoir building, plus a restoration of a guardhouse. A museum in the brick guardhouse explains the quiet history of a fort from which no soldier ever fought an Indian.

The recreational side of the park includes a 57-site campground, boat launches, a swimming beach, and picnic lawns.

Colville National Forest. The forest splits into two main halves, one on each side of Roosevelt Lake. They look like incomplete jigsaw puzzles.

The west half largely covers the rugged Kettle Mountains. There are 13 National Forest Service campgrounds in the forest, with 122 sites among them. All but two are on fishable lakes or streams in which trout are the prime quarry. Several are not far west of Roosevelt Lake, and on or close to State 20 leading from Colville or Kettle Falls to the old gold mining town of Republic. The two campgrounds on State 20 serve as trailheads.

Connoisseurs of back roads give high marks to a route starting at Gifford. From there a toll ferry crosses to Inchelium on the west bank. A gravelled road runs north from there along Roosevelt Lake to State 20, which heads west over 5,575-foot Sherman Pass, through Republic, then west to Tonasket in the Okanogan.

Along this route, Sherman Creek and the Sanpoil River rank high as fly-fishing streams.

The eastern half of the national forest has 13 widely scattered campgrounds. Again, the emphasis is on fishable waters, notably the remote Deep Lake out of Northport and Bayley Lake north of Chewelah.

For winter sports, 49° North, with a 1,700-foot vertical drop, has three chairlifts, a day lodge, and overnight accommodations. The ski area is just east of Chewelah.

The forest supervisor's headquarters is at Colville. District rangers are located at Republic, Kettle Falls, and Newport.

Useful Addresses in the Inland Empire

- Umatilla National Forest
  2517 S.W. Hailey
  Pendleton, OR 97801
- Whitman Mission National Historic Site
  Rte. 2
  Walla Walla, WA 99362

Chambers of Commerce

- P.O. Box 94, Chewelah, WA 99109
- 749 Sixth St., Clarkston, WA 99403
- P.O. Box 267, Colville, WA 99114
- P.O. Box 631, Newport, WA 99156
- P.O. Drawer O, Othello, WA 99344
- P.O. Box 298, Pomeroy, WA 99347
- N. 151 Grand Ave., Pullman, WA 99163
- P.O. Box 2147, Spokane, WA 99210
- P.O. Box 644, Walla Walla, WA 99362

Index

Aberdeen, 58
Adam East Museum, 106
Alaska ferries, 12
Alki Beach Park, 24
Alpine Lakes, 84
Anacortes, 37
Ape Cave, 67, 81
Apples, 115
Art, 12, 17, 18, 21, 39, 40, 41, 48, 49, 98, 122
Auburn, 42

Backpacking. See Hiking
Baker Lake, 89
Ballard Locks, 27
Banks Lake, 105
Battleground Lake State Park, 67
Bay Center, 64
Beacon Rock, 95, 97
Beacon Rock State Park, 97
Bellingham, 40–41
Bicycling, 8, 25–26
Bingen, 98
Birch Bay, 39–40
Bird Creek Meadows, 83
Blue Mountains, 121–122
Boating, 9, 18, 31, 33, 35, 43, 63, 67, 84, 92–93, 97, 102, 103, 108, 114, 115
Boeing Airplane Company, 40
Bogachiel State Park, 56
Bonneville Dam, 97, 99
Borst Historic Park, 70
Bremerton, 47
Brewster, 112
British Columbia Ferry System, 15
Bruceport County Park, 64
Bush-Pacific Pioneer State Park, 64

Callam Bay, 50
Camano Island, 39
Camano Island State Park, 39
Camping, 8, 75, 82, 84, 86, 91–92
Camp Six Logging Museum, 41–42
Cannonball Island, 53
Cape Alava, 53
Cape Disappointment, 63
Cape Flattery, 52–53
Cape Horn, 97
Capitol Lake Park, 58
Carkeek Park, 24
Cascades, 72–95
Cashmere, 109–111
Cathlamet, 64–65
Causland Park, 37
Cedar Creek Grist Mill, 67
Center for Asian Arts, 16

Central Cascades, 83–86
Centralia, 70
Central Washington, 104–115
Charbonneau, 103
Chateau Ste. Michelle, 17–18
Chehalis, 70
Cheney Cowles Memorial Museum, 119
Chewelah, 124
Chinook, 67
Chittenden Locks, 18, 25, 27
Chuckanut Drive, 39
Clamming, 20, 45, 61, 62, 68
Clark County Historical Museum, 69
Clark Mansion, 119
Cle Elum, 84
Climbing, 75, 77, 78, 81, 82, 94
Colonial Creek Campground, 91–92
Columbia River Gorge, 95, 96–102
Columbia River map, 100
Colville, 124
Colville National Forest, 124–125
Conconully, 112
Concrete, 91
Copalis Beach, 56
Coulee City, 105
Coulee Dam, 104–105, 107
Coulee Dam National Recreation Area, 124–125
Coulee region, 104–108
County fairs, 29
Countyline Park, 65
Coupeville, 36
Cowlitz County Museum, 70
Cowlitz River, 67–69
Crescent Bar, 111
Crow Butte State Park, 98–100
Crystal Mountain, 77, 79

Diablo Lake, 91
Discovery Park, 23
Dorothy Lakes, 86
Dosewallips River, 47
Dry Falls, 105–106
Duncan Gardens, 119
Dungeness, 49–50

Early Winters, 93
Ellensburg, 114
Elwha River, 50
Ephrata, 106
Esther Short Park, 69
Ethnic Cultural Center, 17
Everett, 40
Evergreen Point Floating Bridge, 18
Expo '74, 119

Fairhaven, 40
Federation Forest State Park, 77

Ferries, 6, 12, 15, 35, 36, 42, 65
Fidalgo Island, 37
Finch (John A.) Arboretum, 119
Fishing,
   fresh-water, 9, 31, 47, 50, 56, 92, 103, 108, 125
   salt-water, 9, 13, 31, 33, 37, 50, 62, 63–64
Fort Canby State Park, 61–63
Fort Casey State Park, 36
Fort Columbia State Park, 65
Fort Flagler State Park, 49
Fort Nisqually, 41–42
Fort Okanogan State Park Museum, 111
Fort Simcoe, 114
Fort Vancouver, 69
Fort Walla Walla Park, 120–121
Fort Worden State Park, 49
Foss Lakes, 86
Freeway Park, 16, 22
Friday Harbor, 33

Gasworks Park, 23, 30
Ghost towns, 112
Gifford Pinchot National Forest, 78, 83
Gig Harbor, 47–48
Ginkgo Petrified Forest State Park, 111
Glacier Peak Wilderness Area, 94
Goat Rocks Wilderness Area, 78
Golf, 8, 26, 29, 31, 86, 103
Grand Coulee Dam, 104–105, 107
Grand Coulee map, 108
Grant County Historical Museum, 106
Grays Harbor, 56, 63
Green Lake, 23, 30, 31

Hamma Hamma Recreation Area, 47
Hanford Atomic Energy Works, 100
Hanford Science Center, 101
Harts Pass, 93
Heart of the Hills Campground, 50
Henry Art Gallery, 17
Hiking, 8, 45–47, 53, 55, 74, 75–78, 80, 84, 86, 94, 95
Hing Hay Park, 16
Hoh River rain forest, 56
Hood Canal shoreline, 45
Hoodsport, 45
Hoquiam, 58
Horseback riding, 56, 78, 83, 93, 94
Horseshoe Basin, 94
Horsethief Lake State Park, 98
Hovander County Park, 41
Hurricane Ridge, 50, 51

Ice Harbor Dam, 122
Ilwaco, 63, 66
Indians, 39, 55, 83, 85, 101, 106, 109, 110, 119, 120, 122, 124

Industrial tours, 17–18, 40, 57, 70, 101, 111, 113, 114
Information sources, 31, 42, 58, 70, 85, 94, 103, 114, 125
Ingalls Lake, 84
Inland Empire, 116–126
International District Arts and Crafts Cooperative, 16

Jackson House, 68
Jogging, 25–26
John Day Dam, 98

Kalaloch, 55
Kamiak Butte, 124
Kelso, 70
Kennewick, 100–103
Kettle Mountains, 116, 125
Kingdome, 16
Kitsap Peninsula, 47–48

La Conner, 38, 39
Lake Chelan, 108, 115
Lake Chelan National Recreation Area, 93–94
Lake Chelan State Park, 108
Lake Crescent, 50
Lake Cushman State Park, 47
Lake Ozette, 53
Lake Padden Park, 40–41
Lake Quinault, 55
Lake Sacajawea Park, 70
Lake Sammamish State Park, 24
Lake Sylvia State Park, 58
Lake Union, 31
Lake Washington Floating Bridge, 18
Lake Wenatchee, 86
Lake Wynoochee, 58
La Push, 55
Leadbetter State Park, 63
Leavenworth, 86, 90
Lewis and Clark, 63
Lewis and Clark State Park, 68
Lewis River, 67
Lewisville County Park, 67
Lincoln Park, 24
Little Goose Dam, 122
Logging, 89
Long Island, 63
Longmire, 75
Longview, 70
Loomis, 112
Lopez Island, 34
Lower Granite Dam, 122
Lower Monumental Dam, 122
Luther Burbank Park, 24

McNary Dam, 100
Manito Park, 118
Marblemount, 91
Maryhill Museum, 98
Marymoor County Park, 24
Mayfield Lake, 67
Merwin Lake, 67
Molson, 112
Monte Cristo, 91
Moses Lake, 106–108
Mt. Adams Wilderness Area, 83
Mt. Baker, 38, 89

The mighty hand of man

Mile after mile of rolling Palouse Hills have been manicured by generations of large-scale wheat growers.

Mt. Baker Lodge, 89
Mt. Baker-Snoqualmie
    National Forest, 84
Mount Constitution, 33
Mt. Erie, 37
Mt. Pilchuck, 91
Mt. Rainier, 14, 73–77
Mt. Rainier map, 76
Mt. Rainier National Park,
    73–77
Mt. St. Helens, 81
Museum of Science and
    Industry, 18
Music, 21

Nahcotta, 61
Neah Bay, 50
Newhalem, 91
North Beach Peninsula, 60–64
North Bend, 84
North Cascades, 86–94
North Cascades Highway, 73,
    91–93
North Cascades National Park,
    89, 93
Northcentral Cascades map, 88
Northcentral map, 109
Northeast map, 124
North Head lighthouse, 71
Northwest Trek, 77

Ocean Shores, 56
Ohanapecosh, 75
Ohme Gardens, 109
Okanogan, 111
Old Fort Spokane, 125
Olmstead Place, 114
Olympia, 57–58
Olympia Brewing Company, 57
Olympia city map, 57
Olympia Oyster Company, 57
Olympic Game Farm, 49
Olympic National Park, 44, 59
Olympic Peninsula, 44–59
Olympic Peninsula map, 52
Omak Stampede, 110
Orcas Island, 33
Oysterville, 61

Pacific Beach, 56–57
Pacific Crest Trail, 78, 80, 83, 93
Pacific Northwest Indian
    Center, 119, 121
Pacific Science Center, 11–12
Pack trips. See Horseback
    riding
Packwood, 78–80
Packwood Lake, 78
Palouse, 122–124
Palouse Falls, 122
Palouse Hills, 126
Palouse River, 123
Paradise, 75
Park Lake, 106
Pasayten Wilderness, 89, 94
Pasco, 100–103
Peace Arch State Park, 41
Pharmaceutical garden, 25
Pike Place Market, 12, 19
Pioneer Square, 15, 19
Plants and gardens, 24–25, 41,
    45, 57, 70, 75, 77, 79, 83, 91,
    109, 119

Plymouth, 100
Point Defiance Park, 41
Port Angeles, 49
Port Gamble, 48
Port Townsend, 46, 48–49
Poulsbo, 48
Puget Sound, 6, 32–43
Puget Sound map, 37
Pullman, 122–124
Puyallup, 42

Queets River rain forest, 55–56
Quillayute Indian Reservation,
    55

Rain forests, 54, 55–56
Rainier Brewery, 18
Rainy Pass, 93
Razor clams, 68
Republic, 124
Reynolds Metals Company, 70
Rialto Beach, 53
Richland, 100–103
Rimrock Lake, 80
Rockport, 91
Rocky Reach Dam, 109
Rodeos, 110, 113
Roosevelt (Franklin D.) Lake,
    124–125
Roslyn, 84
Ross Lake, 92–93
Ross Lake National Recreation
    Area, 89
Ruby Beach, 55
Ruby Mine, 112

Sacajawea State Park, 101
Salmon Bay Terminal, 18
Salmon fishing, 9, 13, 31, 33,
    62, 63, 64
Saltwater State Park, 24
Sand Point, 53
San Juan Island, 33
San Juan Island National
    Historic Park, 33
San Juan Islands, 32–36
San Juan Islands map, 34
Schafer State Park, 58
Seal Rock, 45
Seahurst (Ed Munro) Park, 24
Seattle, 3, 10–31
    aquarium, 15
    Asian community, 16
    ferries, 12, 15
    harbor tour, 15
    neighborhoods, 16–18
    underground tour, 15
    urban core, 11–16
    waterfront, 12–15
Seattle Art Museum, 12, 21
Seattle Center, 11–12
Seattle maps, 12, 28
Seattle-Tacoma International
    Airport, 17
Sekiu, 50
Sequim, 49–50
Seward Park, 24
Shaw Island, 34, 36
Shelton, 47
Shi-Shi Beach, 53
Skamokawa, 64–65
Skiing, 9, 75, 77–80, 84–86, 87,
    89, 91, 93, 120, 125

Skykomish, 86
Slocum House, 69
Snake River, 100, 122
Snohomish, 85
Snoqualmie Falls, 84
Snoqualmie Pass, 84, 87
Snoqualmie Pass Highway, 73
Soap Lake, 106
South Cascades, 77–83
South Cascades map, 81
Southcentral map, 112
Southeast map, 124
Southwest corner, 60–71
Southwest corner map, 65
Space Needle, 11
Spirit Lake, 81
Spokane, 116–120
Spokane House Interpretive
    Center, 120
Spokane map, 117
Spokane River, 117
Sports, 21, 23, 89, 103, 113
Staircase Campground, 45–47
State Capitol Museum, 57
Steamboat Rock State Park,
    105
Stehekin, 93–94
Steilacoom, 42
Steptoe Butte, 124
Stevenguamish River, 91
Stevenson, 97
Stevens Pass, 85–86
Stevens Pass Highway, 73, 85
Summer Falls State Park, 106
Sun Lakes State Park, 105–106
Sunrise, 75
Swift, 67
Swift Reservoir, 81

Tacoma, 41–42
Teawhit Head, 55
Tennis, 8, 26, 103
Theater, 17, 21
The Dalles Dam, 98
Thomas Burke Memorial—
    Washington State
    Museum, 17
Tieton River, 80–81
Timber carnivals, 89
Tokeland, 64
Tri-Cities, 100–103
Tri-Cities map, 101

Umatilla National Forest, 121
University of Washington, 17, 23

University of Washington
    Arboretum, 25
Upper Grand Coulee, 105

Vancouver, 69
Vantage, 111
Vashon Island, 42
Volunteer Firemen Museum,
    39
Volunteer Park, 24–25

Walk-In Wild Zoo, 120
Walla Walla, 120–121
Wanapum Dam, 111
Wanapum State Park, 111
Washington Pass, 93
Washington state map, 4–5
Washington State University,
    122
Waterfront Park, 16, 18
Waterfront Trail, 25
Wenatchee, 108–109
Westport, 63–64
Weyerhauser sawmill, 70
Whatcom Museum of History
    and Art, 40
Whidbey Island, 36
Whistler Basin Viewpoint, 93
White Pass, 78–81
White Pass Highway, 73
White Pass Ski Area, 78–80
White River Valley Historical
    Society Museum, 42
Whitman College, 120–121
Whitman Mission, 120
Wildflowers. See Plants
Willapa Bay, 9
Willapa Bay Shellfish
    Laboratory, 61
Willapa Harbor, 64
Willis Carey Museum, 111
Wind River, 83
Wing Luke Museum, 16
Winter sports, 9, 75, 77–80,
    84–87, 89, 91, 93, 120, 125
Winthrop, 93
Woodland Park, 23, 25

Yakima, 112–114
Yakima River Canyon, 114
Yakima Valley, 112–114
Yakima Valley Museum, 113
Yale Lake, 67

Photographers

Dave Barnes: 9. **Ed Cooper:** 6 top, 38 top, 46 bottom, 54, 107, 115 bottom, 123, back cover. **Keith Gunnar:** 14, 35 top, 46 top, 62 top, 74, 82, 90 bottom, 95 top, 118 top. **L. J. Linkhart:** 30 bottom, 102, 118 bottom. **Don Normark:** 38 bottom. **Jim Poth:** 16. **Jim Scolman:** 25. **Harald Sund:** 3, 6 bottom, 19 bottom, 22, 35 bottom, 43, 51, 59, 66, 90 top, 99, 110, 126. **Harolyn Thompson:** 30 top. **Bob Waterman:** 95 bottom, 115 top. **Doug Wilson:** 19 top, 27, 62 bottom, 79. **Art Wolfe:** 71. **Craig Zwicky:** 121.

Cartography by Roberta Edwards, Tim Kifune, Ells Marugg, and Jack Doonan.